MIXED METAPHORS

ALSO AVAILABLE FROM BLOOMSBURY

Political Metaphor Analysis, by Andreas Musolff
More WordCrime, by John Olsson
Linguanomics, by Gabrielle Hogan-Brun

MIXED METAPHORS

Their Use and Abuse

By Karen Sullivan

BLOOMSBURY ACADEMIC
LONDON • NEW YORK • OXFORD • NEW DELHI • SYDNEY

BLOOMSBURY ACADEMIC
Bloomsbury Publishing Plc
50 Bedford Square, London, WC1B 3DP, UK
1385 Broadway, New York, NY 10018, USA

BLOOMSBURY, BLOOMSBURY ACADEMIC and the Diana logo are trademarks of
Bloomsbury Publishing Plc

First published in Great Britain 2019
Reprinted 2019 (twice)

Copyright © Karen Sullivan, 2019

Karen Sullivan has asserted her right under the Copyright, Designs and Patents Act, 1988, to be identified as Author of this work.

Cover design by Olivia D'Cruz
Cover images: Fish: © Alamy Stock Photo/Patrick Guenette and Quagga Media, Moon: Alamy Stock Photo/David Cole

All rights reserved. No part of this publication may be reproduced or transmitted in any form or by any means, electronic or mechanical, including photocopying, recording, or any information storage or retrieval system, without prior permission in writing from the publishers.

Bloomsbury Publishing Plc does not have any control over, or responsibility for, any third-party websites referred to or in this book. All internet addresses given in this book were correct at the time of going to press. The author and publisher regret any inconvenience caused if addresses have changed or sites have ceased to exist, but can accept no responsibility for any such changes.

A catalogue record for this book is available from the British Library.

Library of Congress Cataloging-in-Publication Data

Names: Sullivan, Karen, 1980- author.
Title: Mixed metaphors : their use and abuse / By Karen Sullivan.
Description: London ; New York : Bloomsbury Academic / Bloomsbury Publishing Plc, 2018. | ePDF: 978-1-3500-6606-9 | eBook: 978-1-3500-6605-2 |
Includes bibliographical references and index.
Identifiers: LCCN 2018007407 (print) | LCCN 2018016087 (ebook) |
ISBN 9781350066052 (ePub) | ISBN 9781350066069 (ePDF) |
ISBN 9781350066045 (hardback) | ISBN 9781350066038 (pbk.)
Subjects: LCSH: Metaphor. | Paradox. | Ambiguity. | Metaphor–Psychological aspects.
Classification: LCC P301.5.M48 (ebook) |
LCC P301.5.M48 S845 2018 (print) | DDC 808/.032–dc23
LC record available at https://lccn.loc.gov/2018007407

ISBN:	HB:	978-1-3500-6604-5
	PB:	978-1-3500-6603-3
	ePDF:	978-1-3500-6606-9
	eBook:	978-1-3500-6605-2

Typeset by Integra Software Services Pvt. Ltd.
Printed and bound in Great Britain

To find out more about our authors and books visit www.bloomsbury.com and sign up for our newsletters.

For my parents,
who were by my side, standing behind me,
every step of the way.

CONTENTS

List of Figures viii

1 Perfect Mix or Perfect Mess? 1
2 Conceptual Metaphor Theory 25
3 The Main Reasons Metaphors Mix 47
4 More Exotic Mixes 63
5 Metaphor or Not? How Ambiguity Causes 'Mixing' 85
6 Malaphors and Other 'Ducks Out of Water' 117
7 Why We Need Multiple Metaphors 147
8 Mixing Metaphors for Fun and Profit 171
9 Making the Most of Your Metaphors 187
   Appendix: Index of Metaphors 191

Bibliography 220
Index 226

LIST OF FIGURES

1. It may be difficult to imagine lightning that looks like a drunken ballerina 9
2. How many mice are in this picture? 30
3. Burning eyes and fiery hair can be hazardous 31
4. Parents are larger than children, which encourages kids to develop IMPORTANCE IS SIZE. In addition, physical contact between parents and children leads to the metaphor AFFECTION IS WARMTH. Photograph by Bill Sullivan 34
5. When we open the box and SEE the kitten, we UNDERSTAND that we'd better buy cat food, make a vet appointment, and think of something to tell the landlord 35
6. Eels are hard to get your head around 41
7. Covered wagons on the Oregon Trail faced many dangers, but not alligators 51
8. Carrots don't make good bait 57
9. Most canaries don't care if a pot boils over 58
10. If I had a car, this would be my bumper sticker 59
11. A rabbit is not a good substitute for a fig leaf 65
12. A Facebook post describes friends as bras 71
13. This meme could be inspiring – unless you're a tree. Photograph by Bill Sullivan 74

14 Another inspiring quotation has been sabotaged by its background image 74

15 Few people want to see their children carried off by kites 88

16 Trains are better off if they don't venture off their tracks 90

17 This meme critiques the proverb *When life hands you lemons, make lemonade* 91

18 Cues such as the textured background encourage readers to first interpret this meme metaphorically 92

19 This message of hope appeared on a billboard, photographs of which were circulated online 101

20 Glow sticks are activated by shaking, but human comprehension is not 106

21 Talking mantises might bite each other's heads off either literally or figuratively 107

22 'Ducks out of water' seem fine 126

23 This man needs to 'hold his lid' 128

24 The Earth is carried by a giant turtle. Underneath that, it's turtles all the way down 137

25 The nuclear genie is here to stay – and he brought friends 138

26 Molecules are often represented as balls on sticks (left) or as attached bubbles (right) 152

27 These two characters have different metaphors for happiness 157

28 Empty minds fill up with monsters 166

29 Many frog species are threatened and some are poisonous, so it's not recommended to eat wild frogs 173

30 This meme compares two horrific experiences 179

31 Information is mapped from a source domain, such as ACQUIRING A DESIRED OBJECT, to help understand a target domain, such as ACHIEVING A PURPOSE 194

32 ACHIEVING A PURPOSE can be understood as either REACHING A DESTINATION or ACQUIRING A DESIRED OBJECT. In our lives, we have to both go places and get objects, in order to achieve even simple goals such as eating 195

33 BUSINESS COMPETITION IS BASEBALL allows us to think about the workers in a company as the members of a baseball team 199

34 BUSINESS COMPETITION IS AMERICAN FOOTBALL lets us consider employees in a company as a team in American football 199

35 STATUS IS VERTICALITY lets us think about dominance as being located 'above' other people 214

36 UNDERSTANDING IS GRASPING supplements UNDERSTANDING IS SEEING by giving us another way of thinking about cognition 217

37 UNDERSTANDING IS SEEING is a frequently encountered metaphor in English 218

1 PERFECT MIX OR PERFECT MESS?

Lightning pirouetted like a drunken ballerina across purpling clouds and a sky the colour of regret.[1]

What makes the 'ballerina' sentence painful to read? Its spelling, grammar, and punctuation are flawless, yet the passage is awkward, unconvincing, and would have no place in a literary classic (though it did manage to be published in a contemporary novel).

The problem with the sentence is its metaphors. First of all, lightning moves in straight or jagged lines and cannot 'pirouette'. Second, most of us haven't had the privilege of seeing a ballet dancer perform while drunk, so we may have trouble imagining what this looks like. Finally, we have no way of knowing whether the colour of 'regret' is green, grey, black, or orange. The pirouetting lightning, the ballerina, and the regret-coloured sky make the passage hard to understand.

Compare the 'ballerina' passage with a metaphoric phrase from *Sons and Lovers* by D. H. Lawrence:

> Another old shop whose small window looked like a cunning, half-shut eye.[2]

We've all seen a half-shut eye and can easily compare this image to the half-closed window of a shop. The shopfront can be understood as a face, and the 'cunning' expression of the eye hints at a secretive, ominous attitude. We immediately suspect that the shop is old and mysterious. Each word in the metaphor conveys imagery and emotional impact.

Both the 'ballerina' and the 'half-shut eye' metaphors have the form of *similes*. That is, they introduce metaphoric comparisons with the word *like*, as in more familiar similes such as *her cheeks are like roses* or *we're like two peas in a pod*. However, labelling these examples as similes doesn't help explain why many critics would be horrified by the 'ballerina' example but delighted by the 'half-shut eye'. The examples are metaphoric similes because they include the word *like*. If *like* is removed and *a drunken ballerina* is instead offset with commas, in the first example, and *looked like* is replaced with *was* in the second example, the two passages are no longer similes. Removing *like* or *looked like* is also a useful exercise because it shows that these words have a relatively small effect on how the metaphors are understood.[3] If these words are changed, the 'ballerina' passage is still confusing and the 'half-shut eye' description is still expressive.

In general, the specific words in metaphoric language are less important than the *concepts* that the metaphors are comparing. Critics often pay attention to metaphoric words instead of concepts, simply because words are easier to identify. It's straightforward to decide that a metaphor includes the word *like* and therefore is a simile. It's harder to pinpoint what's wrong with lightning that pirouettes or what's interesting about a window that resembles an eye.

Even though metaphoric words are easier to study, metaphoric concepts tell us much more about how metaphors work. Every metaphor has conceptual structure that hides certain facts and forces others to our attention.[4] Well-chosen metaphors help us imagine people who never lived and events that never happened. Metaphors let us think about black holes, authoritarianism, death, and thousands of other things we can't see or touch.

We could say that metaphors allow us to 'grasp' otherwise nameless notions, 'tackle' difficult problems, and 'move forward' in our understanding of the world. Language is 'full' of metaphors once we 'open our eyes'. Yet metaphors are almost imperceptible unless something brings them to our attention. For the most part, we notice metaphors only when they go wrong or when they seem so exceptional that we marvel at what they can do.

English speakers often know intuitively that there's something amiss with a metaphor, like those in the 'ballerina' passage, but can't pinpoint the problem. Many English speakers are happy to call these 'mixed metaphors' even if they can't tell exactly what's wrong with them.[5] Most linguists, on the other hand, define mixed metaphor more narrowly. They tend to consider a metaphor mixed only if it combines, or 'mixes', two different, incompatible metaphors.[6] Rugby coach Craig Bellamy produced a mixed metaphor of this strictly defined type when he complained about a colleague, 'He's gone behind my back, right in front of my face!' Nobody could be behind Bellamy (as in the first metaphor) and also in front of him (as in the second metaphor), so these two metaphors are contradictory and are 'mixed' in every sense of the term.

For most English speakers, though, the definition of mixed metaphors has been extended to encompass individual metaphors that are simply hard to imagine, like a drunken ballerina, and those that are internally inconsistent, like spinning lightning. These mixed metaphors cause as much trouble as the more traditional kind, so they'll be included in this book along with the metaphors that linguists usually consider mixed.

Human intuitions about metaphors are not limited to whether or not metaphors are mixed. As human beings, we have the ability to use and understand metaphoric language without conscious awareness of the metaphoric concepts involved. There are nevertheless advantages to making ourselves consciously aware of the metaphors around us. If we know how metaphors work on a conceptual level, we can control their effects. We can avoid using metaphors that are confusing or distracting, and we can design metaphors that do exactly what we want. When we encounter metaphoric language, we can analyse what makes it effective or not. We can avoid being manipulated by subconscious metaphors, and we can accept the benefits of a metaphor while rejecting any aspects we find unhelpful or inaccurate.

It's only recently that the conceptual underpinnings of metaphoric language have been recognized at all. From Aristotle's time until the last decades of the twentieth century, metaphor was generally considered a poetic embellishment rather than an essential part of everyday cognition. In 1980, the linguist George Lakoff and the philosopher Mark Johnson published *Metaphors We Live By*, a book that changed how many people think about metaphor. Lakoff and Johnson showed that metaphor pervades all language use, not just poetry or literature. Most metaphors, they argued, are so effortless and natural that we use them all the time without noticing. We don't usually think of everyday sentences such as *I'm planning ahead* as metaphoric. However, it's apparent that the word *ahead* is not strictly literal in this sentence, because the future that we're planning for isn't physically ahead of us. Lakoff and Johnson argue that examples such as *I'm planning ahead* are metaphoric, even though they're less noticeable than some of the clever, original metaphors found in poetry. Today, there is disagreement over which words and phrases should be considered metaphoric,[7] but even conservative metaphor researchers agree that metaphors occur in everyday language as well as literary language.

Lakoff and Johnson also found that metaphor is anything but superficial embellishment. Metaphors are primarily ways of thinking, not ways of speaking. When we use metaphoric language, it activates complex cognitive (i.e. thought-based) structures called *conceptual metaphors*. This is what gives metaphoric language its power. For instance, when we say that we 'see' what someone means, that their meaning is 'clear' to us, or that their explanation 'sheds light' on a topic, we use words and phrases related to vision, such as *see, clear*, or *shed light*, to talk about the comprehension of ideas. According to Lakoff and Johnson, we use words related to vision because we actually think about comprehension in terms of vision. The concepts of vision and comprehension are cognitively connected. The next chapter introduces further evidence for conceptual associations of this kind and describes how these connections affect human language and thought.

If metaphors are conceptual structures, this helps explain why they are sometimes used in ways that can seem confusing or awkward, such as in mixed metaphors. Conceptual metaphors, according to Lakoff and Johnson, are mostly subconscious and unintentional. Since we're not consciously aware of most of our metaphors, we sometimes use them in ways that won't make sense to other people. We might, for example, say that we 'see' what someone is saying, 'see' that a dog is smelly and needs a bath, or otherwise claim to 'see' attributes that are actually perceived by other senses. Usually, audiences will understand even an imperfect metaphor.[8] Our listeners won't be confused if we say we 'see' that a fabric feels soft or 'see' how a concerto is structured. Using this wording does, however, suggest that we're not paying attention to our choice of metaphors, and it may distract a listener from the point we're trying to make.

This book employs research from linguistics and cognitive science to explore why some metaphors seem confusing or peculiar, whereas others are memorable and marvellous. The absurd examples are usually produced by speakers and authors who are apparently unaware of the metaphors they're using, as in the 'drunken ballerina' passage. The more meaningful examples come from people who consciously and skilfully craft their metaphors, as in the 'half-shut eye' quotation. Finally, some mixed metaphors are used by people who are aware of their metaphors but pretend not to be, for devious reasons of their own.

This last class of metaphors is in many ways the most revealing because it shows how metaphors can be pushed to their limits. Skill with metaphors doesn't always mean making them effortless for the reader.[9] Certain speakers and authors like to challenge their readers with unusual metaphor combinations, which can make language memorable, effective, and often humorous. When classical guitarist Andrés Segovia describes the piano as 'a monster that screams when you touch its teeth', this evocative combination of metaphors wouldn't normally be considered mixed. Even though the toothy image and the sound of screaming come from two different metaphors (specifically, two *image metaphors*, which are discussed in the next chapter), with a little imagination we can visualize a toothy monster screaming, and Segovia's delightful description is worth the effort this takes.

Other skilled speakers and writers use the power of metaphor for more nefarious ends. That is, they intentionally mangle their idioms and metaphors to create malicious humour, such as when Texas State Treasurer Ann Richards described US presidential nominee George H. W. Bush as 'born with a silver foot in his mouth'. Richards intentionally mixed metaphors by combining the idioms *born with a silver spoon in one's mouth* 'be born wealthy and privileged' and *put one's foot in one's mouth* 'misspeak', in order to suggest that Bush was both privileged and prone to speech errors. By presenting her comment in the guise of a speech error itself (specifically, a malaphor; see Chapter 6), Richards mocked Bush's own speech errors and added humour to make the insult more memorable.

About 150 years before Richards, another US politician, Congressman John Randolph, made a clever metaphoric criticism of his colleague Senator Edward Livingston:

> He is as a man of splendid abilities, but utterly corrupt. He shines and stinks like rotten mackerel by moonlight.[10]

A great politician might metaphorically be said to 'shine', and a corrupt one could metaphorically 'stink'. These metaphoric uses of *shine* and *stink* involve conceptual metaphors that are traditionally called GOODNESS IS LIGHT and MORALITY IS PURITY (metaphor naming conventions are discussed in the next chapter). Although Randolph's description has never been called 'mixed', other combinations of these two metaphors could easily attract this label, as in *his filthy, luminous mind* or *the idea was stained with shame but shone with genius*. Dirty, stinky objects usually shine less than clean ones, so these two metaphors are difficult to use together in a meaningful way. However, Randolph makes the metaphors work by comparing his colleague specifically to a dead fish, which might well both 'shine' and 'stink' in the light of the moon. This clever choice allows Randolph to use the two metaphors together in a way that makes perfect sense and is unlikely to be criticized as mixed.

We often need more than one metaphor to communicate an idea, such as the notion that a politician 'shines and stinks'. Particularly, when we use conceptual metaphors to solve problems or reason about abstract issues, we frequently require multiple metaphors (see Chapter 7). Fortunately, there are numerous ways to use several metaphors together without giving the impression of mixed metaphor. First, we can present two metaphors as separate structures that should be understood individually, rather than together.[11] For example, we could say that a politician 'stinks' and several sentences later explain how he 'shines', and no one would consider this a mixed metaphor. Chapters 3 and 4 outline a number of strategies for keeping metaphors separate. Second, we can carefully design two metaphors so that they don't have to be separate, but nevertheless make sense, as in Randolph's quotation, in which a dead fish might logically both stink and shine. Chapter 7 talks about this option. Finally, we can intentionally choose illogical metaphors that might seem mixed, but which also come across as clever and original. Richards's 'silver spoon' quotation is an example of this strategy (covered in Chapter 8). However, not every writer or speaker uses metaphors as elegantly as Randolph and Richards, which is how mixed metaphors get their bad reputation.

What are mixed metaphors?

Style manuals don't usually define mixed metaphors, and when they do, the definitions often aren't of much help. For example, one guide to public speaking suggests that 'a mixed metaphor makes illogical comparisons between two things'.[12] This definition could describe any comparison that's hard to understand, such as 'penguins are like bagpipes', so it isn't a practical tool for identifying mixed metaphors.

Most linguists' and psychologists' definitions of mixed metaphors specify that two metaphors are necessary in order to form a mixed metaphor and that these metaphors must differ from each other in some way.[13] Some definitions additionally require that these two metaphors must occur together within a sentence, clause, or other unit.[14] Indeed, most of the mixed metaphors discussed in this book do involve two or more distinct metaphors, and normally these metaphors occur within the same sentence, so the mixed metaphors examined here will largely follow the definitions previously suggested by psychologists and linguists.

Nevertheless, it should be noted that the specialists' definitions of mixed metaphor diverge from the popular understanding of the concept in two ways. First, a surprising number of 'mixed metaphors' only involve one metaphor, as in the 'drunken ballerina' example. This phenomenon will be discussed in Chapters 5 and 6. Second, some mixed metaphors occur in two different clauses or sentences, as shown in Chapters 3 and 4.

Before exploring the full range of mixed metaphors, however, let's look at what happens in the classical examples. In traditional mixed metaphors, two metaphors are put together in a way that conflicts with what we know about the world. The following news headline describing Iranian politician Mahmoud Ahmadinejad involves this type of mixing:

Ahmadinejad wields axe to cement his position.[15]

A politician can 'wield an axe' to metaphorically 'chop away' unwanted employees from his team (SOCIAL GROUPS ARE COMPLEX STRUCTURES) and can 'cement' his position to keep it metaphorically 'stable' (PERSISTING IS REMAINING ERECT). However, no one can cement anything using an axe. The way the metaphors are put together causes us to imagine an impossible scenario, which inspired *The Independent* to choose this headline as one of its top ten mixed metaphors. Because of the implausibility of cementing with an axe, the metaphor combination is not particularly helpful for understanding Ahmadinejad's actions and motivations, and is exactly the kind of usage that is most often considered a mixed metaphor.[16]

It's important to notice that each of the two metaphors in the Ahmadinejad headline would be fine on its own. A politician can either 'wield an axe' or 'cement his position' without any hint of mixing. The 'axe' and 'cement' metaphors in the headline seem mixed because they look like they ought to be considered together rather than separately. The metaphors occur side by side in the same headline, and they both describe physically modifying things (by chopping or cementing them), so most readers will try to make sense of both at once.

In order for two metaphors to seem mixed, they have to be combined or *compounded*.[17] Metaphors that are spoken on two different days, or written in two different books, will never seem mixed because everybody will have forgotten the first metaphor by the time they encounter the second one. The need for metaphors to compound prior to mixing is the reason that many definitions of mixed metaphor require the metaphors to occur within the same sentence or clause. Readers who encounter two metaphors in the same clause, for example, are more likely to put the metaphors together because the first one is still fresh in their minds when they encounter the second one.

Metaphors don't need to be in the same clause or sentence in order to combine, but when they're this close together, their combination is more likely. Keeping metaphors in separate sentences, or otherwise discouraging them from compounding, is the simplest way to keep them from mixing. Chapters 3 and 4 discuss this and other factors that encourage metaphors to combine. It's also possible for metaphors to combine gracefully, without mixing (see Chapter 7), but two metaphors must always first combine in order to mix. Any strategy that inhibits compounding will therefore prevent mixing.

Of course, not all mixed metaphors result from the combination of two metaphors. In fact, 28 per cent of the time, the term *mixed metaphor* refers to expressions that involve only one metaphor, according to a recent study by linguist Elena Semino.[18] These so-called 'mixed metaphors' include ambiguous expressions, malapropisms, and metaphoric imagery that's simply hard to visualize – such as drunken ballerinas or the colour of regret (Figure 1).

In this book, the following phenomena will be considered mixed metaphors:

1. Two or more metaphors that combine, but result in contradictions, inconsistencies, or strange scenarios that are hard to imagine, like 'wielding an axe to cement a position' (Chapters 3 and 4; metaphoric idioms are discussed in Chapter 6).

2. One metaphor that is internally inconsistent or hard to imagine, such as lightning that looks like a drunken ballerina (Chapter 8).

3. One metaphor that results in contradictions, inconsistencies, or ambiguities with non-metaphoric concepts, such as when a restaurant advertises, 'order anything from our menu and we'll step on it!' (Chapter 5).[19]

FIGURE 1 It may be difficult to imagine lightning that looks like a drunken ballerina.

Of course, some people may notice contradictions that others miss, and some people are better than others at imagining unusual scenarios. This means that a metaphor that is mixed for one person may not be mixed for

PERFECT MIX OR PERFECT MESS?

someone else. Unintentional mixed metaphors occur when speakers and writers use metaphors that seem fine to them, but appear mixed to others.

Metaphors that are considered mixed in this book may not be mixed for all people all the time, but all have either been called mixed by at least one critic or else share properties with metaphors that have received this criticism. Occasionally, critics identify 'mixed metaphors' that do not belong to the types in the above list. Some of these cases will be mentioned in the text. However, in this book, the term *mixed metaphor* applies only to the above types and is applicable whenever these metaphors are encountered by people who perceive them as contradictory, inconsistent, ambiguous, or hard to imagine.

Usually, speakers and writers want to avoid contradictions and ambiguities, so they often try to avoid mixed metaphors. Style guides offer tips in this regard, such as 'use only a single metaphor per paragraph'.[20] Unfortunately, advice like this would be nearly impossible to follow. Writing that followed this rule would not only sound stilted, but also be limited in the topics it could cover.

Instead of offering arbitrary rules or guidelines for metaphor use, then, the current book will describe how and why metaphors function. These explanations, informed by findings from linguistics, will make it possible to maximize the effective use of metaphors and idioms in any context, for any purpose, and in any genre of writing.

We'll see why, from a cognitive perspective, multiple metaphors are necessary and useful, and why it is counterproductive (and usually impossible) to follow the advice in writing guides, such as limiting yourself to a single metaphor per paragraph. We'll also see how traditional definitions of mixed metaphor in linguistics and psychology fail to capture the range of phenomena that are often criticized as mixed metaphors.

Linguistics and style

In general, linguists avoid taking a stance on mixed metaphors or other stylistic issues. Even in the field of stylistics, which is dedicated to applying linguistic concepts to the study of literature, linguistics scholars try to remain agnostic regarding the relative value of one stylistic choice over another. Linguists who work on stylistics describe writers' style choices and discuss the effects of these choices, but don't usually voice an opinion about what constitutes good or bad style. To most linguists, the idea of calling any language use 'bad' or 'good' is as absurd as a geologist saying that a particular rock is either 'bad' or 'good'. Like other scientists, linguists collect and analyse data without passing judgement on the data itself.

In linguistics, this non-judgemental approach is called *descriptivism*. Descriptivists are interested in objectively documenting and studying the language that speakers produce, and attach equal value to the speech of an illiterate child and the Queen of England. Linguists are wary of *prescriptivists*, that is, grammarians who tell speakers how to use their language and who designate one form as more 'correct' than another. From the perspective of mainstream descriptivist linguistics, a 'double negative', as in *I didn't do nothing*, is not wrong. Past participles such as *caughten* and *boughten* as in *I've caughten a cold* or *I've boughten all the ingredients* (as opposed to *I've caught a cold* or *I've bought all the ingredients*) are non-standard but not incorrect. In fact, these newer participle forms are more regular than the standard uses, in that they employ the regular participle suffix *-en* following the pattern set by most other English past participles. Descriptive linguists do not pass judgement on non-standard uses, so they are rarely grammar pedants or even punctuation enthusiasts.

Linguists have good reasons to be wary of prescriptivism. Considerations of style have probably held back the study of language more than they have advanced it. Throughout history, certain ways of speaking have been artificially privileged as 'better' than others. Until very recently, nobody studied dialects such as Cockney English, African American English, or Australian Aboriginal English because these dialects were considered 'bad English'. The stigma attached to these dialects was based on classism and racism, and had no linguistic basis whatsoever. From a linguistic standpoint, all dialects of English are equally interesting, equally regular in their grammar and pronunciation, and equally correct for speakers of that dialect. Modern linguists try to consider all dialects because every dialect has something to tell us about how human language works.

Similarly, all languages are equal from a linguistic standpoint. Every language has some areas that are simpler and some that are more complex. For example, a language with few restrictions on word order (syntax), such as Finnish, might have relatively complex rules of word formation (morphology). A language with simple rules of word formation, such as English, might have many grammatical restrictions. No languages are 'simple' or 'primitive'.

Indeed, the concept of language was apparently invented only once, around 80,000 years ago, so all present-day languages descend from one common ancestor language and all have had the same amount of time to develop.[21] Even constructed languages like Esperanto were based on languages that already existed, not invented from scratch by people who didn't speak any language. In this sense, no language is older than any other, and no language is more primitive than any other.

Finally, all languages and dialects are equal in that all can express the same concepts. When a language lacks a word for a concept, speakers of the language can still think about the concept and can still describe it using their language. For example, English lacks a single word for 'mother's sister' or 'father's sister'. Both of these concepts are called *aunt*. A second word must be added to *aunt* to distinguish between *paternal aunt* 'father's sister' and *maternal aunt* 'mother's sister'. Many languages have separate words for 'father's sister' and 'mother's sister'. In Hindi, for example, these concepts are *bua* and *mausii*, respectively. Even though English lacks distinct words for 'father's sister' and 'mother's sister', English speakers can still tell apart their Aunt Emily (their father's sister) and their Aunt Sue (their mother's sister). Speakers are aware of the difference between the aunts even though both are referred to by the same word *aunt*. The lack of a single word for a concept in a language does not mean that the concept is missing for speakers of the language.

It's fortunate that we can have thoughts for which we lack words. If human beings needed a specific word in order to think or talk about a concept, then corrupt leaders could limit people's vocabulary in order to control their thoughts, as in George Orwell's dystopian novel *1984*. In the fascist world of *1984*, the evil government Big Brother hires linguists to selectively destroy vocabulary, beginning with words for concepts like *democracy* and *freedom*, and eventually eradicating simple vocabulary such as *excellent* and *bad*, to create the thought-controlling language Newspeak. 'It is a beautiful thing, the destruction of words', says Syme, one of the linguists employed on this ominous task.

Unfortunately for Syme, Newspeak would never work. Without a word for 'democracy', speakers could still imagine the concept and describe it, even using the limited vocabulary of Newspeak. Speakers of the language would quickly invent or borrow new words. Within a generation, Newspeak would have a rich and complex vocabulary and all of Syme's work for Big Brother would be wasted.

Although all languages are equally expressive, individual humans are not necessarily equally adept at exploiting the possibilities of the languages that they speak. For example, some politicians are famous for their eloquence, while others are renowned for their confusing circumventions or odd-sounding metaphors. Whatever language or dialect you speak, you can use it effectively or poorly. In fact, since any language or dialect is suitable for expressing any thought, the poor or ineffectual use of one's native dialect might be considered evidence of muddy thinking. Any language is rich enough to convey a speaker's thoughts, but if those thoughts are themselves disorganized or simplistic, that, too, is likely to be communicated when language is used. It may be useful to distinguish between dialectal differences on the one hand and individual differences that correlate with particular (possibly unwanted) effects on the other hand. We can, perhaps, respect a friend's dialect when says he has 'boughten' a new camera and still criticize his lack of detail in describing the type of camera he bought.

Linguists' views on mixed metaphors

For hundreds of years, prescriptivist grammarians have condemned mixed metaphors as bad style. When linguists became interested in mixed metaphors, it was natural for them to disagree with the prescriptivists, simply because they'd been fighting prescriptivists for years. In this case, opposing prescriptivism meant that some linguists were inclined to argue that mixed metaphors were a good thing.

One of the earliest linguistics papers on mixed metaphor 'challenges the view of mixed metaphor as awkward language usage', arguing that it is both 'frequent and … hardly ever results in incoherent discourse'.[22] Subsequent linguistic studies have tended to agree. Mixed metaphors 'rarely pose problems to the listener', according to one author. 'Instead, they should be admired.'[23] Mixed metaphor 'offers testimony to the cognitive flexibility that is the hallmark of human intelligence and creativity', writes the editor of *Mixing Metaphor*, a recent collection of linguistic essays on mixed metaphor.[24] Other contributors to the volume describe 'the "problem" of mixed metaphor' as 'mostly an illusion',[25] or claim that at most, 'Mixing metaphor appears problematic from a normative and collective view on language use, not from a subjective point of the speaker.'[26] '"Mixing" … is a natural process of figurative meaning construction', writes another contributor.[27] Some linguists even object to the derogatory term 'mixed metaphor': 'The use of metaphor along with other metaphors and stylistic patterns is a natural discourse phenomenon', one linguist writes. 'That is why I view the traditional notion of "mixed metaphor" (and hence the term) as inappropriate.'[28]

Many linguists argue that mixed metaphors are natural, comprehensible, and creative. Indeed, most of the examples in this book support this view. The majority of the quotations included here are naturally occurring and are creative insofar as they are innovative uses of language that have never been used before by another human being. In addition, the intended meanings of the mixed metaphors are usually not difficult to figure out. From an academic perspective, these mixed metaphors could indeed be seen as evidence of the human creative and communicative potential.

On the other hand, most language users are neither academics nor linguists. Many people feel that unintended mixed metaphors reflect poorly on the speakers and writers who use them. For speakers and writers, making a good impression can be just as important, if not more important, than merely being understood. If you are attempting to give a political speech or write a novel, you will not be satisfied with simply communicating information. Politicians, novelists, and other professional users of language need to convey data, but they also strive to present that information in a way that is clear, amusing, sympathetic, inspiring, or otherwise effective at achieving a particular impression. If your hearers or readers are annoyed, bored, confused, or amused at your expense, you will probably not consider your speech a success even if the audience understood your intent, nor will you deem your novel a triumph just because readers managed to follow the plot. Unless there is a dramatic change in the public opinion of mixed metaphors, many speakers and writers cannot afford to ignore the negative effect these metaphors can have on their audiences.

Why, then, do mixed metaphors often seem clumsy, ignorant, or unprofessional? When are they useful, and when are they a problem? We can begin to find answers to these questions by comparing critics' and linguists' evaluations of metaphors called 'mixed'.

What's wrong with mixing metaphors?

Grammarians have ranted against the use of mixed metaphors since the 1700s. Even today, textbooks, writing manuals, guides to public speaking, and dictionaries decry mixed metaphors as 'ludicrous'.[29] Secondary school textbooks introduce metaphor with the caution: 'Warning! Don't mix metaphors',[30] and dictionaries define mixed metaphor as 'incongruous and ludicrous'.[31] Prescriptivists illustrate the horror of mixed metaphors with examples apparently of their own invention, such as *To succeed you must keep your nose to the grindstone and your head held high*[32] or *That loose cannon is a wet blanket*.[33] In every case, mixed metaphors are poorly defined but criticized as 'ludicrous' and 'illogical'.

Considering the prescriptivists' panic over mixed metaphors, linguists' defence of these structures is a brave departure from tradition. But are all mixed metaphors worth defending? Is the prescriptivists' terror totally unjustified? One possibility is that the prescriptivists' concerns are well motivated, but are not based on the sort of issues that linguists usually worry about. Linguists who defend mixed metaphors argue that they have a bad reputation due to 'a normative and collective view on language use', that is, due to prescriptivist biases.[34] Linguists love language variation because it creates more phenomena to study. If mixed metaphors occur naturally and don't result in incoherence, then from a linguist's perspective, they look like an asset rather than a problem.

Although most linguists aren't particularly bothered by mixed metaphors, it is nevertheless research in linguistics that helps explain why mixed metaphors might sometimes be an issue. First, mixed metaphors are associated with a lack of control. Linguists observe that metaphor combinations may be used intentionally to express a sense of helplessness, such as when medical patients describe health problems they can't control. UK linguist and metaphor researcher Jonathan Charteris-Black found that people experiencing chronic pain used mixed metaphors to convey the intensity of their pain.[35] For example, one patient described leg pain as *wearing burning barbed wire pantyhose*. Of course, barbed wire pantyhose doesn't exist. But far from being nonsense, the mixed metaphor functions perfectly to convey the uncontrollable horror of the chronic pain.

When patients talked about having control over their pain, they tended to reuse the same metaphor rather than mixing metaphors. For instance, one patient repeatedly used variations on the phrase *keeping the pain to a dull roar* to describe the careful prescription of medication for pain management. Charteris-Black offers the generalization that mixed metaphors 'typically occur when a strong opinion is being voiced and speakers' emotions inhibit clear and effective communication – though in some types of writing, such as dialogue, they may be used for poetic effect'.[36]

This 'poetic effect' can include descriptions of chaotic, out-of-control situations, as noted by English professor and stylistics researcher Andrew Goatly.[37] He cites a passage by D. H. Lawrence as an example, which reads in part as follows:

> And all the sky was teeming and tearing along, a vast disorder of flying shapes and darkness and ragged fumes of light and a great brown circling halo, then the terror of a moon running liquid-brilliant into the open for a moment, hurting the eyes before she plunged under cover of cloud again.[38]

Although this passage contains a host of metaphors, Goatly focuses on the expression *ragged fumes of light*, in which the 'light' is compared to both a ragged fabric and gaseous fumes. He also notes that the moon is described both as *liquid* and as diving *under cover* like an animal. Furthermore, the moon is referred to as *she*, which suggests that it is compared to a woman as well as an animal and a liquid. Why did Lawrence choose to mix these metaphors? And, why is the result dramatic rather than ridiculous? Goatly guesses 'that the disorder being described by Lawrence here is the very motivation for this metaphorical mixing – to mirror a rapid succession of physical impressions and their accompanying emotions.'[39]

It's not surprising that strings of mixed metaphors are particularly effective at expressing emotional experiences. In general, metaphors excel at describing the emotions.[40] For example, psychologist Lynn Fainsilber and computer scientist Andrew Ortony found that speakers used more metaphors when they were describing their feelings than when they were reporting their actions. They also found that more metaphors were used to describe intense emotions than mild emotions. If a greater number of metaphors indicates more intense emotions and mixed metaphors also suggest a lack of control, then it's no wonder that authors choose sequences of mixed metaphors to describe overwhelming emotional experiences.

Mixed metaphors, then, are ideal for communicating chaos, helplessness, and emotional unbalance. These applications of mixed metaphors suggest why they might be undesirable in contexts such as political speeches. Most political leaders want to show that they are in charge and have a coherent plan. Mixed metaphors instead give the impression of disordered thinking and emotional desperation, which are usually undesirable qualities in a politician. This may be one reason why politicians are so often criticized when they mix metaphors.

This criticism is undoubtedly also due to the fact that politicians give a lot of speeches, and reporters keep close records of everything they say, so any mixed metaphors will be noted. These metaphors are then likely to be repeated by political opponents, precisely because they give an impression of helplessness and desperation that is potentially damaging for politicians. This type of impression might not threaten the career of other professionals, such as plumbers or graphic designers, so these professionals' mixed metaphors generally draw less attention than those of politicians. Many of the mixed metaphors in this book are from politicians, simply because these are so often recorded and repeated.

How mixed metaphors can indicate ignorance

Mixed metaphors not only indicate helplessness, but also can suggest that a speaker is naïve, ignorant, or stupid. To understand this potential problem, consider how sports metaphors can be mixed by speakers who are unfamiliar with the relevant sports. 'Grammar girl' Mignon Fogarty discusses this issue in the following excerpt from her blog entry 'Mixed Metaphors':

> Sports metaphors tend to be popular and they're also easy to mix. For example, if you tried to motivate your co-workers by saying, 'It's our turn at bat, so let's make this touchdown for the company', you'd have mixed baseball and American football metaphors, and if you try to imagine the image that goes with the metaphor, you don't know whether to put your players on a baseball field or a football field.

A speaker who knows little about either baseball or American football might produce a mixed metaphor as in Fogarty's example, because the speaker doesn't understand how the two sports are played, nor which involves a turn at bat as opposed to a touchdown. An unmixed metaphoric sentence with baseball metaphors might read, *It's our turn at bat, so let's hit a homerun for the company*, whereas one about American football might run, *Our team's on offence, so let's make this touchdown for the company*. Each of these examples uses one metaphor throughout, without mixing. Either of these unmixed examples makes more sense than the combination of two metaphors in Fogarty's example.

A similar sports example is found in the newspaper headline *Step up to the plate and fish or cut bait*, which combines two metaphoric idioms and possibly shows a lack of familiarity with both baseball and fishing. Charles Schulz, the author of the classic comic 'Peanuts', has his character Lucy produce a diatribe of mixed sports metaphors:

> You, Charlie Brown, are a foul ball in the line drive of life! You're in the shadow of your own goal posts ... you are a miscue ... you are three putts on the eighteenth green ... you are a seven-ten split in the tenth frame ... a love set! You have dropped a rod and reel in the lake of life ... you are a missed free throw, a shanked nine iron and a called third strike!

The 'Charlie Brown' example was, of course, not produced naturally in unplanned speech. The author Schulz was presumably familiar with all of the referenced sports. Nevertheless, the passage shows how severely sports metaphors can be mixed and demonstrates that this mixing is associated with ignorance of the sports in question.

Although sports metaphors may be the most frequently repeated mixed metaphors, metaphors related to other specialized interests also mix easily. When this happens, it can usually be attributed to unfamiliarity with the relevant interest or hobby. For example, *I'm tired of being a pawn in your game of checkers* suggests ignorance of the fact that pawns are game pieces in chess, not checkers.[41] Replacing the word *checkers* with *chess* would result in a sentence with unmixed chess metaphors, but the speaker apparently doesn't know or care that the two games are different.

Science metaphors can be misused by those unfamiliar with the relevant scientific concepts. For example, a *Business Insider* article begins: *Stockton, California is one of many flash points of the housing bubble.* The author of this piece probably was unaware that a 'flash point' is the lowest temperature at which the vapours of a fluid will ignite. Bubbles cannot normally be set on fire at any temperature. In addition, since *flash point* refers metaphorically to the stage at which a crisis 'flares up', a metaphoric 'flash point' must be an event, and cannot be a city in California. All the potential problems with this mixed metaphor result from the author's ignorance regarding the scientific sense of *flash point*.

Other metaphors are mixed not out of ignorance, but because the speaker hasn't noticed that the literal meanings of the metaphors are incompatible. For instance, an MSNBC reporter criticized a Republican claim by calling it *awfully thin gruel for the right wing to hang their hats on*. Obviously, no one can hang a hat on gruel. It seems safe to assume that the reporter knew what gruel is, knew what a hat is, and would not attempt in real life to hang a hat on gruel. This mixed metaphor was not due to unfamiliarity with the relevant concepts, but rather to inattentiveness to the literal meanings of *gruel* and the idiom *to hang one's hat on something*.

The following passage by a US journalist is similar:

> The coattails of a successful favourite son can serve as a ladder to lift all with access into the perfumed White House atmosphere of perks and power.[42]

This author probably knew the literal meanings of *coattails* and *ladder*, and recognized that actual coattails would not make a very good ladder. Nevertheless, readers of this passage are likely to visualize a political candidate literally attempting to climb up coattails as if they were a ladder.

Unfortunately for the speakers who produced the 'gruel' and 'coattails' examples, mixed metaphors *can* be produced out of ignorance, so even an inattentive speaker who mixes metaphors may appear ignorant. We have no evidence besides common sense that the MSNBC reporter was not genuinely confused over whether a hat could be hung on gruel, for example. The 'gruel' and 'coattails' mixed metaphors therefore suggest that the authors don't know much about gruel and coattails. Indeed, both gruel and coattails are less frequent in everyday life than they were back when the relevant metaphors became popular. However, most English speakers know the difference between gruel and a hat rack, and between coattails and a ladder. If the authors of the above metaphors were indeed this ignorant about these concepts, then they would be unusually ill-informed. Unfortunately for the authors, then, their metaphors might give an impression of ignorance even if the metaphors were in fact due to lapses in attention, rather than genuine ignorance about coattails and gruel. In fact, mixed metaphors that arise from inattentiveness can make a speaker sound even worse than a genuinely ignorant speaker, because the speaker may seem ignorant about everyday objects such as coats and ladders, not just specialized topics like baseball or chess. A person may be forgiven for not knowing the rules of baseball, but won't be excused for thinking that gruel is a good place to hang a hat.

Another reason to be careful about mixing metaphors is that mixed metaphors are particularly likely to be noticed. When mixed metaphors are used intentionally to express helplessness or emotional crisis, they can be particularly moving and memorable. When they are produced by accident, they are likely to be remembered in less favourable ways. Professor of cognitive stylistics Anita Naciscione, a defender of mixed metaphor, notes that mixed metaphors inexorably draw the reader's attention. A mixed metaphor 'becomes the centre of interest: it is outside the reader's experience, as it has not been encountered before', she writes. 'It is a focal point, attracting attention and increasing emotional suspense.'[43]

Mixed metaphors can be powerful rhetorical devices for expressing complex concepts such as chronic pain or despair, but they can also be suggestive of incompetence and ignorance. The potential problem with mixed metaphors is not that they are incomprehensible. As numerous linguistics researchers have observed, mixed metaphors are generally easy to understand. However, defending mixed metaphors on the basis of their comprehensibility is fighting a straw man. When speakers and writers want to convey competence, control, or emotional stability, mixed metaphors can undermine these goals.

Notes

1   Edna Buchanan, *Cold Case Squad* (New York: Simon & Schuster, 2004), 77. Examples throughout the book have been adapted to conform to Oxford spelling and punctuation.
2   D. H. Lawrence, *Sons and Lovers* (New York: Dover Publications, 2002), 82.
3   George Lakoff and Mark Turner, *More than Cool Reason* (Chicago, IL: The University of Chicago Press, 1989). Andrew Goatly, *The Language of Metaphors* (London: Routledge, 1997). Carol Moder, 'It's Like Making a Soup: Metaphors and Similes in Spoken News Discourse', in *Language in the Context of Use: Discourse and Cognitive Approaches to Language*, ed. Andrea Tyler, Yiyoung Kim, and Mari Takada (Berlin: Mouton de Gruyter, 2008). Peter Stockwell, 'The Metaphorics of Literary Reading', *Liverpool Papers in Language and Discourse* 4 (1992): 52–80. Peter Stockwell, *Cognitive Poetics* (New York: Routledge, 2002). Karen Sullivan, *Frames and Constructions in Metaphoric Language* (Amsterdam and Philadelphia, PA: John Benjamins, 2013), 110–13.
4   Raymond W. Jr. Gibbs, *The Poetics of Mind: Figurative Thought, Language, and Understanding* (Cambridge: Cambridge University Press, 1994). Jonathan Charteris-Black, *Politicians and Rhetoric. The Persuasive Power*

of Metaphor (Basingstoke: Palgrave-Macmillan, 2011). Andreas Musolff, 'What Role Do Metaphors Play in Racial Prejudice? The Function of Antisemitic Imagery in Hitler's Mein Kampf', *Patterns of Prejudice* 41, no. 1 (2007): 21–43. Andreas Musolff, 'Dehumanizing Metaphors in UK Immigrant Debates in Press and Online Media', *Journal of Language of Aggression and Conflict* 3, no. 1 (2015): 41–56. Christian Burgers, Elly A. Konijn, and Gerard J. Steen, 'Figurative Framing: Shaping Public Discourse through Metaphor, Hyperbole, and Irony', *Communication Theory* 26, no. 4 (2016): 410–30, and many others.

5 Elena Semino, 'A Corpus-Based Study of "Mixed Metaphor" as a Metalinguistic Comment', in *Mixing Metaphor*, ed. Raymond W. Jr. Gibbs (Amsterdam and Philadelphia, PA: John Benjamins, 2016), 203–222.

6 George Lakoff and Mark Johnson, *Metaphors We Live By* (Chicago, IL: University of Chicago Press, 1980), 92. George Lakoff and Zoltán Kövecses, 'The Cognitive Model of Anger Inherent in American English', in *Cultural Models in Language and Thought*, ed. Dorothy Holland and Naomi Quinn (Cambridge: Cambridge University Press, 1987), 201. John Barnden, 'Communicating Flexibly with Metaphor: A Complex of Strengthening, Compounding and Unrealism', *Review of Cognitive Linguistics* 14, no. 2 (2016): 454. John Barnden, 'Mixed Metaphor: Its Depth, Its Breadth, and a Pretence-Based Approach', in *Mixing Metaphor*, 76. Zoltán Kövecses, 'A View of "Mixed Metaphor" within the Conceptual Metaphor Theory Framework', in *Mixing Metaphor*, 3. Lynne Cameron, 'Mixed Metaphors from a Discourse Dynamics Perspective: A Non-Issue?', in *Mixing Metaphor*, 17–18. Jonathan Charteris-Black, 'The "Dull Roar" and the "Burning Barbed Wire Pantyhose": Complex Metaphor in Accounts of Chronic Pain', in *Mixing Metaphor*, 156–58. Charles Forceville, 'Mixing in Pictorial and Multimodal Metaphors?', in *Mixing Metaphor*, 223.

7 For instance, Max Black 'More about Metaphor', in *Metaphor and Thought*, ed. Andrew Ortony (Cambridge: Cambridge University Press, 1993). The metaphoricity of examples in Lakoff and Johnson, *Metaphors We Live By*, is challenged by Gerard J. Steen and Raymond W. Jr. Gibbs, 'Introduction', in *Metaphor in Cognitive Linguistics*, ed. Raymond W. Jr. Gibbs and Gerard J. Steen (Amsterdam and Philadelphia, PA: John Benjamins 1999); and Cornelia Müller. 'Why Mixed Metaphors Make Sense'. In *Mixing Metaphor*, edited by Raymond W. Gibbs Jr, 31–56. Amsterdam and Philadelphia, PA: John Benjamins, 2016. Cornelia Müller, 'Why Mixed Metaphors Make Sense', in *Mixing Metaphor*.

8 Michael Kimmel, 'Why We Mix Metaphors (and Mix Them Well): Discourse Coherence, Conceptual Metaphor, and Beyond', *Journal of Pragmatics* 42 (2010): 97–115. Charles Denroche, *Metonymy and Language: A New Theory of Linguistic Processing* (New York: Routledge, 2015).

9 Stockwell, 'The Metaphorics of Literary Reading'. Peter Stockwell, *The Poetics of Science Fiction* (Harlow: Longman, 2000). Stockwell, *Cognitive Poetics*.

10 Robert Remini, *Henry Clay: Statesman for the Union* (New York/London: W. W. Norton & Company, 1991), 83, note 32.

11 As 'replacements' rather than 'compounding', according to Barnden, 'Communicating Flexibly with Metaphor', 442–73.

12 Cindy L. Griffin, *Invitation to Public Speaking* (Boston, MA: Wadsworth, Cengage Learning, 2008), 255.

13 Lakoff and Johnson, *Metaphors We Live By*, 92. Lakoff and Kövecses, 'The Cognitive Model of Anger Inherent in American English', 201. Barnden, 'Communicating Flexibly with Metaphor', 454. Barnden, 'Mixed Metaphor', 76. Kövecses, 'A View of "Mixed Metaphor" within the Conceptual Metaphor Theory Framework', 3. Cameron, 'Mixed Metaphors from a Discourse Dynamics Perspective: A Non-Issue?', 17–18. Charteris-Black, 'The "Dull Roar" and the "Burning Barbed Wire Pantyhose"', 156–58. Forceville, 'Mixing in Pictorial and Multimodal Metaphors?', 223. Douglas Hofstadter and David Moser, 'To Err Is Human; To Study Error-Making Is Cognitive Science', *Michigan Quarterly Review* 28, no. 2 (1989): 185–215.

14 Julia E. Lonergan, 'Understanding Mixed Metaphor and Conceptual Metaphor Theory' (PhD diss., University of California, Santa Cruz, 2009), vii. Julia E. Lonergan and Raymond W. Jr. Gibbs, 'Tackling Mixed Metaphors in Discourse: New Corpus and Psychological Evidence', in *Mixing Metaphor*. Kimmel, 'Why We Mix Metaphors (and Mix Them Well)', 98. Hofstadter and Moser, 'To Err Is Human', 189.

15 Kim Sengupta, 'Ahmadinejad Wields Axe to Cement His Position', *The Independent*, 14 December 2010. Available online: http://www.independent.co.uk/news/world/middle-east/ahmadinejad-wields-axe-to-cement-his-position-2159595.html (accessed 24 May 2017).

16 Semino, 'A Corpus-Based Study of "Mixed Metaphor"'.

17 Barnden 'Communicating Flexibly with Metaphor'.

18 Semino, 'A Corpus-Based Study of "Mixed Metaphor"'.

19 These non-metaphoric concepts consist of target domains and metonymic vehicles, which will be introduced in Chapters 2 and 5, respectively.

20 Laurie E. Rozakis, *The Complete Idiot's Guide to Grammar and Style* (New York: Penguin Group, 2003), 132.

21 Gilles Fauconnier and Mark Turner, 'The Origin of Language as a Product of the Evolution of Double-Scope Blending', *Behavioral and Brain Sciences* 31, no. 5 (2008): 520–21.

22 Kimmel, 'Why We Mix Metaphors (and Mix Them Well)', 97–8.

23 Denroche, *Metonymy and Language*, 22.

24 Raymond W. Jr. Gibbs, ed., *Mixing Metaphor*, ix.

25. Cameron 'Mixed Metaphors from a Discourse Dynamics Perspective', 29.
26. Müller, 'Why Mixed Metaphors Make Sense', 39.
27. Anita Naciscione, 'Extended Metaphor in the Web of Discourse', in *Mixing Metaphor*, 264.
28. Naciscione, 'Extended Metaphor in the Web of Discourse', 243.
29. Alan Horsfield, *Creative Writing Years 7–8* (Glebe, NSW: Pascal Press, 2004), 125. Laurie Rozakis, *The Complete Idiot's Guide to Grammar and Style* 132. Webster's New World Dictionary, *Webster's 2 New College Dictionary* (Boston, MA: Houghton Mifflin Co., 2005), 720.
30. Horsfield, *Creative Writing*, 125.
31. Webster's New World Dictionary, *Webster's 2 New College Dictionary*, 720.
32. Horsfield, *Creative Writing*, 125.
33. Rozakis, *The Complete Idiot's Guide to Grammar and style*, 132.
34. Müller, 'Why Mixed Metaphors Make Sense', 39.
35. Charteris-Black, 'The "Dull Roar" and the "Burning Barbed Wire Pantyhose"'.
36. Charteris-Black, 'The "Dull Roar" and the "Burning Barbed Wire Pantyhose"', 159.
37. Andrew Goatly, *The Language of Metaphors* (London: Routledge, 1997), 288.
38. D. H. Lawrence, 1915, *The Rainbow* (Harmondsworth, Middlesex: Penguin Books, 1949): 49.
39. Goatly, *The Language of Metaphors*, 189.
40. Andrew Ortony, 'Why Metaphors Are Necessary and Not Just Nice', *Educational Theory* 25 (1975): 45–53.
41. Russell D. Scott, 'Mixed Metaphors', *The Russler*, 2016. Available online: http://therussler.tripod.com/dtps/mixed_metaphors.html (accessed 11 December 2016), attributed to Vinnie Faducci.
42. *The New Yorker Magazine*, 'Block That Metaphor!', 16 October 2000, 246.
43. Naciscione, 'Extended Metaphor in the Web of Discourse', 261.

2 CONCEPTUAL METAPHOR THEORY

It's hard to find an example of writing or speech that's completely non-metaphoric. Any use of language that's more complex than 'stop' on a street sign will probably include at least a few metaphors. Metaphors abound in everyday conversation, newspapers, scientific articles, and almost every other spoken or written use of language. Conceptual metaphors are so natural that we think and speak metaphorically all the time without even being aware of it.

You don't have to be an expert writer or speaker to use metaphors. For example, *Baywatch* actress Pamela Anderson describes one of her many marriages using a string of metaphors:

I'm moving on … I feel like I'm finally free … I'm in love.

Here, Anderson metaphorically describes her life changes in terms of physically moving from one location to another. That is, she is metaphorically 'moving' from an oppressive place in her life to a state that is 'free' of constraints and where she is 'in' love.[1] The words *moving, free,* and *in* refer literally to physical motion but metaphorically describe life situations. Anderson's metaphors are not particularly original. All of us talk about our life experiences in terms of physical movement. As it turns out, the reason we do this is because we actually *think* about our lives this way.

The 1980 book *Metaphors We Live By* showed that examples like the Anderson quotation can be explained in terms of human cognition. According to this model, called Conceptual Metaphor Theory, metaphors are primarily ways of thinking, not ways of speaking. Since metaphoric language comes from metaphoric thought, the patterns in metaphoric language are clues to the conceptual metaphors underneath. For example, speakers talk about life experiences in terms of physical movement because there is a conceptual metaphor, called LIFE IS A JOURNEY, that allows life experiences to be understood and described as journey events.

The titles of specific conceptual metaphors like LIFE IS A JOURNEY are traditionally written in small caps to show that they designate concepts, rather than words. Metaphoric language that involves a conceptual metaphor such as LIFE IS A JOURNEY usually doesn't include the words in the metaphor's title, such as *life* or *journey*. When Anderson says she is *free*, *moving on*, and *in love*, all of these expressions involve LIFE IS A JOURNEY even though they don't use the words *life* or *journey*. Conceptual metaphors need some kind of title so that we can refer to them, but the words in these titles should never distract us from the conceptual structure of the metaphors that they describe. It can be a useful exercise to glance through the list of metaphor titles and examples in the appendix at the end of this book. The example sentences in each metaphor entry rarely include the words that are in the metaphor's title, such as *life* and *journey* for LIFE IS A JOURNEY. Although it is usually possible to use the title words in a sentence that involves the relevant metaphor, as in *Her life has been one hell of a journey*, in practice these examples are rare. A metaphor's title isn't usually a good indication of what the metaphor will look like when it appears in language.

Rather than connecting individual words such as *life* and *journey*, LIFE IS A JOURNEY and other conceptual metaphors establish systems of connections between general concepts like LIFE and JOURNEY.[2] When a word or phrase related to JOURNEY is used in an appropriate context, the connections between JOURNEY and LIFE allow the word or phrase to be understood as metaphorically applying to LIFE. For example, Anderson talks about herself as metaphorically 'moving on' with her JOURNEY, with the intended meaning that she is progressing with her LIFE. The expression *moving on* makes us think about motion, which brings up the concept JOURNEY.[3] We know from the context that Anderson is talking about her life decisions, so LIFE IS A JOURNEY allows us to understand that *moving on* metaphorically refers to LIFE and specifically indicates making progress with LIFE.

Because JOURNEY and LIFE are connected at a conceptual level, any words related to JOURNEY, such as *free* or *moving on*, can metaphorically refer to LIFE. Words that literally describe JOURNEYS are understood as metaphorically applying to LIFE when it's clear from the context that the words indicate life situations rather than the literal experience of moving through space. For instance, when Anderson says she is 'free' of her previous relationship, she means that the relationship was metaphorically an obstacle that kept her from 'moving on'. It's clear that Anderson didn't break 'free' from a trap or other physical obstacle. Instead, she became metaphorically 'free' from a situation she didn't like.

According to LIFE IS A JOURNEY, the situations that 'hold us back' and keep us from being 'free' in LIFE are metaphorically the obstacles that can block our progress on a JOURNEY and keep us from going where we want. This connection between LIFE and JOURNEY is apparent in many other English words and phrases, such as when we talk about life problems as physical obstacles that we can 'overcome', 'get through', or 'find a way around'. For example, we can 'overcome' an illness, 'get through' a divorce, or 'find a way around' a disagreement. This is just one of many correspondences between LIFE and JOURNEY, some of which are listed in the appendix under LIFE IS A JOURNEY. The first section of the appendix describes how to interpret these lists.

For the purposes of this book, we won't need to keep track of the specific correspondences between concepts such as LIFE and JOURNEY. As long as we're aware that metaphors take information from one domain and apply it to another, we should be able to recognize mixed metaphors and classify them into the types discussed in the previous section. However, it will be important to keep in mind that the two domains in a metaphor have different roles.

The domain that provides the information, such as JOURNEY in LIFE IS A JOURNEY, is called the *source* domain. The JOURNEY domain is the source of the real-world knowledge that we metaphorically use to understand LIFE, such as moving around and encountering obstacles. The domain that we're trying to understand, such as LIFE, is called the *target* domain. We take our knowledge about the source domain and apply it to the target domain. For example, we use our source-domain experience of getting past obstacles on a JOURNEY to understand the target-domain experience of resolving problems in LIFE, which is why we can say we've 'gotten over' the flu or 'worked around' a lack of materials.

Source domains like JOURNEY tend to be *concrete*, insofar as they can be perceived by the body and the senses.[4] Since source domains can be seen, touched, or otherwise directly experienced, we usually understand them well and know a lot about them. The JOURNEY domain, for example, is based on our physical experience of moving through space.[5] Everyday experiences of motion, such as walking to the shops, are physical journeys that teach us about motion and space. For example, they show us that obstacles can stop us or slow us down. They tell us that choosing the right path will help us reach a particular destination and even teach us that we can use a map to stay on a particular path. Simply by going about our daily business, we learn all the various components that make up a JOURNEY and we understand how they fit together.

Target domains like LIFE are usually more *abstract* than source domains. For example, LIFE cannot be physically seen or touched. As a result, LIFE may be more difficult to reason about than a more concrete domain such as JOURNEY. It may be easier to decide how to overcome a physical obstacle on a journey than how to resolve a difficulty in one's life. Metaphors such as LIFE IS A JOURNEY are useful because they help us reason about abstract concepts such as LIFE in terms of more concrete ones such as JOURNEY. If we think about a life difficulty (such as an illness) in terms of a physical obstacle on a journey (such as a mountain), we can use reasoning from JOURNEY to deal with LIFE. A mountain is difficult to climb, but if we keep going, we get past it, and then travel becomes easier again. If we think about an illness as a mountain, then we can reason that even though it may be 'tough going' for a while, we'll 'overcome it' and then life will be easier. Metaphoric reasoning of this kind carries over into our speech and writing, which is why Anderson is able to say that she is 'moving on' from a bad relationship.

There are hundreds, perhaps thousands, of conceptual metaphors that fit the pattern of LIFE IS A JOURNEY. Some of these are listed in the appendix.

Image metaphors

The first metaphors we acquire as children are not complex systems like LIFE IS A JOURNEY. Instead, these early metaphors are simple comparisons between how two things look, sound, or feel. A young child might notice that a cloud is shaped like a puppy or that a red apple is the same colour as a red crayon. Later in life, we might imagine that someone's eyes look like sapphires or say that loud snoring sounds like thunder. These metaphors, called *image metaphors*, compare two images, sounds, or other sensations.[6] They are often invented on the spot and used only once.[7] Because they don't occur repeatedly across an entire population of speakers, they aren't given individual names like LIFE IS A JOURNEY.

Non-image metaphors, such as LIFE IS A JOURNEY, are called *conceptual metaphors* to distinguish them from image metaphors like the ones in *her eyes are sapphires* or *his snoring was thunder*.

If metaphors like *her eyes are sapphires* sound poetic to you, you're absolutely right. Image metaphors are particularly frequent in poetry and literature, where they add originality and vividness to descriptions.[8] Many common misconceptions about metaphor, such as the notion that metaphors are literary ornaments, may have been based on observations of image metaphors. It's only in the past few decades that these two types of metaphor have been distinguished at all. Before this, any generalizations about one type were applied to both. Even today, most writing instructors and style guides use the word *metaphor* indiscriminately for both image metaphors and conceptual metaphors, which is misleading for writers who want to use either kind of metaphor effectively.

Historically, most of the false generalizations about metaphors have been founded on truths about image metaphors. As mentioned previously, prior to Conceptual Metaphor Theory, metaphors were considered poetic, decorative, individual, and unsystematic. All of these are qualities that describe image metaphors better than conceptual metaphors.

Image metaphors have probably had a disproportionate effect on opinions about metaphor because they are so noticeable and memorable. Conceptual metaphors, in contrast, are subtle and subconscious. When we use image metaphors, we often try to design one that's novel and interesting. When we use a conceptual metaphor, we usually don't even know that we're doing it. As a result, conceptual metaphors have, until recently, received less attention from researchers and critics, and have had relatively little influence on popular and critical views of metaphor overall.

Image metaphors also differ from conceptual metaphors in that they don't help us understand abstract concepts such as LIFE. Neither domain in an image metaphor is more abstract or concrete than the other. The source and target domains in these metaphors are always equally concrete because both are visual, like sapphires and eyes, or because both are sounds, like thunder and snoring. The image metaphor *her eyes are sapphires* may allow us to appreciate the value and beauty of someone's eyes, but it won't help us make LIFE decisions, or allow us to reason about abstractions such as time, ageing, or quantum physics. Similarly, an image metaphor that compares two sounds, such as *his snoring was thunder*, doesn't give us information that allows us to think about a difficult abstract concept. The sentence just means that the snoring was abnormally loud.

Most image metaphors are visual, so they work well in 'visual puns' such as the following cartoon. The computer mouse was named for its resemblance to a living mouse. That is, it was named on the basis of an image metaphor. The two types of 'mice' look similar and have the same name, so they can interact in scenarios such as the cartoon in Figure 2.

This scene is a type of visual *zeugma*, where the metaphoric and non-metaphoric senses of a word (such as *mouse*) are juxtaposed in a way that's so jarring it can be humorous. An example of zeugma in language would be *I have four mice – two computer mice and two pet mice*. Computer mice and living mice are so different that it sounds strange to group them together in one plural expression such as *four mice*. Zeugma is discussed in Chapter 5.

Image metaphors are often used together with other metaphors, which means that they have the potential to form mixed metaphors. They may combine with conceptual metaphors, as in *Her burning eyes and fiery hair set his heart alight*. Here, *burning eyes* involves an image metaphor that compares the eyes' brightness and intensity to that of fire, and *fiery hair* is another image metaphor comparing red hair and red flames. The expression *set his heart alight*, however, involves the conceptual metaphor PASSION IS HEAT. The expression sounds awkward because readers may try to interpret the metaphors together, rather than separately, and may imagine that the sparks from the eyes and hair set fire to someone's heart, possibly causing injury (Figure 3). Readers who interpret the sentence this way will probably consider it a mixed metaphor.

FIGURE 2 How many mice are in this picture?

FIGURE 3 Burning eyes and fiery hair can be hazardous.

Where do conceptual metaphors come from?

After image metaphors, the next metaphors we acquire as children are basic conceptual metaphors called *primary metaphors*.⁹ We learn these metaphors by experiencing the source and target domains at the same time. For example, we acquire the metaphor UNDERSTANDING IS SEEING, as in the metaphoric sentence *I see what you mean*, because we often see things and simultaneously understand something as a result. Every time we see the milk in the fridge we understand that it's there. When we watch a glass of milk fall off the table, we understand that it's fallen off the table. When we see milk moustaches on people's faces, we understand that they have been drinking milk. We learn about the world through vision. The domains of UNDERSTANDING and SEEING are connected in the real world, so it is natural to use SEEING when we need to think and talk about UNDERSTANDING.

All primary metaphors are based on real-world connections like the one between SEEING and UNDERSTANDING. As children, we learn dozens of other primary metaphors in much the same way as UNDERSTANDING IS SEEING, each of which is based on a different set of real-world overlaps between the source domain (e.g. SEEING) and the target domain (such as UNDERSTANDING). For instance, the metaphor QUANTITY IS VERTICALITY underlies expressions such as *stocks rose* or *funds are getting low*. Stocks and funds don't really go anywhere and don't literally rise or fall. Nonetheless, the metaphor QUANTITY IS VERTICALITY allows us to talk and think about changes in stock prices and other quantities that would be hard to reason about without the help of the metaphor. Like other primary metaphors, QUANTITY IS VERTICALITY comes from experiences in which the target domain (QUANTITY) is associated with the source domain (VERTICALITY). When we pour sugar into a heap, as we add more sugar, the heap gets higher. When we stack up books, more books make a higher pile. As we add water to a glass, the water level rises. In many real-world situations, height (VERTICALITY) increases along with quantity (QUANTITY). This connection forms the basis of the metaphor QUANTITY IS VERTICALITY. The concepts QUANTITY and VERTICALITY don't always occur together, but since they often do, we can think of QUANTITY in terms of VERTICALITY even when no literal VERTICALITY is involved, such as when colder temperatures are called 'falling' or increased prices are said to be 'rising'.

The connection between QUANTITY and VERTICALITY feels so real that it's easy to forget it's a metaphor. Sometimes when I'm teaching about metaphor, my students argue that stocks physically go up and down. They point out that graphs and charts of stocks show them 'moving up' and 'moving down'. Of course, these graphs are not evidence that stocks actually 'go' anywhere. They're created by humans using the metaphor QUANTITY IS VERTICALITY. They help prove the basic point of Conceptual Metaphor Theory, that metaphors are ways of thinking, not just ways of speaking. Even when we're reasoning without using language, such as when we're representing a concept visually in a graph, we tend to use the same conceptual metaphors that we use when talking.

Let's look at the origins of IMPORTANCE IS SIZE, which we'll see later in some mixed metaphors. This metaphor allows us to use expressions related to SIZE, such as *big* and *small*, to talk about IMPORTANCE, as in *he's a big man in the used car business* or *don't think small – think big!* Since IMPORTANCE IS SIZE is established in childhood like all primary metaphors, it's based on real-world correspondences that are especially relevant for children.[10] For kids, SIZE and IMPORTANCE are related in meaningful ways. To children, their adult caretakers are both big and important. Big animals are often more dangerous than small ones. A big piece of cake is more satisfying than a small one. Furthermore, visual perspective makes closer objects seem bigger, and closer objects are more likely to be important. These real-world correspondences eventually develop into the primary metaphor IMPORTANCE IS SIZE.

Another primary metaphor, AFFECTION IS WARMTH, also clearly has its basis in childhood experiences. This metaphor leads to expressions such as *warm welcome*. Children learn to associate AFFECTION with WARMTH through physical contact that indicates that they are cared for, such as when they are hugged by their parents or caretakers (Figure 4). This metaphor doesn't develop in every human language. However, like all primary metaphors, it does occur across unrelated languages. It can even occur among people who live in very hot climates, where warmth might not necessarily be considered something positive.[11]

Primary metaphors may be found everywhere in the world, across unrelated languages, because they are based on human experiences that we all share.[12] These fundamental metaphors seem to be part of what makes us human. When we consider how few features all languages have in common, it's impressive that primary metaphors show up in so many unrelated languages. The search for 'language universals' (i.e. attributes that all human languages share) has not been very successful. Supposed universals, for example that all languages have adjectives,[13] have turned out to be true only for well-known languages like English, not for less-studied languages elsewhere in the world.[14] It turns out that languages don't need adjectives when they use verbs or nouns instead, so that *the big dog* in English would be expressed more like *the dog (that's being) big* in a language that uses a verb to express large size or *the dog, the big (one)* in a language that uses a noun for this purpose. Nevertheless, it seems true that all languages have metaphors, and many have the same metaphors.

Often primary metaphors emerge from our physical experiences fully formed and ready to use. We don't necessarily need to add anything, or put multiple metaphors together, in order for the metaphors to be useful. For example, our real-world experiences offer us a lot of connections between UNDERSTANDING and SEEING that give us cognitive benefits without requiring any work or adaptation. To illustrate how real-world experiences can lead to multiple connections, imagine we're opening a

FIGURE 4 Parents are larger than children, which encourages kids to develop IMPORTANCE IS SIZE. Physical contact between parents and children leads to the metaphor AFFECTION IS WARMTH. Photograph by Bill Sullivan.

box to see what's inside. Let's say it's a kitten. When we open the box, we SEE the kitten and we UNDERSTAND there's a kitten (Figure 5). When the box was closed, we couldn't see the kitten and we didn't understand it was there. In this experience, every stage of UNDERSTANDING occurred at the same time as an equivalent stage in the process of SEEING. The two concepts were basically the same thing.

Other aspects of UNDERSTANDING and SEEING don't occur together in the real world, but are added on to the metaphor UNDERSTANDING IS SEEING anyway. For example, we metaphorically think about good ideas, interesting books, or smart people (all of which help us understand things) as lights (which help us see things). In cartoons, a light bulb represents an idea. University logos often depict books with rays of light coming out of them, to show how books can make people more knowledgeable. We

FIGURE 5 When we open the box and SEE the kitten, we UNDERSTAND that we'd better buy cat food, make a vet appointment, and think of something to tell the landlord.

can talk about a news report as 'shedding light on' a situation or describe a conversation as 'illuminating'. We refer to intelligent people as 'bright' or 'brilliant' and call less intelligent people 'dim'. Of course, books and conversations don't actually emit light, and neither do people. If they did, we could tell at a glance who was smart and who wasn't, which would be extremely useful. Unfortunately, this particular correspondence exists only in UNDERSTANDING IS SEEING and not in the real world. Some metaphoric connections come directly from experience, whereas others are added on later.

Let's look at one more example of how we build on to the structure of a primary metaphor. AFFECTION IS WARMTH is based on our real-life associations between increased AFFECTION and increased WARMTH. In general, hugs make us feel loved. However, the WARMTH scale is limited by the fact that human bodies produce heat, but cannot produce cold. Unless we have superpowers that allow us to freeze water and shoot ice bolts, we can't make people feel cold, no matter how little affection we feel for them. We can only warm them up by embracing or touching them. The part of AFFECTION IS WARMTH that allows us to describe unfriendliness as cold, as in *chilly attitude, icy glance*, or *cold personality*, has been added on to AFFECTION IS WARMTH to make it apply to more situations.

Compound metaphors

Although primary metaphors like AFFECTION IS WARMTH can be extended to make them more effective, the most important way we amplify the power of metaphors is by putting two or more metaphors together. When we combine two or more metaphors, the result is called a *compound metaphor*.[15] For example, English has the primary metaphor ANGER IS HEAT, which is based on the physical rise in body temperature that accompanies anger. ANGER IS HEAT underlies expressions such as *hot under the collar* 'angry' and *to stay cool* 'not get angry'. English also has the metaphor THE BODY IS A CONTAINER (FOR THE EMOTIONS), as in expressions such as *she was full of passion* or *he was brimming with delight*. The structures of these two metaphors fit together neatly. The source domains (HEAT and CONTAINER) are compatible because substances can be physically inside containers. The target domains

(ANGER and BODY) can also be combined, because human bodies can show signs of anger.

When the two metaphors are put together, a person's anger is metaphorically a hot liquid that's contained by the person's body, as part of the compound metaphor ANGER IS THE HEAT OF FLUID IN A CONTAINER. This compound metaphor allows us to think of anger as 'boiling inside' someone, causing a person to 'steam' or even making the person 'explode' with rage. The compound metaphor has a richer structure than any of the metaphors that it incorporates. The complex structure of ANGER IS THE HEAT OF FLUID IN A CONTAINER is apparent in the wide variety of phrases and sentences that use the compound metaphor, and can also be seen in the complexity of the metaphor's structure as listed in the appendix.

Unlike primary metaphors, compound metaphors are seldom the same across languages and cultures.[16] Even when compound metaphors are built entirely out of universal primary metaphors, they're unlikely to be universal themselves, because there are so many different ways that metaphors can be put together. Factors outside of language, such as culture and climate, can shape the compound metaphors in a particular society.[17] These differences become apparent when metaphoric words and phrases are translated into a language that doesn't have the relevant compound metaphor. The words and phrases then have to be replaced by ones that aren't metaphoric or ones that involve a different metaphor.[18] For example, the Japanese expression *harawata ga niekurikaeru* 'one's intestines are boiled' metaphorically means 'to be angry'. Even though Japanese has the primary metaphors ANGER IS HEAT and THE BODY IS A CONTAINER (FOR THE EMOTIONS), as in English, the metaphors don't combine in exactly the same way in the two languages. In Japanese, the anger is metaphorically 'contained' in the bowels, whereas in English the anger is 'inside' the head. The Japanese expression could potentially be translated with an English expression that describes anger as a fluid within the head, such as *flip one's lid, blow one's top*, or *have steam coming out one's ears*. However, a literal English translation of the Japanese expression doesn't make sense.[19]

In sum, all humans are given the same set of primary-metaphor building blocks, but different language and cultural groups put the blocks together in different ways. Some individuals even force the blocks together in ways that don't fit – which is the major reason we get mixed metaphors.

Dead metaphors

Some words once evoked metaphors, but now are no longer metaphoric for people who don't know their history. Words and expressions that used to evoke metaphor but no longer do so are called 'dead' metaphors.[20] For example, the English word *comprehend* comes from Latin *comprehendere* 'grasp'. The Latin origin of *comprehend* is still apparent in the meanings of related English words such as *apprehend* 'capture' and *prehensile* 'capable of grasping'. Despite the existence of words like these, few English speakers associate *comprehend* with physical grasping. Consequently, *comprehend* no longer involves the metaphor UNDERSTANDING IS GRASPING, and instead simply means 'understand'. The word *comprehend* is a dead metaphor.

Even though *comprehend* is a dead metaphor, the conceptual metaphor UNDERSTANDING IS GRASPING itself is far from dead. The conceptual metaphor is now conveyed by other words, such as *grasp* 'understand' or *get* 'understand', as in *she grasped the situation* or *he got the point*. The 'death' of a metaphor is the loss of a connection between a metaphor and a specific word, not the loss of the conceptual metaphor itself. 'Dead' metaphors are words and phrases that were previously metaphoric, not conceptual metaphors that have disappeared. Conceptual metaphors generally 'outlive' the specific words and expressions that involve them.

As another example of dead metaphor, consider the English word *broadcast* 'send information by radio or television'. This verb once meant to 'throw widely'. For example, a farmer could sow seeds by 'broadcasting' them into his field. This older meaning is still apparent insofar as *broadcast* contains *cast*, which still means 'throw', and *broad*, which still has the meaning 'wide'. The word *broadcast* obtained its modern meaning from COMMUNICATING IS OBJECT TRANSFER, which allows us to metaphorically think about communication to a large populace, such as by television or radio, in terms of the wide distribution of objects. Now the 'throw widely' meaning of *broadcast* is gone, and the word simply means 'send information by radio or television', without any need for COMMUNICATING IS OBJECT TRANSFER.

Dead metaphors are especially frequent in idiomatic phrases because these fixed expressions frequently preserve old words that are no longer in common usage. For example, the idiom *to be on tenterhooks* 'to experience painful suspense or impatience' includes the word *tenterhooks*, which is unfamiliar to most present-day English speakers. A tenter is a wooden framework for stretching newly milled cloth to dry. The cloth is attached to the tenter by tenterhooks. In medieval times, tenters were also used to hang up prisoners who were scheduled to be tortured. The physical agony of hanging from hooks, while dreading worse torture yet to come, metaphorically represented the mental agony of expecting a momentous event (THE MIND IS A BODY). Most present-day speakers understand *to be on tenterhooks* as meaning 'to experience painful suspense or impatience' without using the metaphor THE MIND IS A BODY. For these speakers, the metaphor in this idiom is dead.

Of course, the 'living/dead' nomenclature is itself a metaphor, in that it personifies metaphors as living beings that can 'live' and 'die'. Like all metaphors, this personification metaphor is helpful in some ways but imperfect in others. It is useful because it allows us to think about 'living' metaphors as having some of the traits of living beings. That is, 'living' metaphors can be thought of as active, having effects, and able to cause changes. The personification metaphor also lets us effortlessly reason that 'dead' metaphors will *not* have effects or instigate changes. Nonetheless, in other respects the metaphor misrepresents the actual situation, because metaphors can be partly dead and partly alive.

The linguist Cornelia Müller extended the personification metaphor by introducing the terms *sleeping* and *waking* to describe metaphors that are inactive but potentially active and those that are active but potentially inactive, respectively.[21] This distinction is important for mixed metaphors, which often result when a metaphor is dead (or sleeping) for a speaker but living (or awake) for a hearer. For instance, the verb *follow* metaphorically means 'understand' via THINKING IS MOVING. However, *follow* 'understand' seems to have been a dead metaphor for musician Devin Townsend when he said the following:

I understand very well why people wouldn't follow where I'm coming from.[22]

When Townsend made this comment, he wasn't thinking about the impossibility of following a place that someone has come from. He meant that people wouldn't understand where he was coming from (i.e. they wouldn't know about the past experiences that have informed his music, via LIFE IS A JOURNEY). Townsend probably was subconsciously aware of the LIFE IS A JOURNEY metaphor in the phrase *where I'm coming from*, but did not notice the incompatible metaphor THINKING IS MOVING in *follow* 'understand'. For some English speakers, the metaphor in *follow* 'understand' is alive, so these speakers may criticize examples such as Townsend's as 'mixed metaphors'.[23]

The living/dead status of metaphors is important for the study of mixed metaphor because the degree to which words represent living metaphors affects their ability to combine with other metaphoric language. Simply put, dead metaphors can't be mixed. This is apparent if we compare pairs of words that have similar meanings, but which involve dead and living metaphors. The dead metaphor *comprehend* has near-synonyms that are living instances of the metaphor UNDERSTANDING IS GRASPING, such as the words *grasp* or *get*. These living metaphors can seem mixed if there is ambiguity between the metaphoric and non-metaphoric senses, as in the following (invented) example: *Why is this eel so slippery? I can't grasp it!* If *grasp* is replaced with *comprehend*, the potential for confusion disappears, as in *Why is this eel so slippery? I can't comprehend it!* (Figure 6). Mixed metaphors of this type, in which there is ambiguity or conflict between the source- and target-domain content of a metaphor, are discussed in Chapter 5.

Living metaphors – but not dead ones – can be considered mixed when they combine with other metaphors that have related target domains, such as the living metaphor in the word *grasp* (UNDERSTANDING IS GRASPING) and in the word *chew* (UNDERSTANDING IS DIGESTING) in the following sentence: *David had to chew on that idea for a while before he could grasp it*. Here, it sounds like David had to spit out the chewed-up idea before he could grab it, which is not something humans normally do. The sentence sounds better with a dead metaphor: *David had to chew on that idea for a while before he could comprehend it*. Of course, it also works well with two instances of the same metaphor UNDERSTANDING IS DIGESTING: *David had to chew on that idea for a while before he could swallow it*, in which both *chew* and *swallow* relate to DIGESTING.

As metaphors die, or go to 'sleep' in Müller's terminology, they become more acceptable with incompatible metaphors. For example, the sense of the verb *see* meaning 'understand' has become so conventional that it doesn't usually evoke UNDERSTANDING IS SEEING. When it doesn't evoke this metaphor for a speaker, the speaker may well use it together with other metaphors that are technically incompatible, as in the following example overheard by a friend of mine:

We'll keep an ear to the ground and see what happens.[24]

FIGURE 6 Eels are hard to get your head around.

In this case, my friend considered the metaphor to be mixed because he noticed that you can't see with your ear. But for a listener who didn't notice that *see* 'understand' was metaphoric – that is, for whom the metaphor was dead or sleeping – the sentence would be fine. In a hundred years, perhaps *see* 'understand' will be thoroughly dead, and examples such as the above won't be mixed at all or will only be mixed for a few prescriptivists who happen to know the etymology of *see*.

Mixed metaphors with two source domains that don't make sense together, as in the 'chew ... grasp' example above, are the structures that most deserve the name 'mixed metaphors'. Unlike many of the structures that are given this name, they actually combine two distinct metaphors.[25]

Even though they are the 'best' mixed metaphors, in the sense that they are most deserving of this name, they give rise to some of the worst results in terms of confusing, awkward prose. The next two chapters show what makes these mixed metaphors the best of the worst.

Notes

1. Marla Lehner and Lesley Messer, 'Pamela Anderson and Kid Rock to Wed', *People Magazine*, 18 July 2006. Available online: http://people.com/celebrity/pam-anderson-kid-rock-to-wed (accessed 16 March 2018).
2. Lakoff and Johnson, *Metaphors We Live By*.
3. See Chapter 2 in Sullivan, *Frames and Constructions in Metaphoric Language* for a detailed explanation of this process.
4. Lakoff and Johnson, *Metaphors We Live By*. Alice Deignan, *Metaphor and Corpus Linguistics* (Amsterdam and Philadelphia, PA: John Benjamins, 2005).
5. Many metaphoric connections have a real-world basis; see Joseph E. Grady, 'Foundations of Meaning: Primary Metaphors and Primary Scenes' (PhD diss., Department of Linguistics, University of California, Berkeley, 1997). Joseph E. Grady and Chris Johnson, 'Converging Evidence for the Notions of Subscene and Primary Scene', in *Metaphor and Metonymy in Comparison and Contrast*, ed. René Dirven and Rolf Pörings (Berlin and New York: Mouton de Gruyter, 2002).
6. Lakoff and Turner, *More than Cool Reason*, 90.
7. George Lakoff, *Women, Fire and Dangerous Things* (Chicago, IL: University of Chicago Press, 1987), 219–21.
8. Sullivan, *Frames and Constructions in Metaphoric Language*. Elisabet El Refaie, 'Reconsidering "Image Metaphor" in the Light of Perceptual Simulation Theory', *Metaphor and Symbol* 30, no. 1 (2015): 63–76.
9. Grady, 'Foundations of Meaning'. Joseph E. Grady, 'Theories are Buildings Revisited', *Cognitive Linguistics* 8, no. 4 (1997): 267–90. Grady, 'The Conduit Metaphor Revisited: A Reassessment of Metaphors for Communication', in *Discourse and Cognition: Bridging the Gap*, ed. John-Pierre König (Stanford, CA: CSLI, 1998), 205–18. Joseph E. Grady, 'Primary Metaphors as Inputs to Conceptual Integration', *Journal of Pragmatics* 37 (2005): 1595–614. Grady and Johnson, 'Converging Evidence for the Notions of Subscene and Primary Scene'.
10. Grady and Johnson, 'Converging Evidence for the Notions of Subscene and Primary Scene'.

11 Maria Koptjevskaja-Tamm, ed. *The Linguistics of Temperature* (Amsterdam and Philadelphia, PA: John Benjamins, 2015).

12 Grady, 'Foundations of Meaning'. Joseph E. Grady, Sarah Taub, and Pamela Morgan, 'Primitive and Compound Metaphors', in *Conceptual Structure, Discourse, and Language*, ed. Adele E. Goldberg (Stanford: CSLI, 1996). George Lakoff and Mark Johnson, *Philosophy in the Flesh* (New York: Basic Books, 1999).

13 Steven Pinker and Paul Bloom, 'Natural Language and Natural Selection', *Behavioral and Brain Sciences* 13 (1990): 707–26.

14 Nicholas Enfield, 'Adjectives in Lao', in *Adjective Classes: A Cross-Linguistic Typology*, ed. R. M. W. Dixon and Alexandra Aikhenvald (Oxford: Oxford University Press, 2004). Nicholas Enfield, 'The Myth of Language Universals: Language Diversity and Its Importance for Cognitive Science', *Behavioral and Brain Sciences* 32 (2009): 429–92.

15 Grady, 'Foundations of Meaning'. Grady, 'Primary Metaphors as Inputs to Conceptual Integration', 1595–614. Grady et al., 'Primitive and Compound Metaphors'. Compound metaphors are also called *complex metaphors*, as in Lakoff and Johnson, *Philosophy in the Flesh*.

16 Ning Yu, 'Metaphor from Body and Culture', in *The Cambridge Handbook of Metaphor and Thought*, ed. Raymond W. Gibbs, Jr (New York: Cambridge University Press, 2008). Zoltán Kövecses, *Metaphor in Culture: Universality and Variation* (Cambridge: Cambridge University Press, 2005). Lakoff and Johnson, *Philosophy in the Flesh*.

17 Antonio Barcelona and Cristina Soriano, 'Metaphorical Conceptualization in English and Spanish', *European Journal of English Studies* 8 (2004): 295–307. Jonathan Charteris-Black, 'Speaking with Forked Tongue: A Comparative Study of Metaphor and Metonymy in English and Malay Phraseology', *Metaphor and Symbol* 18 (2003): 289–310. Alice Deignan, 'Metaphorical Expressions and Culture: An Indirect Link', *Metaphor and Symbol* 18 (2003): 255–71.

18 Raymond Van Den Broeck, 'The Limits of Translatability Exemplified by Metaphor Translation', *Poetics Today* 2, no. 4 (1981), 73–87. Peter Newmark, *Approaches to Translation* (Oxford: Pergamon Press, 1981). Gideon Toury, *Descriptive Translation Studies and Beyond* (Amsterdam and Philadelphia, PA: John Benjamins, 1995). Christina Schäffner, 'Metaphor and Translation: Some Implications of a Cognitive Approach', *Journal of Pragmatics* 36 (2004): 1253–269. Karen Sullivan and Elena Bandín, 'Censoring Metaphors in Translation: Shakespeare's *Hamlet* under Franco', *Cognitive Linguistics* 25, no. 2 (2014): 177–202.

19 For an impressive variety of metaphors for anger and other emotions, across a wide range of languages, see the following: Zoltán Kövecses, *Metaphor: A Practical Introduction* (Oxford: Oxford University Press, 2002).

Zoltán Kövecses, *Language, Mind and Culture* (Oxford: Oxford University Press, 2006).

20 Ivor Armstrong Richards, *The Philosophy of Rhetoric* (Oxford: Oxford University Press, 1965). Lakoff and Johnson, *Metaphors We Live By*. Cornelia Müller, *Metaphors Dead and Alive, Sleeping and Waking: A Dynamic View* (Chicago, IL/London: University of Chicago Press, 2008).

21 Müller, *Metaphors Dead and Alive*.

22 *Noisefull*, 'Devin Townsend', 19 October 2012. Available online: http://noisefull.com/interviews/devin-townsend (accessed 4 November 2017).

23 Scott, 'Mixed Metaphors'.

24 B. Godfrey Lee, Facebook post, 1 December 2013.

25 For simplicity, only 'parallel' metaphors occurring in sequence, rather than 'serial' metaphors in which one is embedded in the other will be discussed in this category of metaphor. See Mark G. Lee and John A. Barnden, 'Reasoning about Mixed Metaphors within an Implemented AI System', *Metaphor and Symbol* 16, no. 1 – 2 (2001), 29–42. More specifically, these metaphors will belong to the type Barnden terms 'same-target parallel compounding' in 'Communicating Flexibly with Metaphor', 453.

Further Reading on Conceptual Metaphor

Accessible readings recommended for non-specialist readers are designated by an image of a door:

▌Bergen, Benjamin. *Louder than Words: The New Science of How the Mind Makes Meaning*. New York: Basic Books, 2012.

▌Dancygier, Barbara and Eve Sweetser. *Figurative Language*. Cambridge: Cambridge University Press, 2014.

▌Feldman, Jerome A. *From Molecule to Metaphor: A Neural Theory of Language*. Cambridge, MA: MIT Press, 2006.

Jr. Gibbs, Raymond W. ed. *Mixing Metaphor*. Amsterdam and Philadelphia, PA: John Benjamins, 2016.

Grady, Joseph E. 'Theories are Buildings Revisited'. *Cognitive Linguistics* 8, no. 4 (1997): 267–90.

Grady, Joseph E. 'The Conduit Metaphor Revisited: A Reassessment of Metaphors for Communication'. In *Discourse and Cognition: Bridging the Gap*, edited by John-Pierre König, 205–18. Stanford, CA: CSLI, 1998.

Grady, Joseph E. and Chris Johnson. 'Converging Evidence for the Notions of Subscene and Primary Scene'. In *Metaphor and Metonymy in Comparison and Contrast*, edited by René Dirven and Rolf Pörings, 533–54. Berlin and New York: Mouton de Gruyter, 2002.

Grady, Joseph E., Sarah Taub, and Pamela Morgan. 'Primitive and Compound Metaphors'. In *Conceptual Structure, Discourse, and Language*, edited by Adele E. Goldberg, 177–87. Stanford, CA: CSLI, 1996.

Kimmel, Michael. 'Why We Mix Metaphors (and Mix Them Well): Discourse Coherence, Conceptual Metaphor, and Beyond'. *Journal of Pragmatics* 42 (2010): 97–115.

Kövecses, Zoltán. *Metaphor: A Practical Introduction*. Oxford: Oxford University Press, 2002.

Kövecses, Zoltán. *Language, Mind and Culture*. Oxford: Oxford University Press, 2006.

Lakoff, George and Mark Johnson. *Metaphors We Live By*. Chicago, IL: University of Chicago Press, 1980.

Lakoff, George and Mark Johnson. *Philosophy in the Flesh*. New York: Basic Books, 1999.

Müller, Cornelia. *Metaphors Dead and Alive, Sleeping and Waking: A Dynamic View*, Chicago, IL: University of Chicago Press, 2008.

3 THE MAIN REASONS METAPHORS MIX

If a company's boss sends a memo on Monday urging employees to 'buckle your seat belts!' and at a Friday meeting encourages everyone to 'grab the bull by the horns!', the employees won't be confused. On Monday, they'll understand that the boss wants them to get ready for a challenging time, and on Friday they'll recognize that the boss now wants them to directly take on the challenge. They won't try to put the two metaphors together and imagine driving around in a car trying to catch a bull. However, if the boss tells everyone, 'Fasten your seatbelts and grab that bull by the horns!' the employees won't know whether to think about driving or bullfighting, and might even imagine doing both at once.

Any two random metaphors, such as the 'seat belts' and 'bullfighting' examples, are unlikely to make sense if we try to understand them together. This usually isn't a problem. We can use one metaphor on Monday and another one on Friday and never worry about mixing. Incompatible metaphors only mix if we put them together and try to understand them as if they were a single, compound metaphor. What, then, incites us to combine metaphors rather than understanding them separately?

There are three major factors that seem to make us more likely to combine metaphors, and this chapter will consider each of these in turn. First, metaphors are more likely to combine if they're spoken one after the other, as in 'fasten your seatbelts and grab that bull by the horns!', or if they're close together in a text. Second, metaphors are also more likely to mix if they are more similar. That is, when metaphors involve related topics, readers will be more inclined to combine them. Finally, readers are more likely to put metaphors together if the metaphors are more alive or 'awake', in contrast to metaphors that are closer to death or more deeply 'asleep'.

Proximity

Can we avoid mixing just by keeping our metaphors far enough apart? Many analysts have suggested that mixed metaphors result only when two metaphors are close together in a text or spoken one right after the other. As mentioned, one writing guide suggested that we could avoid mixed metaphors by using only one metaphor per paragraph. In practice, this advice would be difficult or impossible to follow.[1] However, the writing guide seems to be correct that separating metaphors will prevent mixing. Linguists who study metaphor have claimed variously that mixed metaphors happen when metaphors are combined within a single clause,[2] when they occur within a short sentence,[3] or when they're within 'one relevant grammatical or discursive frame' (which in practice often also means a sentence).[4]

Linguist Elena Semino studied which metaphors were actually called 'mixed' by users or observers.[5] She found that 86 per cent of the metaphors that were criticized this way occurred within one sentence. Of these, approximately equal numbers occurred within one clause (40 per cent) and across clauses (46 per cent). It's apparently rare for metaphors to seem mixed when they occur in different sentences, which suggests that a little bit of distance will often keep incompatible metaphors from combining and clashing.

Incompatible metaphors do seem particularly obvious when they occur close together, such as within the same clause:

> What father would anoint his child with such a leaden armour of expectations?[6]

The mixing in this passage is probably due to the author's unfamiliarity with the concept of anointing. Indeed, anointing isn't frequent in most modern societies. When anointing does happen, oil is applied to the body, usually for ritual purposes such as consecration or designation for a sacred role. The reference to 'anointing' in this passage lets us think about a child who is chosen for a task as 'anointed' for the task. It should be noted that the 'anointing' in this example is not technically a metaphor, but is instead a closely related structure called GENERIC IS SPECIFIC, which is discussed in the appendix.[7] Although GENERIC IS SPECIFIC is not a metaphor, it behaves like a metaphor in its interactions with other structures, so mixed structures that include GENERIC IS SPECIFIC will here be considered mixed metaphors.

In the 'anointing' sentence, the GENERIC IS SPECIFIC structure in the first part of the sentence mixes with the LIFE IS A JOURNEY metaphor in the phrase about 'armour'. Whereas anointing someone assigns that person a sacred role, putting someone in heavy armour gives that person a continual burden. In this example, the heavy armour weighs down the child and makes it more difficult for him to progress (LIFE IS A JOURNEY). Both the 'anointing' and the 'armour' suggest that the father's expectations are severe and harsh.

Because GENERIC IS SPECIFIC and LIFE IS A JOURNEY are in close proximity in this example, many readers will try to imagine the 'anointing' and the 'armour' in a single scene. They might imagine that the father is somehow smearing leaden armour onto his child, for example. Since this is impossible, the passage can readily be considered a mixed metaphor. A sentence that consistently used the 'armour' metaphor, instead of two incompatible structures, would fix this potential problem. For example, there is no mixing in the sentence *What father would burden his child with such a leaden armour of expectations?*

A similar issue arises when a journalist describes the iPhone's trajectory to success as leaving *roadkill in its wake*.[8] Only water vehicles leave a wake and only land vehicles result in roadkill, so these special cases of LIFE IS A JOURNEY aren't compatible – unless we imagine carcasses being thrown off the back of a boat, for example. Because the references to *roadkill* and *wake* are both within the same clause, it's especially hard not to put the metaphors together.

The next passage combines the metaphoric idiom *funny bone* with two other metaphors within the same clause.

(She writes) at night when her inner funny bone is fully unleashed.[9]

The phrase *funny bone* means 'sense of humour' (THE MIND IS A BODY). In this example, the sense of humour is described as *inner* because it's not 'visible' all the time (UNDERSTANDING IS SEEING). Bones are literally inside the body, so *inner … bone* may seem redundant. There's nothing unusual about an 'inner bone' – that's where bones are supposed to be. But then the bone is *unleashed*, so it's set free to do as it likes (LIFE IS A JOURNEY). This is harder to imagine. Is the bone somehow alive and able to act on its own? Does the bone break through the person's skin? How was the 'leash' attached when the bone was inside the person? It's difficult to form a mental image of the situation, so readers are likely to perceive the example as mixed. The mixing might have been avoided if the phrase *funny bone* and the verb *unleashed* weren't in the same clause.

Unfortunately, keeping metaphors in separate clauses doesn't always prevent them from mixing. In Semino's study described above, 46 per cent of mixed metaphors occurred in different clauses, but within one sentence. That is, about half of the mixed metaphors in the study shared the pattern of the following example by US Republican radio personality Rush Limbaugh:

> I knew enough to realize that the alligators were in the swamp and it was time to circle the wagons.

The metaphors in this sentence occur in different clauses conjoined by *and*. Even though the metaphors are in separate clauses, critics seem to find the sentence a particularly egregious example of mixed metaphor. It appears, for example, in multiple Internet lists of mixed metaphors.[10]

It's not clear exactly which political issue is the target domain in the 'alligators' example, but it's likely that the 'alligators' are Democrats and the 'wagon train' is inhabited by Republicans. In the target domain (i.e. in the real world), Democrats do not dismember and eat their Republican opponents. As 'alligators', however, the Democrats physically 'attack' the Republicans instead of verbally challenging them. This is a special case of ARGUMENT IS PHYSICAL COMBAT, in which verbal disagreements by humans, such as Democrats, are conceptualized specifically as physical attacks by wild animals.

The Republicans' verbal strategies to rebut the Democrats' argumentation are then understood as 'circling their wagons'. In the early United States, colonists travelling west in wagon trains would arrange their covered wagons in a defensive circle in order to repel attackers. In the 'alligators' passage, Republicans are metaphorically the colonists and Democrats are the attackers (a version of ARGUMENT IS PHYSICAL COMBAT in which all participants are human).

Both the 'alligator' and 'wagon' metaphors are special cases of ARGUMENT IS PHYSICAL COMBAT, but the PHYSICAL COMBAT in the metaphors is of different types. Together, the metaphors are distracting. Covered wagons didn't move south into alligator country, and wagon trains weren't ever circled to fend off alligator attacks (Figure 7). A more consistent sentence might read, *I knew enough to realize that the bandits were planning an ambush and it was time to circle the wagons*, or,

FIGURE 7 Covered wagons on the Oregon Trail faced many dangers, but not alligators.

alternatively, *I knew enough to realize that the alligators were in the swamp and it was time to strengthen our fences.* Neither sentence has exactly the meaning of the original, but both avoid mixed metaphors.

The Limbaugh quotation shows that it's possible for metaphors to mix even if they're in different clauses. This is more likely if the metaphors are unusual, colourful, or otherwise memorable, as in the Limbaugh sentence, because hearers are more likely to remember the first metaphor when they encounter the second one. Metaphors that are separated by clause or sentence boundaries tend to mix only when this is encouraged by other factors. One of these factors is memorability, as in the 'alligators' example. However, the most effective factor for stimulating longer-distance mixing is similarity between the metaphors in question.

Similarity

When two jigsaw puzzle pieces are of the same colour, we're more likely to try to put them together. Likewise, when two metaphors seem related, we'll probably check to see if they fit. There are several ways in which two metaphors can resemble each other, and all of these seem to lead to mixing.

We've already seen mixes between related metaphors, such as *It's our turn to bat, so let's make this touchdown for the company*, in which the BASEBALL and AMERICAN FOOTBALL source domains both are special cases of the same SPORT domain. Readers will always be tempted to put together references to two related source domains, such as two team sports, even if they are contradictory.

This tendency is also apparent in the following example, in which Chicago security attorney Andrew Stoltmann gives his opinion of high-frequency stock traders.

> They're the barnacles on the wheels of progress, and I would like to see them eliminated.[11]

Both metaphors in *barnacles on the wheels of progress* are special cases of LIFE IS A JOURNEY that involve vehicles. The problem is that barnacles afflict water vehicles, whereas wheels are part of land vehicles. Because these vehicles are otherwise similar, but barnacles are specific to one and wheels to the other, the metaphors seem mixed.

The following metaphor, which was featured in 'Block That Metaphor!' in *The New Yorker*, describes the experience of entering a New York subway:

> The moment that you walk into the bowels of the armpit of the cesspool of crime, you immediately cringe.[12]

A filthy subway can metaphorically be an armpit, bowels, or a cesspool, but can't be all three at once. All three references involve image metaphors that compare the stench and perhaps the appearance of the subway to a stinky part of the body or other smelly location. However, these similarities practically guarantee that readers will try to put the metaphors together, and ensure that some readers will notice that bowels can't also be an armpit or a cesspool.

The metaphors in the 'bowels' passage illustrate another feature that seems to draw attention to the incompatibility of the metaphors. The metaphoric words in the sentence make it particularly obvious that the metaphors can't all be understood at once. The three words *bowels*, *armpit*, and *cesspool* all metaphorically describe the subway. These words metaphorically represent the same thing (the subway), but literally designate three different concepts (bowels, armpits, and cesspools). The difference between these concepts is what makes the metaphors mixed in the first place. Directly naming these incompatible concepts in the sentence, by using the words *bowels, armpit,* and *cesspool,* may make the mixing more obvious.

Mixed metaphors can be particularly apparent when metaphoric words name the clashing parts of the metaphors, such as *bowels, armpit,* and *cesspool* in the previous example. To see how this might work, compare the 'bowels' sentence with the 'touchdown' example discussed at the start of this chapter. In the 'touchdown' sentence, the problem is that the touchdown in AMERICAN FOOTBALL is treated as if it were the same thing as a home run in BASEBALL. Both metaphorically represent success in a BUSINESS COMPETITION. Yet *home run* doesn't appear in the sentence. We have to infer the possibility of a home run from *turn at bat*. If we don't fully complete this step, for example if we're not familiar with the sports in question, we might not be bothered by the potential mixed metaphor. A sentence such as *A home run against this company will be a real touchdown for us,* which directly presents a home run and a touchdown as the same thing, makes the incompatibility more apparent and is more obviously mixed.

It's rare for authors to draw attention to the parts of their metaphors that don't work, as in the 'bowels' example and the invented 'touchdown' example. Perhaps, the mixing in this kind of example is so obvious that authors notice it and avoid it. Compare the first sentence below, a quotation from the singer/actress Cher, with the second sentence, an invented example where the contradiction is more obvious. For most readers, the metaphors in the second sentence will seem more mixed than those in the first sentence.

> I've been up and down so many times that I feel as if I'm in a revolving door.

> I've been up and down in this elevator so many times that I feel as if I'm in a revolving door.

In the first example, Cher is presumably discussing her career and prestige as a singer and actress. She talks about the 'ups and downs' of her career (STATUS IS VERTICALITY) and her alternating progress 'forwards and backwards' as if in a revolving door (LIFE IS A JOURNEY). Of course, a revolving door can't move you up and down, so the metaphor is mixed. Still, the mixing may be more apparent in the second sentence because the elevator and the revolving door are presented as if they were the same conveyance carrying Cher along and determining her life's path.

The 'revolving door' quotation again shows how easily mixing can occur across clauses, particularly in the presence of other factors like similarity between the metaphors and the inclusion of words that make the mixing more obvious. As in Limbaugh's 'alligators' example, the two metaphors in the Cher quotation are found in different clauses, but this doesn't protect them from mixing.

In fact, similarity can encourage mixing not only between clauses, but even across sentence boundaries. This is apparent in the next example, which was spoken by Robert Taylor in his role as the host of *Death Valley Days*[13]:

> The future of the church depends on passing the torch to the next generation. Tonight's speaker is one who has taken hold of the baton.

Both sentences in this example describe church leadership as a physical object that is 'carried along' through time and 'passed on' to the next generation via LIFE IS A JOURNEY. In the first sentence, the object is a torch, and in the second, it has become a baton. As in the 'bowels' example, the sentence emphasizes the incompatible part of the metaphors, in this case by using the words *torch* and *baton* as if these words referred to the same object. The torch and baton metaphorically represent the same thing, church leadership, but naming the two objects makes the inconsistency between the metaphors even more noticeable.

Given that the 'torch' and 'baton' sentences involve extremely similar metaphors, an audience could reasonably expect the relevant details of the metaphor in the 'torch' sentence to be the same in the following sentence. The unexpected change to a 'baton' suggests that the speaker doesn't remember that his baton was a torch a second ago or doesn't know the difference between a torch and a baton. Either way he looks incompetent.

The conceptual metaphors in the following example are not as closely related, but both involve trains, which is enough to convince most readers to try to put the metaphors together. The manager of the Florida Tomato Committee, Reggie Brown, reacts to a crisis in tomato farming with this statement:

We're not totally clueless. We've seen this train coming. We've tried every alternative and put every engine on the track, but none of them run.[14]

The second and third sentences both describe the crisis in terms of trains, but the metaphors in the sentences are otherwise different and conflicting. The second sentence in the passage represents the imminent crisis as a train hurtling towards the tomato farmers, which will cause damage when it arrives. Notice that in this metaphor the train is moving towards the farmers.

The third sentence presents trains as potential solutions, which the farmers are trying to get moving so that they can progress forward to a solution. In this metaphor, the trains are moving away from the farmers' position, probably with the farmers riding along. That is, the trains in the two sentences are moving in opposite directions.

The relevant metaphor in the sentence *We've seen this train coming* is TIME IS A MOVING OBJECT, which allows us to think about future events as objects that are moving towards us. In English speakers' version of TIME IS A MOVING OBJECT, events approach us from in front. That is, when the holidays are 'coming', we conceptualize them as approaching from in front of us, arriving, and then going away into the past behind our backs.

The third sentence in the passage, *We've .... put every engine on the track*, presents time in a different and contradictory way via LIFE IS A JOURNEY. In LIFE IS A JOURNEY, we move forward into the future. That is, we're travelling on an outgoing train instead of watching an incoming train. In fact, TIME IS A MOVING OBJECT and LIFE IS A JOURNEY cannot be combined in English.[15] If we try to put the metaphors together, for instance in order to understand the 'trains' example, the result makes little sense. In this quotation, the 'moving' event in TIME IS A MOVING OBJECT is specifically an approaching train. The tomato farmers are on a metaphorical JOURNEY and want to 'move forward' in their own trains. The two metaphors produce a scenario in which the inbound and outbound trains collide, resulting in a worse situation than if the tomato farmers had done nothing at all. Of course, Brown did not intend for his audience to interpret TIME IS A MOVING OBJECT and LIFE IS A JOURNEY together. Regardless, he includes 'trains' in both metaphors, which makes them look like they should fit together.

When two metaphors are less obviously similar, fewer readers will perceive them as mixed. For example, the metaphors in the following passage describe two different species of animal, and so are less likely to mix than two metaphors that are both about trains.

> The carrot was now far chunkier than the stick, and given the state of things at home ... He slipped with ease upon the hook.[16]

Here, the main character in the novel *The Unhappy Medium* is offered a better job and is urged on like a donkey by a carrot and a stick. Some animals can be encouraged forward by a combination of incentives (carrots) and threats (whipping with a stick). These methods can metaphorically lead a human in a particular direction via LIFE IS A JOURNEY. In the second sentence of the passage, the character is described as a fish that his new employer 'catches' on a 'hook' via a special case of ACHIEVING A PURPOSE IS ACQUIRING A DESIRED OBJECT, in which hiring the character is understood as catching a fish. Many readers will not put these two metaphors together because they involve donkeys and fish, which are very different types of animals. The unlucky readers who do combine the metaphors will imagine some kind of scenario that includes a carrot and a hook (Figure 8).

Readers may or may not mix two metaphors about different kinds of animals. Similarly, they may or may not mix metaphors involving two types of objects that can be put in the mouth:

> But Republican leaders weren't willing to bite that bullet. What they came up with instead was a dog's breakfast ...[17]

Instead of biting a bullet (undertaking a brave, necessary act via an idiom involving GENERIC IS SPECIFIC), Republicans apparently cooked up a dog's breakfast (IDEAS ARE FOOD). This 'breakfast' sounds scarcely more appetizing than a bullet. However, when we 'bite a bullet' we don't usually eat it, whereas we do usually expect a breakfast to be edible, so the two metaphors are not as similar as they could be. Readers will only put the metaphors together if they compare biting a bullet and biting into one's breakfast, which some readers may not do.

Any type of similarity in two metaphors or in their presentation seems to encourage readers to combine the metaphors, whereas dissimilarities seem to discourage this process. For comparison, let's consider an example with none of the similarities found in the earlier metaphors, and which also presents its metaphors in two separate sentences. The metaphor can

FIGURE 8 Carrots don't make good bait.

still be read as mixed, but the mixing is less obvious because it lacks the proximity and similarity of any of the previously presented metaphors.

> We're like the canary down the mine. We're the first people who pick up what's going on out there and what we're seeing at the moment is a boiling pot whose lid is coming off.

In this example, the representative of a UK Citizens Advice Bureau is describing his group's awareness of the effects of government funding cuts. In the first sentence, he compares his bureau's foresight regarding the dangers of the cuts with a canary's ability to recognize the dangerous lack of oxygen in a mine, which it signals by dying. The 'boiling pot' in the second sentence is the budgetary issue which is 'heating up' and about to 'boil over' and make a mess. If we try to fit these metaphors together, we end up imagining a canary that finds a boiling pot in the depths of a mine. This would be bizarre (Figure 9). But many readers won't bother to combine the 'canary' and 'boiling pot' metaphors because they are so different and are separated by several clauses and a sentence boundary.

If the two metaphors were in the same sentence, as in the following, the potential for mixing would be greater:

We're like the canary down the mine, seeing a boiling pot whose lid is coming off.

Because the metaphors have so little in common and they're separated by a sentence boundary, many readers won't feel inclined to try to force them together. More stringent critics could nevertheless call the metaphors 'mixed'. Indeed, they have done so, since the above quotation comes from a list of mixed metaphors published in a UK newspaper.[18] Nevertheless, the example is arguably on the milder end of the spectrum of mixing.

FIGURE 9 Most canaries don't care if a pot boils over.

Sleeping and waking

Dead metaphors don't mix. As we saw, the word *comprehend* once meant 'grasp' via UNDERSTANDING IS GRASPING, but now is a dead metaphor for almost all English speakers. It is therefore safe to use the word *comprehend* together with any metaphors, even those that clash with UNDERSTANDING IS GRASPING, without mixing metaphors (Figure 10). For most speakers, *comprehend* simply means 'understand'. This metaphor isn't just sleeping – it's totally defunct.

Although almost nothing can awaken a metaphor like *comprehend* 'understand', many sleeping metaphoric words and phrases wake up when the conditions are right. For example, when the verb *see* 'understand', as in *I see what you mean*, is asleep, the speaker doesn't think about vision or the metaphor UNDERSTANDING IS SEEING. Words and phrases that are deeply asleep aren't understood as metaphors. However, *see* 'understand' can wake up when it occurs with other words related to UNDERSTANDING IS SEEING, as in *You tried to cover up your plan with lies, but everybody could see what you were hiding*, in which the words *cover up* and *hiding* evoke UNDERSTANDING IS SEEING. In this context, the verb *see* 'understand' may awaken and be understood via UNDERSTANDING IS SEEING like the other metaphoric words in the sentence. Readers of the 'cover up' sentence are more likely to think about the visual meaning of *see* than readers of *I see what you mean*, in which no other words help readers think of the relevant metaphor.

Similarly, the sense of *hard* meaning 'difficult' historically involved the metaphor DIFFICULTY IS HARDNESS, but now is often understood non-metaphorically. Nonetheless, in a sentence like *That task was so hard I couldn't make a dent in it*, the metaphor is likely to wake up because physical hardness keeps surfaces from denting via DIFFICULTY IS HARDNESS.

Again, in modern English the sense of *stop* meaning 'prevent' doesn't always evoke LIFE IS A JOURNEY, but in a context such as *I had to stop him from throwing himself over an emotional cliff*, the reference to 'motion off

☠ Dead metaphors don't mix. ☠

FIGURE 10 If I had a car, this would be my bumper sticker.

a cliff' revitalizes the metaphor and causes *stop* to be associated with both stopping motion (as in a JOURNEY) and preventing an action (in LIFE).

Other factors besides context help determine whether a metaphor is asleep or awake. Some speakers may be better at spotting metaphors than others. Some may know more about the history of a word or phrase, including whether it arose via metaphor. Even speakers' recent experiences can cause them to experience a metaphor as asleep or awake. We don't yet know all the factors that cause sleeping metaphoric words and phrases to awaken.[19]

The fact that metaphors can sleep and wake is both bad news and good news for speakers and writers who want to avoid mixed metaphors. The bad news is that when a metaphoric word or phrase is sleeping for us, we probably won't notice if we use the word or phrase in ways that are inconsistent with its source-domain meaning. A writer or speaker who thinks of *see* as simply meaning 'understand' won't notice the potential mixing in a sentence such as *We'll keep an ear to the ground and see what happens.* For someone else who reads or hears this sentence, the metaphor UNDERSTANDING IS SEEING might be awake. This person will notice that you can't 'see' with your 'ears' and will probably think that the metaphor is mixed.

The good news is that it's probably safe to use words and phrases that were formerly metaphoric but which now are unlikely to awaken. Novel, original metaphors will always be more active than well-established ones. For example, the mixing in the 'alligators in the swamp' quotation stands out because the metaphors are unusual and are expressed in an original way. This makes them noticeable and active. Novel or unusual metaphors are the most 'alive', in that they never sleep and will always mix if they are in close proximity to incompatible metaphors. Deeply asleep or dead metaphors will not have these properties.

Sleeping metaphors such as *see* 'understand' are not entirely dead, but are still far less likely to mix than 'waking' metaphors. Other words that are usually sleeping metaphors include *way* 'method', as in *This is the way to cook quinoa* or *You're doing it the wrong way!*, which once involved LIFE IS A JOURNEY. Another example is *get* 'understand', as in *I get it now*, from UNDERSTANDING IS GRASPING. Similarly, *obscure* 'esoteric', as in *That's an obscure reference*, which evolved via UNDERSTANDING IS SEEING, is usually a sleeping metaphor.

Words such as *way* and *get* have been used so often with their extended meanings that we may be able to access these meanings without thinking about the underlying conceptual metaphors. Since we can understand *way* 'method' without LIFE IS A JOURNEY, for example, we're unlikely to activate LIFE IS A JOURNEY when we hear *way* 'method', and we therefore won't be able to combine LIFE IS A JOURNEY with any other metaphors that happen to be around. Most of the time, *way* 'method' is sleeping so deeply it might as well be non-metaphoric.

We can get a sense for whether metaphoric words are sleeping or dead just by looking at the entries in a dictionary. Any word for which the target-domain meaning is listed first in the dictionary is likely to be dead or sleeping. For example, the first meaning listed for *way* in most English dictionaries is the metaphoric meaning 'manner, mode, or fashion', rather than the source-domain meaning 'route'. Words such as *way* are not likely to awaken and unlikely to mix, because they are too near death.

In sum, it seems that we can avoid mixed metaphors by keeping incompatible metaphors separate, by choosing metaphors that are as different as we can make them, and by selecting dead or sleeping metaphors if this is an option. On the other hand, if we want to write glaringly obvious mixed metaphors, we're likely to achieve this if we put metaphors in the same sentence, choose metaphors that are similar, and use novel, living metaphors that readers will be sure to notice.

There are several other ways to draw attention to mixed metaphors. Let's look now at some of the more unusual factors that encourage metaphors to combine.

Notes

1   Gerard J. Steen, *Finding Metaphor in Grammar and Usage* (Amsterdam and Philadelphia, PA: John Benjamins, 2007). Gerard J. Steen, *A Method for Linguistic Metaphor Identification from MIP to MIPVU* (Amsterdam and Philadelphia, PA: John Benjamins, 2010).
2   Kimmel, 'Why We Mix Metaphors (and Mix Them Well)', 110.
3   Barnden 'Mixed Metaphor', 102. Hofstadter and Moser, 'To Err Is Human', 189.
4   Steen 2016, 115.
5   Semino, 'A Corpus-Based Study of "Mixed Metaphor"', 216.
6   Melvyn Bragg, *The Maid of Buttermere* (London: Hodder and Stoughton, 1987).

7   Karen Sullivan and Eve Sweetser, 'Is "Generic Is Specific" a Metaphor?', in *Meaning, Form and Body*, ed. Fey Parrill, Vera Tobin, and Mark Turner (Stanford, CA: CSLI, 2009).

8   Michael Liedtke, 'Apple Proved a Phone Can Change the World in 10 Years', *The Register-Guard*, 10 January 2017.

9   South Coast Writers Conference 2016, 4.

10 Jim Carlton, 'My Favorite Mixed Metaphors', *Jim Carlton.comedy*, 2016. Available online: http://www.jimcarlton.com/my_favorite_mixed _metaphors.htm (accessed 11 December 2016). Scott, 'Mixed Metaphors'.

11 Jeff Cox, 'This Is the Worst Thing about Fake-Tweet Stock Dive', *CNBC*, 24 April 2013. Available online: www.cnbc.com/id/100669021 (accessed 31 August 2016).

12 *The New Yorker Magazine*, 'Block That Metaphor!', 27 March 2000, 118.

13 Forceville, 'Mixing in Pictorial and Multimodal Metaphors?', 225–26.

14 Rita Beamish, 'US Drags Its Feet in Phasing Out Banned Pesticide'. *The Seattle Times*, 28 November 2005. Available online: http://www.seattletimes.com/nation-world/us-drags-its-feet-in-phasing-out-banned-pesticide/ (accessed 12 December 2016).

15 Kevin E. Moore, 'Frames and the Experiential Basis of the Moving Time Metaphor', *Constructions and Frames* 24 (2011): 80–103.

16 T. J. Brown, *The Unhappy Medium,* Kindle edition, 2014, Loc. 650.

17 Paul Krugman, 'GOP Health Care Plan a Half-Baked Disaster', *The Register-Guard*, 12 March 2017.

18 John Rentoul, 'The Top Ten: Mixed metaphors', *The Independent*, 16 March 2014. Available online: http://www.independent.co.uk/arts-entertainment /books/features/the-top-ten-mixed-metaphors-9191302.html (accessed 4 October 2016).

19 Additional factors are discussed in Müller, *Metaphors Dead and Alive.*

4 MORE EXOTIC MIXES

Metaphors can be made to mix even if they're different, far apart, and near death. That is, they can combine and mix even if they lack all of the factors discussed in the previous chapter. When these factors are missing, though, other conditions have to be right. For example, metaphors can be encouraged to mix if they're repeated often enough or if they're put in the context of many other metaphors.

Two metaphors are more likely to mix if the combination is repeated a second time, as in the following sentence.

> While we are ingesting the author's valuable insights, we may also be swallowing his blind spots.[1]

The word *insight* isn't used to refer to visual sight anymore, so it's a dead or sleeping metaphor for many speakers. The clause *While we are ingesting the author's valuable insights* therefore might not come across as mixed if it occurred on its own. However, as we've seen, dying or sleeping metaphors can be awakened by other uses of the same metaphor. The reference to *blind spots* in the next clause is likely to awaken the UNDERSTANDING IS SEEING metaphor that underlies the meaning of *insights*. If the metaphor awakens, this results in two consecutive clauses in which UNDERSTANDING IS SEEING interacts with UNDERSTANDING IS DIGESTING (evoked by *ingesting* and *swallowing,* respectively). Of course, neither 'blind spots' nor 'insights' can be literally eaten, so the metaphors in both clauses will mix if they're combined. Here, this is a problem, because the two repeated metaphors make readers more likely to combine the incompatible metaphors and notice that they're mixed.

In general, an increased number of metaphors makes nearby metaphors more apparent. When readers have recently encountered several metaphors, they will be on the lookout for new ones. This effect is strongest when the same conceptual metaphor is repeated, as in the 'ingesting … insights' example. However, the addition of any new metaphor seems to draw attention to other metaphors and encourage the metaphors to combine. The odds of incompatibilities between the metaphors increase with each additional metaphor, as the following example illustrates.

> Out of the hat on Monday night the Home Secretary produced the rabbit, the temporary provisions Bill, as her fig leaf to cover her major U-turn.[2]

Covering one's nudity with a rabbit is already strange (Figure 11). But then we learn that the rabbit is covering not private parts, but a 'major U-turn'. The revelation of the 'U-turn' is metaphorically understood as the sudden emergence of a rabbit via a special case of UNDERSTANDING IS SEEING. The distraction from the embarrassing 'U-turn' is metaphorically represented as a fig leaf covering nudity, via a second special case of UNDERSTANDING IS SEEING that is incompatible with the first one. We can tell that these special cases are incompatible, because when we try to combine them, the provisions bill is a rabbit in one metaphor but a fig leaf in the other. Finally, the Home Secretary's complete change of plan is understood as a U-turn via LIFE IS A JOURNEY. Neither a fig leaf nor a rabbit can cover a U-turn, so this is another inconsistency in the metaphor combination. Any two of these metaphors would probably mix, but the combination of three is certain to be noticed. The repeated mixing suggests that the speaker is either out of control emotionally or unusually ignorant about rabbits, U-turns, and nudity.

Sometimes, when writers and speakers simply use a lot of metaphors, these are criticized as mixed. Sequences of metaphors may attract this critique even if no two of the metaphors on their own would probably be labelled as mixed. The following passage, for example, was reprinted in *The New Yorker*'s mixed metaphor column 'Block That Metaphor!'

> It distracts from the goal, and the goal is so big – we're hunting elephants with a BB gun. If we don't all get behind fixing the hole in the hull, we're all going down. And that team spirit isn't there.[3]

The 'goal' in the first two clauses is apparently a sports reference, which is followed by a hunting metaphor, then one about ships, followed by

FIGURE 11 A rabbit is not a good substitute for a fig leaf.

another sports metaphor. The phrase *get behind fixing the hole in the hull* can be readily criticized as mixed, since a hull breach isn't the kind of problem that can be fixed by 'getting behind it' (ASSISTANCE IS SUPPORT). Otherwise, the metaphors are fairly distinct and are presented individually in separate sentences. Since the metaphors are so different and are divided by sentence boundaries, most readers wouldn't try to put them together if there weren't so many. The sheer number of different metaphors makes readers more likely to notice them, try to combine them, and recognize them as mixed.

The metaphors in the following example also seem to have received attention mostly for their sheer quantity. In this 2016 quotation, US presidential candidate Hillary Clinton criticizes her opponent Donald Trump's slogan 'Make America Great Again'.

> America never stopped being great. We have to make America whole. We have to fill in what's been hollowed out. We have to make strong the broken places, restitch the bonds of trust and respect.

The metaphors in this passage were too much for newspaper columnist Dana Milbank, who wrote, 'Filling holes, stitching bonds, breaking barriers: Is this an election or a public works project?'[4] Indeed, in Clinton's long sequence of metaphors describing America as a broken object (THE NATION IS AN OBJECT), it's hard to tell what kind of object America could be. It's almost a riddle. What requires stitching, making whole, strengthening, and filling in, all at once? Some kind of mattress, perhaps? A porcelain doll with a cloth body? It's difficult to combine the metaphors in a satisfactory way. Nevertheless, the metaphors don't involve obvious conflicts like a rabbit that's also a fig leaf, so many readers might overlook their inconsistencies if they weren't confronted with such a large number of metaphors all at once. Clinton's metaphors might have escaped criticism if she'd stopped at two.

If any of the metaphors in a string do come across as mixed for the reasons noted above, readers are especially likely to notice any further mixing. For example, the following passage, which featured in the *New Yorker*'s 'Block That Metaphor!' column, starts off with an obvious mixed metaphor in the first sentence:

> The committee was tired of stoking public outrage with fortnightly gobbets of scandal. It decided to publish everything it had left, warts

and all. Now everyone is tarred with the same ugly brush, and the myth that forever simmers in the public consciousness – that the House shelters 435 parasitic, fat-cat deadbeats – has received another shot of adrenalin.[5]

Public outrage is first presented as a fire that can be 'stoked', then as an animal that can be fed 'gobbets' of meat. Both fuelling a fire and feeding an animal encourage the fire/animal to grow and become more dangerous, so both serve as appropriate source domains for making a bad situation worse. However, nothing can be both a fire and an animal, and few materials can serve both as fuel and as food, so the resultant metaphor is mixed. The metaphors in the next few clauses of the passage are relatively distinct and might not combine if any two of them occurred together on their own. But the metaphors just keep coming. Even readers who don't bother to combine all these metaphors may decide that they're mixed, just because there are so many. Since the first metaphors in the passage were clearly mixed, readers will be particularly inclined to expect additional mixed metaphors and will probably see the long sequence of metaphors as fulfilling this expectation.

The following description of the Trump Tower lobby builds a coherent, complicated compound metaphor, but since it begins with an incompatible metaphor the whole thing may come across as mixed:

> Outside this 1980s-chic aquarium, cable news has become a dog pack chasing the brightly coloured balls that Mr. Trump throws in every direction.[6]

Distracting the press can be metaphorically understood as throwing balls to dogs via a novel combination of LIFE IS A JOURNEY (i.e. the dogs run in random directions, so won't accomplish their goals) and ACHIEVING A PURPOSE IS OBTAINING A DESIRED OBJECT (the colourful balls seem like desirable objects, but are actually unimportant). This novel compound metaphor is wasted, however, because the initial description of the lobby as an aquarium (an image metaphor) has nothing to do with dogs and doesn't fit well with the novel metaphor. This flaw may make the whole passage come across as mixed.

In general, it's safe to assume that a long string of metaphors will contain some contradictions. Few authors are skilled enough to put together more than two or three metaphors without creating contradictions.

Consequently, when we see a lot of metaphors in one passage, the odds are good that some will be mixed. Unless metaphors have been intentionally designed to be compatible (see Chapter 7), any two random metaphors that are combined will usually mix. In the 'gobbets of scandal' example, for instance, we can't sensibly combine the metaphor about warts and the one about adrenalin, because the author didn't design these metaphors to be compatible. If we try to invent a non-mixed metaphor that includes these two concepts, we find that it's impossible to create any compound metaphor that involves both warts and adrenaline. Any two arbitrary concepts, such as warts and adrenaline, are unlikely to fit together in a meaningful way. As a result, most accidental metaphor combinations will be mixed.

A passage full of metaphors can be a literary triumph. More often, though, large numbers of diverse metaphors simply result in mixing.

Lengthy metaphors

When a passage is thick with metaphors, readers are more likely to notice them. Another context that increases readers' awareness of metaphor is when the same metaphor is extended over the course of a passage. In general, it's an excellent strategy to reuse the same metaphor multiple times because it lets the metaphor become more active in readers' minds and allows the writer to build up more detailed inferences about the target domain. Readers understand passages better and more quickly if the same metaphor is used repeatedly.[7] However, if the metaphor is badly designed or mixed, increased activation of the metaphor makes these glitches more apparent.

The following passage describes a plausible source domain that might be familiar to some readers. The passage asks us to imagine going to a bar, having some drinks, and flirting with someone we wouldn't normally be interested in. The 'bar' source domain is easy to visualize and is consistent throughout the passage. The problem here is that the two political candidates in the target domain have different roles in the source-domain bar scene. One candidate is represented as a flirtatious drunk, and the other is described as a cocktail.

> It's 2 a.m. The bar is closing. Republicans have had a series of strong and nasty Donald Trump cocktails. Suddenly Ted Cruz is beginning

to look kind of attractive. ... Well, Republicans, have your standards really fallen so low so fast? Are you really that desperate? ...

Back in the early evening, before the current panic set in, Republicans understood that Cruz would be a terrible general election candidate, at least as unelectable as Trump and maybe more so.[8]

In this passage, Trump's ideas are understood as nasty cocktails via IDEAS ARE FOOD. Republicans 'swallowed' these ideas, but this made them feel unwell and lowered their standards, much in the way that drinking alcohol can make you feel poorly and cause you to be more easily attracted to people.

Ted Cruz, in contrast, is metaphorically described as an individual who looks appealing only when you've had enough drinks. Cruz's attractiveness is understood as his electability via ALLIANCES ARE LOVE RELATIONSHIPS, in which a full alliance is metaphorically understood as sexual intercourse.

The target-domain meaning of the passage is clear. Republicans are annoyed with Trump and tempted to support Cruz, though he is not a good candidate. The source-domain structure also works, in that drinks can lower your standards. The domains just aren't connected in a consistent way. Normally, two candidates should be metaphorically described as either two drinks or two unattractive barflies, not one of each. The imperfection in the metaphor potentially makes the length and intricacy of the metaphoric passage work against itself. An extended metaphor should justify its length by continually improving our understanding of the target domain. Imperfect metaphors, on the other hand, are less objectionable if they're short.

The metaphor ALLIANCES ARE LOVE RELATIONSHIPS was popular in describing the 2016 US Republican primaries and frequently was extended in long passages. The next example was written two months after the previous one, by a different journalist, when Trump secured the Republican nomination:

A shotgun wedding between GOP leaders and Donald Trump took place Thursday. It was a small, private affair. The marriage has not actually been consummated yet; House Speaker Paul Ryan stopped short of endorsing Trump as the Republican Party's presidential nominee.[9]

This passage doesn't mix metaphors, insofar as it doesn't combine incompatible metaphors or create contradictions. However, it does extend ALLIANCES ARE LOVE RELATIONSHIPS in novel ways that won't work for some readers. It's typical in ALLIANCES ARE LOVE RELATIONSHIPS for an unconditional alliance to be understood as a sexual relationship. In this passage, though, since the nomination was quick and tentative, it is described as an unconsummated shotgun wedding. Apparently, an endorsement by the House Speaker would demonstrate a genuine unconditional commitment and would metaphorically be sexual intercourse, but this didn't happen. The wedding is furthermore described as 'a small, private affair' due to the lack of publicity for the nomination. In sum, the source domain is a specific type of wedding under highly specified conditions. It's not as strange as some of the source domains we've seen, such as covering nudity with a live rabbit. It still may seem unnecessarily specific.

Many people apparently enjoy inventing novel metaphors or adding onto established metaphors. Almost anyone can do this, but it seems that relatively few people can do it well. Poorly planned metaphoric passages often grow longer and longer as the author gropes around for something useful to say. The length of the passage then draws attention to any problems with the metaphor itself.

For example, one of my Facebook friends posted the novel combination of metaphors in Figure 12. The author creatively pieces together several metaphors to create a compound metaphor that represents friends as bras. Like the 'bar' and 'wedding' examples above, the passage is consistent insofar as it draws on one theme, bras, throughout, but is inconsistent in the way it relates the source domain to the target domain.

In the Facebook post, the paragraph about 'good friends' involves ASSISTANCE IS SUPPORT, UNDERSTANDING IS SEEING (according to which social impression is understood as physical appearance), and THE MIND IS A BODY (in which emotional distress is understood as physical harm). These fit together without contradictions and suggest that the relevant traits (being supportive, making you look good, and not hurting you) are metaphorically what you look for when choosing a good friend, just as they're literally what you look for when buying a bra.

The next paragraphs go downhill, metaphorically speaking. Based on the metaphors in the first paragraph, bad friends might be expected to be non-supportive, make you look bad, or hurt you. Instead, the paragraph uses EMOTIONAL INTIMACY IS PHYSICAL PROXIMITY to suggest that bad friends won't 'be there for you', in the way that a bad bra isn't around

 **(Anonymized)**

Thought for the day ...

A good friend is like a good bra – makes you look good and doesn't hurt you ☺

A bad friend is like a bad bra – they're not around when you need them ☹

But all friends are like all bras – if you don't look after them, they'll wear out!

FIGURE 12 A Facebook post describes friends as bras.

when you need it. This works in the target domain, in that bad friends are likely to neglect you when you need them, but it's not a good description of a bad bra. Usually, a 'bad' bra is one that fits poorly, not one you can't find.

Finally, the last paragraph describes friendships as objects that can wear out over time (via FRIENDSHIPS ARE FABRICS). This metaphor is a bit farfetched. Bras eventually wear out whether or not you look after them, and friendships can sometimes last a lifetime even without much work. In addition, when fabric is used frequently, it wears out quickly. Friendships, on the other hand, often become stronger when the friends spend a lot of time together. Author Dorothy Parker neatly points out these inconsistencies in FRIENDSHIPS ARE FABRICS:

> Constant use had not worn ragged the fabric of their friendship.[10]

In this quotation, Parker is not just showing off her awareness of how metaphors work. By pointing out this flaw in FRIENDSHIPS ARE FABRICS, she actually emphasizes the strength, duration, and intensity of the friendship in question. Unlike the author of the 'bra' meme, Parker recognizes the defect in the structure of FRIENDSHIPS ARE FABRICS. Whereas the meme author is hindered by the inconsistency in the metaphor, Parker manages to use it to her own advantage.

There are other ways to deal with the flaw in FRIENDSHIPS ARE FABRICS. For instance, author Austin O'Malley works around the problem by focusing on another part of the metaphor:

> A home-made friend wears longer than one you buy in the market.

Handmade items, such as clothing, often last longer than mass-produced ones. O'Malley's metaphor uses this correspondence to argue that real friendships are more durable than those based on money. By focusing on how friendships are made, not on how they're maintained, O'Malley avoids the problematic part of the metaphor. Both Parker and O'Malley use FRIENDSHIPS ARE FABRICS in original, yet succinct passages, all the while avoiding the strange claim in the 'bra' passage that friendships 'wear out' like fabrics.

Lengthy metaphoric expositions, such as the 'bra' meme, are not only more likely to contain problematic metaphors than shorter passages. Their problems are also more likely to be noticed. In the 'bra' example, the 'make America whole' speech, and the 'Republicans in a pub' critique, the extended metaphor is the whole point of the passage. Readers have to pay attention to these metaphors, or the passages won't make sense. This attentiveness ensures that any defects in the metaphors will also be noticed.

Choice of visual images

Throughout history, language has been accompanied by visual imagery, from the gilded illustrations in medieval manuscripts to the visual gestures that accompany spoken language. In the modern world, language and visual communication are increasingly interdependent. Text messages and online posts are sprinkled with emoticons or emojis, as in the 'bra' example in Figure 12. Billboards combine text and pictures. The visuals on TV are often as important as the dialogue. Even in university lectures, PowerPoint slides have become all but ubiquitous.

This new multimodal world is exciting for linguists because it offers many creative ways to use language. Emojis, visual advertising, and internet memes are popular research topics in linguistics.[11] On handheld devices around the world, words and images interact with each other in novel ways that linguists are eager to study. These include new ways of evoking metaphor.

Frequently, images and text conspire to communicate metaphors. A picture might evoke the source domain of a metaphor, while a text evokes the target domain, for example.[12] An advertisement for brain teasers might have a background image of computer circuitry, to suggest that your brain will be as efficient as a computer if you play their games (THE MIND IS A MACHINE). A car ad might include a picture of a spaceship, to compare the car's design to the sleek, futuristic shape of a spacecraft (image metaphor).

Like any tools, multimodal media can be used well or poorly. For example, the imagery in multimodal metaphors sometimes undermines the linguistic message. In these cases, the metaphors' authors have paid attention to the text but haven't thought much about the image. This is apparent in internet memes – that is, text-and-image combinations that are posted and repeated across the internet. Memes normally consist of text placed against a background image.

Consider the example in Figure 13, a re-creation of a meme that appeared on my Facebook feed. It might have been inspiring except for the forest background.

The author of the meme apparently didn't consider that trees, when they are knocked down, never stand up again. The author probably wanted to evoke a version of PERSISTING IS REMAINING ERECT in which the erect object is the human body. When a human is knocked down, he or she may get up again and become stronger than ever. However, the image of trees evokes a special case of PERSISTING IS REMAINING ERECT in which it's specifically a tree that remains erect. The two versions of the metaphor in the meme are contradictory, because a HUMAN BODY and a TREE differ in crucial ways. Human bodies become stronger through combat and struggle. But if you're a tree, when you get knocked down, it's all over – your limbs are hacked off and you're sawed up into lumber.

The 'get knocked down' meme is not an isolated case. Figure 14, which is also re-created from a meme on my Facebook feed, includes an inspirational message that is similarly undermined by its background image.

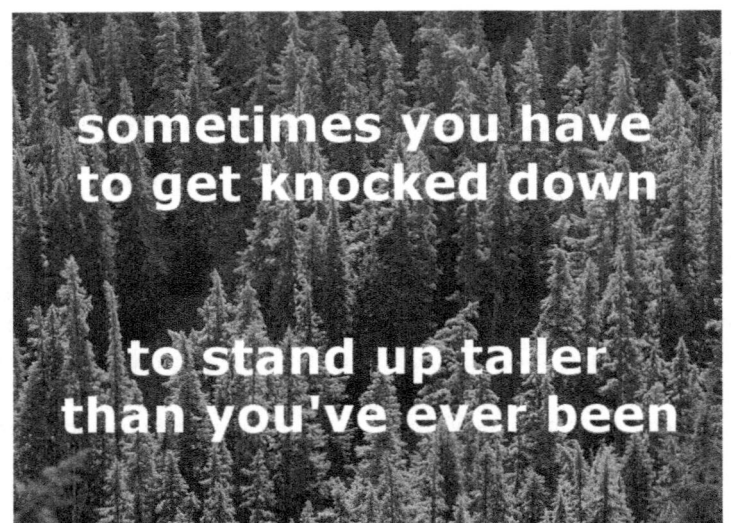

FIGURE 13 This meme could be inspiring – unless you're a tree. Photograph by Bill Sullivan.

FIGURE 14 Another inspiring quotation has been sabotaged by its background image.

As in the 'get knocked down' meme, THE MIND IS A BODY allows us to conceptualize mental development in terms of physical growth. Since the background depicts a plant, we will think of mental improvement specifically in terms of plant growth. So far, this works fine. If we look closer at the image, however, we see that the plant's 'challenge' is a fatal one. It is growing out of a brick wall. Whereas some challenges, such as competing with other plants to reach the sunlight, might encourage a plant to grow tall or large, in this case the 'challenged' plant will be permanently stunted by its unfortunate location.[13] As in the previous example, the particular special case of the metaphor evoked by the visual image doesn't fit logically with the special case that would make the message inspiring.

Unfamiliar scenarios

Some metaphor combinations result in particularly strange source domains. Many mixed metaphors, such as the one that included a 'baton' that was also a 'torch', have source domains that are inherently contradictory. However, the most memorable source domains are not the impossible ones, but the ones that result in a mental image that's possible but bizarre. Sometimes a carefully designed source domain will resonate with an audience even if it's initially unfamiliar, and sometimes an unfamiliar source domain can be used to achieve particular stylistic effects. Both possibilities are discussed in Chapter 8. Usually, however, an unrealistic source domain is just a distraction.

In the following passage, for example, the 'lamp' and 'seesaw' metaphors produce an improbable source domain if they're combined.

> Those systems (of white privilege) persist to this day in some disturbing ways, but the current, vociferous naming and challenging of those systems, the placing of the lamp of truth near the seesaw of privilege and oppression, has provoked a profound sense of discomfort and even anger.[14]

A seesaw is an object that holds one person up high whenever the other person is low. That is, a seesaw is designed so that the two riders are at unequal heights. In this passage, a seesaw is metaphorically a situation where one person has higher status at the expense of another person

(STATUS IS VERTICALITY). The passage also involves UNDERSTANDING IS SEEING because the 'lamp of truth' is 'shedding light on' the unfair system.

At first, the structure of STATUS IS VERTICALITY appears to fit well with UNDERSTANDING IS SEEING. When the metaphors are put together, they create a new source domain in which someone is viewing a seesaw, which metaphorically represents thinking about inequality. But let's take a closer look. If you can, please try to imagine someone placing a lamp near a seesaw. Note that the seesaw is occupied and in motion.

When you imagined the 'seesaw' scene, was it day or night? If it was daytime, then it didn't make much sense for the lamp to be there. If it was night, then maybe you thought it was weird for anyone to be out seesawing at all. Placing a lamp near a seesaw wouldn't provoke 'discomfort and even anger'. It would just be puzzling.

It's not enough to be able to force two metaphors together. Metaphors can seem mixed even if we can imagine a way to fully combine their source domains. A source domain doesn't just need to be physically possible; it should also be a familiar scenario that's easy to understand.

The following sentence discusses the increased use of mobile phones to access the internet:

> And like a horde of aggrieved vultures that has just seen its carrion spirited away to some other part of the savannah, the tech and media business is equally panicked and excited about the vast possibilities for making money from the shift.[15]

This passage uses a combination of ACHIEVING A PURPOSE IS ACQUIRING A DESIRED OBJECT and ACHIEVING A PURPOSE IS REACHING A LOCATION. When these metaphors are put together, the resultant source domain consists of REACHING A LOCATION (another part of the savannah) in order to ACQUIRE A DESIRED OBJECT (carrion). These metaphors normally fit together very well, and there is nothing inherently strange about the source domain REACHING A LOCATION IN ORDER TO ACQUIRE A DESIRED OBJECT. We often go places in order to get things. In this case, however, the source domain is specifically about hungry vultures moving around trying to acquire food.

In practice, source domains are often more detailed than the generic situations described by labels such as *REACHING A LOCATION IN ORDER TO ACQUIRE A DESIRED OBJECT*. This particular label could, after all, describe travelling to a capitol city to get a visa or going to the shed to get a shovel.

Source domains like the 'hungry vulture' scenario are considered *special cases* of more general source domains.[16] Many source domains are special cases of another source domain. For example, we saw that BUSINESS COMPETITION IS BASEBALL is a special case of BUSINESS COMPETITION IS A COMPETITIVE SPORT, precisely because the BASEBALL source domain is more specific than the COMPETITIVE SPORT source domain. Specific source domains like BASEBALL are frequent, so it's not necessarily a problem that the 'vulture' source domain is so detailed. It's more of an issue that the domain doesn't make a lot of sense.

I've never seen even one panicked, excited vulture. Usually, vultures circle at a distance, and they seem relaxed rather than excited. Most readers haven't had close encounters with excited vultures and won't find the vulture metaphor helpful in understanding the tech businesses' situation. Unusual source domains of this kind are less cognitively useful than more routine source domains, and so metaphors that include unfamiliar source domains are often considered mixed metaphors.

Few of us are specialists on vulture behaviour, just as few of us seesaw at night, so almost all of us will have trouble relating to the metaphors in the 'vulture' and 'seesaw' passages. People do, however, have different life experiences. As a result, certain source domains are familiar to some readers but unhelpful to others. These source domains often involve specialized interests or knowledge areas, such as sports or science. A source domain that's relatable for one reader might be confusing for another, even if there's nothing otherwise wrong with it. Even a perfect baseball metaphor won't help a reader who doesn't know anything about baseball.

Metaphors that refer to popular culture are particularly dependent on reader familiarity, as in the following political message that references the British TV drama *Downton Abbey*. (For those who don't know, *kippers* are UK Independence Party supporters and *Greens* are Green Party supporters.)

> In Downton Abbey terms, Greens are a lady upstairs in the dining room; kippers are a footman downstairs in the servants' hall. Indeed, my experience of fanatical Greens … is that many are often very grand indeed, disproportionately hailing (when male) from Eton, Stowe and Westminster, shopping (especially when female) at the most expensive of organic shops, and speaking (when of either sex) in the countiest of accents.[17]

After the first sentence about Downton Abbey and kippers, the rest of the paragraph helps convey the message that supporters of the Green party seem elitist and out of touch. However, this message won't initially be clear to readers unfamiliar with the *Downton Abbey* series. The metaphor isn't mixed, but if a reader doesn't understand the references, the effect is basically the same. The reader can't identify with the source domain and won't benefit from the metaphor.

When authors actively try to write terrible metaphors, these often involve improbable source domains rather than ones with outright contradictions. For example, the following passage describing US Vice President Cheney was probably an attempt to produce the worst mixed metaphor the author could imagine. It appeared in a segment called 'Battle of the Metaphors' on *The Colbert Report*, a political comedy show.

> Dick Cheney is a lioness protecting America's cubs from the laughing hyenas of the left while the poachers of Internationalism sharpen their guns.[18]

If we ignore the obvious fact that guns cannot be sharpened, the metaphor is extravagant but includes little clashing or contradictory information. It involves a special case of THE NATION IS A FAMILY in which the family is specifically a pride of lions. It also includes a special case of ARGUMENT IS PHYSICAL COMBAT where the opponents in the argument are predatory animals, plus another special case of the same metaphor in which the opponents are considered poachers. The source domains of these metaphors fit together nicely, since a family of lions might realistically be threatened by both hyenas and poachers. Still, the high level of detail in the source domain comes across as pretentious. It's also not especially helpful. Like the 'horde of vultures' scenario, the 'lion' situation is unfamiliar to those of us who don't live in the savannah. As such, it won't help our reasoning about America's situation.

In fact, if the metaphor produces any inferences for readers, they're melodramatic and possibly offensive. First, cubs are helpless and dependent on their parents, so the metaphor implies that the American public is inept, naïve, and reliant on Cheney for protection. It also presents the political left as a hungry predator preying on the American public, and proponents of globalization as violent criminals. The metaphors are not outright contradictory, but they create an oddly specific source domain that insults the American public. Of course, the metaphors also insult leftists and globalists, but that is typical of the parodies in *The Colbert Report* and is not particularly noteworthy in this context.

Colbert is not the only humourist to create an intentionally awful source domain. In fact, the winning entries of an annual bad-writing competition, the Bulwer-Lytton Fiction Contest, often are chosen on the basis of their mixed metaphors. The 2011 winner, Sue Fondrie, won with the following entry:

> Cheryl's mind turned like the vanes of a wind-powered turbine, chopping her sparrow-like thoughts into bloody pieces that fell into a growing pile of forgotten memories.

We can easily put these metaphors together. It's not hard to imagine a windmill hacking up small birds into a heap of meat. The scenario combines THE MIND IS A MACHINE (the MACHINE is here specifically a windmill), IDEAS ARE OBJECTS (the OBJECTS are sparrows), and QUANTITY IS VERTICALITY (because the pile of memories becomes higher as memories are added). On the other hand, it's not clear what this combination actually means. Cheryl is apparently processing information quickly and brutally, like a wind turbine, but accomplishing nothing. She violently rejects her own ideas and instantly forgets them. The surreal brutality of the source domain doesn't contribute useful inferences, and as a result seems unjustifiably specific and bloodthirsty.

In short, metaphors with bizarre source domains are just as noticeable as those with self-contradictory source domains. They're likely to come across as puzzling or humorous, whether or not that's what the author intended.

Offensive scenarios

Occasionally, a mixed metaphor results in a mental image that is not just strange, like a lamp by a seesaw, but which is offensive or repugnant. In the following complaint about greedy politicians, a reader who tries to combine the metaphors may end up with an image that equates soldiers and pigs, which could easily be offensive to military personnel or those who support them. (It's also offensive to politicians, but that seems to be more acceptable.)

> Their (the politicians') only interest is feeding at the trough downtown where powerful development interests reward their footsoldiers.[19]

The 'trough' metaphor presents MONEY as FOOD, and greedy politicians as pigs. The development interests are the farmers who feed the pigs. In the 'footsoldiers' metaphor, the developers are seen as commanders and the politicians are footsoldiers (ARGUMENT IS WAR). Both metaphors imply that the politicians are subservient to the developers, which is probably why the author decided the metaphors were compatible even though one compares the politicians to soldiers and the other compares them to pigs. Of course, soldiers do not eat at a trough nor would they fight in exchange for slops. The suggestion that they might do so could be found offensive.

If this example didn't offend you, it's possible that this next one might. Here, the description of a failed political challenge contains sexual imagery that is rendered more grotesque by a mixed metaphor:

> This whole thing is a case of political premature ejaculation and it's backfired.[20]

In this sentence, the stages of the leadership selection process are understood as the stages of sexual intercourse. The over-early attempt to put a new political leader in power is called *premature ejaculation*. Perhaps later on, the leadership challenge might have gone better, but its proponents couldn't wait, according to the metaphor.

The word *backfire*, when used metaphorically, usually draws on the source domain of firearms. It specifically refers to the now-outdated guns and cannons that were ignited from the back, which could accidentally blast backwards and hurt the shooter rather than the target. Since these antiquated guns and cannons aren't now in common use, some speakers might not connect the word *backfire* with this source domain, and for these speakers the metaphor may be dead. Either way, when a strategy 'backfires', it damages the strategist rather than accomplishing its intended purpose.

Unfortunately, sexual intercourse is often described in terms of firearms. When it is, ejaculation is understood as firing a gun. If this 'gun' backfires, it's not clear exactly how this would happen or what it would mean. It's probably better not to speculate. In any case, the source domain is too strange to help us reason about the target-domain political situation.

Improbable source domains, like the 'wind turbine' or 'ejaculation' scenarios, are often more striking than impossible ones, like the 'touchdown' and 'revolving door' examples. When authors try to create the worst mixed metaphors they can imagine, these take the form of bloody windmills, not revolving doors that are also elevators. Surreal or grotesque metaphor combinations are more interesting than the ones we can't imagine at all.

At the other extreme from impossible mixed metaphors, however, some metaphors are confusing because they are all too possible. These metaphors are so much like real life that we may not even notice that they're meant to be metaphors. Oddly enough, these are also often criticized as 'mixed metaphors'. It might seem like a 'mix' would have to include two different metaphors, just as a mixture of liquids has to include at least two liquids, or a cake mix has to include multiple ingredients. For most English speakers, though, *mixed metaphor* seems to denote any metaphor that's odd or funny. As noted in the introduction, a study of the term *mixed metaphor* found that 28 per cent of metaphors with this label involved only one metaphor, rather than two.[21] We'll look at these so-called mixed metaphors next.

Notes

1 Scott, 'Mixed Metaphors' (attributed to Robert K. Oglesby).

2 Rentoul, 'The Top Ten: Mixed metaphors'. This example is attributed to Simon Hughes, UK Lib Dem MP, 2008.

3 *The New Yorker Magazine*, 'Block That Metaphor!', 31 January 2000, 46.

4 Dana Milbank, 'Clinton-Warren Ticket Could Fill "Empathy Gap"', *The Register-Guard*, 7 March 2016, A7.

5 Guy Gugliotta, 'Fallacious "Full Disclosure"', *The Washington Post*, 17 April 1992. Available online: https://www.washingtonpost.com/archive/politics/1992/04/17/fallacious-full-disclosure/97bbcd80-8586-44bf-9205-9b1b8df4a005/?utm_term=.117b664adda4 (accessed 11 December 2016).

6 James Poniewozik, 'The New Reality of TV: All Trump, All the Time', *The New York Times*, 11 December 2016. Available online: http://www.nytimes.com/2016/12/11/arts/television/the-new-reality-of-tv-all-trump-all-the-time.html?smid=tw-nytimesarts&smtyp=cur&_r=0 (accessed 13 December 2016).

7   Naomi Nayak and Raymond W. Jr. Gibbs, 'Conceptual Knowledge in the Interpretation of Idioms', *Journal of Experimental Psychology: General* 119, no. 3 (1990): 315–30. Paul Thibodeau and Frank H. Durgin, 'Productive Figurative Communication: Conventional Metaphors Facilitate the Comprehension of Related Novel Metaphors', *Journal of Memory and Language* 58 (2008): 521–40. Dedre Gentner, Mutsumi Imai, and Lera Boroditsky, 'As Time Goes By: Evidence for Two Systems in Processing Space → Time Metaphors', *Language and Cognitive Processes* 17, no. 5 (2002): 537–65.

8   David Brooks, 'Republicans Must Find a Third Alternative', *The Register-Guard*, 9 March 2016.

9   *The Register-Guard*, '"I do", Sort of: GOP Leaders and Trump Try to Patch Things Up', 13 May 2016.

10 Dorothy Parker, 'The Standard of Living', *The New Yorker*, 20 September 1941, 24. Available online at: https://www.newyorker.com/magazine/1941/09/20/the-standard-of-living (Accessed 10 April 2018).

11 Charles Forceville, *Pictorial Metaphor in Advertising* (London: Psychology Press, 1996). Charles Forceville and Eduardo Urios-Aparisi, eds., *Multimodal Metaphor* (Berlin and New York: Mouton de Gruyter, 2009). Barbara Dancygier and Lieven Vandelanotte, 'Internet Memes as Multimodal Constructions', *Cognitive Linguistics* 28, no. 3 (2017): 565–98. Vyvyan Evans, *The Emoji Code: The Linguistics behind Smiley Faces and Scaredy Cats* (New York: Picador, 2017).

12 Charles Forceville, 'The Identification of Target and Source in Pictorial Metaphors', *Journal of Pragmatics* 34, no. 1 (2002): 1–14.

13 Shortly after I took this photo, the photographed plant indeed died.

14 Charles M. Blow, 'White America's "Broken Heart"', *The New York Times*, 4 February 2016. Available online: www.nytimes.com/2016/02/04/opinion/white-americas-broken-heart.html (accessed 11 December 2016).

15 Farhad Manjoo, 'For Verizon and AOL, Mobile Is a Magic Word', *The New York Times*, 12 May 2015.

16 George Lakoff, 'The Contemporary Theory of Metaphor', in *Metaphor and Thought* (2nd ed.), ed. Ortony, Andrew (Cambridge, England: Cambridge University Press, 1993), 202–51. Zoltán Kövecses, *Metaphor: A Practical Introduction* (Oxford: Oxford University Press, 2002).

17 Matt Ridley, 'Selfish Eco-Snobs Deny the Poor a Chance to Succeed', *The Australian*, 11 November 2014, 10 World.

18 Stephen Colbert, 'Battle of the Metaphors', *The Colbert Report*, 19 April 2007.

19 Ronald Bevirt, 'A Trojan Horse Stirs in South Eugene', *The Register-Guard*, 13 April 2016.

20 Geoff Chambers, 'Plotters Fail to Oust LNP Leader Lawrence Springborg', *The Australian*, 23 February 2016. Available online: http://www.theaustralian.com.au/national-affairs/state-politics/plotters-fail-to-oust-lnp-leader-lawrence-springborg/news-story/5ea552772d6cc8d7875d6b5e83c02193 (accessed 11 December 2016).

21 Semino, 'A Corpus-Based Study of "Mixed Metaphor"'.

Further Reading on Visual Metaphor

Caballero, Rosario. *Re-viewing Space: Figurative Language in Architects' Assessment of Built Space*. Berlin and New York: Mouton de Gruyter, 2006.

Cienki, Alan. 'Metaphoric Gestures and Some of Their Relations to Verbal Metaphoric Expressions'. In *Discourse and Cognition: Bridging the Gap*, edited by Jean-Pierre Koenig, 189–204. Stanford, CA: CSLI, 1998.

Dancygier, Barbara and Lieven Vandelanotte. 'Internet Memes as Multimodal Constructions'. *Cognitive Linguistics* 28, no. 3 (2017): 565–98.

Forceville, Charles. *Pictorial Metaphor in Advertising*. London: Psychology Press, 1996.

Forceville, Charles. 'The Identification of Target and Source in Pictorial Metaphors'. *Journal of Pragmatics* 34, no. 1 (2002): 1–14.

Forceville, Charles and Eduardo Urios-Aparisi, eds. *Multimodal Metaphor*. Berlin and New York: Mouton de Gruyter, 2009.

Ishino, Mika. 'Metaphor and Metonymy in Gesture and Discourse'. PhD diss., Department of Linguistics, University of Chicago, Chicago, 2007.

Mittelberg, Irene. 'Metaphor and Metonymy in Language and Gesture: Discourse Evidence for Multimodal Models of Grammar'. PhD diss., Cornell University, New York, 2006.

Müller, Cornelia and Alan Cienki, eds. *Metaphor and Gesture*. Amsterdam/Philadelphia: John Benjamins, 2008.

Núñez, Rafael and Eve Sweetser. 'With the Future behind Them: Convergent Evidence from Aymara Language and Gesture in the Crosslinguistic Comparison of Spatial Construals of Time'. *Cognitive Science* 30 (2006): 401–50.

Sullivan, Karen and Linh Thuy Bui. 'With the Future Coming up behind Them: Evidence That Time Approaches from behind in Vietnamese'. *Cognitive Linguistics* 27, no. 2 (2016): 205–34.

Whittock, Trevor. *Metaphor and Film*. Cambridge: Cambridge University Press, 1990.

5 METAPHOR OR NOT? HOW AMBIGUITY CAUSES 'MIXING'

Mixed metaphors can be confusing and novel metaphors can be challenging. Yet sometimes it's not even clear whether a metaphor is intended at all. If I tell you, 'I smell a rat around here', you have no way of knowing whether I mean something suspicious or an actual rodent, since I haven't clarified whether the word *rat* should be understood literally or metaphorically. If we're working on a project at a café, and I suggest, 'Let's get moving', I might mean that we should work faster or that we should literally get up and leave. If a hearer has to ask, 'Do you mean that metaphorically or literally?' this is a sign that the metaphor hasn't worked.

Ambiguity between literal and metaphoric meanings

A metaphor that isn't understood as metaphoric fails at its purpose, as in the following line from a novel.

> There was something unpleasing and incongruous about the idea of Bueno shackled to a wife.[1]

Does this sentence mean that Bueno is unlikely to make a good husband? Or does it criticize the idea of literally chaining Bueno to someone's wife? Out of context, the sentence is ambiguous. Examples like this are sometimes criticized as mixed metaphors, even though they involve only one metaphor or no metaphors at all, depending on whether they're interpreted metaphorically or literally.[2]

Ambiguity between metaphoric and non-metaphoric meanings is most likely to be found in news headlines, on Twitter, and in other media where space is limited. Space constraints encourage ambiguity, simply because there is less room to explain what's meant. The following headline is typical.

> Much of gulf dodged the oil but not its taint.[3]

The word *taint* in this example may be misunderstood as literal, since oil can leave behind a physical residue. Even though *taint* is intended to metaphorically refer to political or social stigma via MORALITY IS PURITY, the word's literal meaning may distract from its intended interpretation.

This advertisement for a restaurant is even more confusing:

> Order anything from our menu and we'll step on it![4]

The restaurant doesn't really want readers to think that their staff will step on customers' food. Presumably, the writer intended to convey the metaphoric meaning of *step on it*, by which any kind of rapid activity can be metaphorically understood as the burst of speed that results from stepping on the accelerator in a car (GENERIC IS SPECIFIC).

In the following example, a newspaper writer sets up a complex scenario that ends with an ambiguous statement:

> Big banks aren't the only entities that our country has deemed 'too big to fail'. But our oceans won't be getting a bailout anytime soon ...[5]

Bailing out the oceans does sound difficult. Banks, when they struggle, can be metaphorically 'bailed out' to keep them 'afloat'.[6] The oceans could similarly be saved from threats such as pollution, but when this salvation is described as a *bailout* it makes us consider the absurdity of literally bailing out the ocean.

A local kite festival was announced with the following ambiguous sentence:

> Families will get swept away in the excitement of the annual Redcliffe KiteFest.[7]

When we lose control over our choices due to extreme emotions, we're 'carried away' in a particular direction via LIFE IS A JOURNEY. This can be a good thing if the emotion is excitement or love, or a bad thing if it's anger or fear. However, lightweight humans such as children could be physically 'swept away' by large kites, so the ambiguous sentence seems like a poor choice (Figure 15).

The computer technician who said the following probably did not mean to suggest cannibalism:

> Things are different when you have fifteen people on your plate.[8]

More likely, the technician meant that he needed to solve computer issues for the fifteen people he's responsible for. Unfortunately, the metaphoric idiom *to have on one's plate* (GENERIC IS SPECIFIC, in which things to deal with are specifically food to be eaten) could be interpreted literally.

In the following passage from a novel, the 'dent' in the character's pocketbook is intended to be metaphorical, via QUANTITY IS SIZE:

> So far her Wonderbra had proved to be worth the 500 kroner she had invested. Even though it had left a sizeable dent in her pocketbook.[9]

Nevertheless, the 'dent' could conceivably be damage caused by a physical impact with the Wonderbra.

Ambiguity can lead to all kinds of misunderstandings. English football manager Robert 'Bobby' Gould probably did not feel reassured about the loyalty of his assistant, Stuart Pearson, when Pearson issued the following proclamation:

> Bobby Gould thinks I'm trying to stab him in the back, but I'm right behind him.

Someone who is 'right behind you' metaphorically supports you, via ASSISTANCE IS SUPPORT. Someone who 'stabs you in the back' instead 'betrays you', via ARGUMENT IS PHYSICAL COMBAT. Here, though, both metaphors are ambiguous with literal interpretations – and if Pearson wanted to literally stab Gould in the back, he'd probably do it from behind.

Visual imagery can make it more likely that a metaphor will be misinterpreted. The following caption is more susceptible to misunderstanding because it appears below a large image of an artist at

FIGURE 15 Few people want to see their children carried off by kites.

work, surrounded by curious watchers. I've left the line breaks as they originally appear in the caption because they contribute to the potential for misinterpretation.

> Stan Miller (USA)
> draws an audience
> as he paints fishing
> boats in Samae San.[10]

When readers see the first two lines of the caption, they may read *draws* in its non-metaphoric sense and think that Stan is sketching his audience. The author meant that Stan is metaphorically 'drawing in' an audience, in which the 'pull' sense of the verb *draw* is metaphorically extended via THINKING IS MOVING. Causing others to be interested is conceptualized as pulling them to the source of interest. However, the accompanying image of an artist and audience, and the choice of line breaks, could cause readers to choose a literal interpretation over the intended metaphoric one.

Sometimes, helpful readers point out the availability of a literal meaning, even if the author's intention was clear, as in the Twitter exchange in Figure 16.

If interpreted via LIFE IS A JOURNEY, the Emerson quotation cited by Amtrak California advises readers to choose their own, original, life goal. The literal meaning, of course, instructs readers to bushwhack off-road and make a new trail. The literal reading is of interest here only because the advice comes from a train service and a train that goes off its rails will simply crash. The fact that the quotation is cited by a rail service makes the literal reading more available.

Readers will occasionally latch on to a literal meaning that isn't prompted by context or other cues. The internet meme in Figure 17 incorporates the beginning of the well-known proverb *When life hands you lemons, make lemonade*, which personifies LIFE and allows unpleasant life experiences to be understood as bitter-tasting fruit via THE MIND IS A BODY.

The meme points out the obvious fact that life cannot literally 'hand' you anything. Of course, nobody thinks that the 'lemons' proverb is literal. There is no reason to activate the proverb's non-metaphoric meaning. In fact, the metaphoric reading is so natural that it's unexpected and perhaps humorous to question it – which of course is the meme's point.

 **Amtrak California** @Amtrak_CA

"Do not follow where the path may lead. Go instead where there is no path and leave a trail." Ralph Waldo Emerson

 **(Anonymized)**

@Amtrak_CA With all due respect, this is terrible advice for trains

FIGURE 16 Trains are better off if they don't venture off their tracks.

Many metaphoric readings are so automatic that it's startling when an author invokes a literal interpretation. Writers often use this element of surprise to create humour. In the 'lemons' meme, the author points out the inconsistency of the metaphoric reading with literal reality. In the example in Figure 18, the author pretends that a literal meaning was intended all along, even though the introductory non-metaphoric sentence, font and format, all make it reasonable for a reader to pick up on the metaphoric reading.

When we talk about something serious-sounding 'deep down' or 'inside' us, it's usually an emotion like despair that's metaphorically contained in the body (via THE MIND IS A BODY). In this case, the author thwarts our expectations by giving us a literal container (a shoe) with a familiar, trivial sock problem.

In all of the above examples, only a single metaphor is ambiguous. When more than one metaphor in an expression has a literal reading,

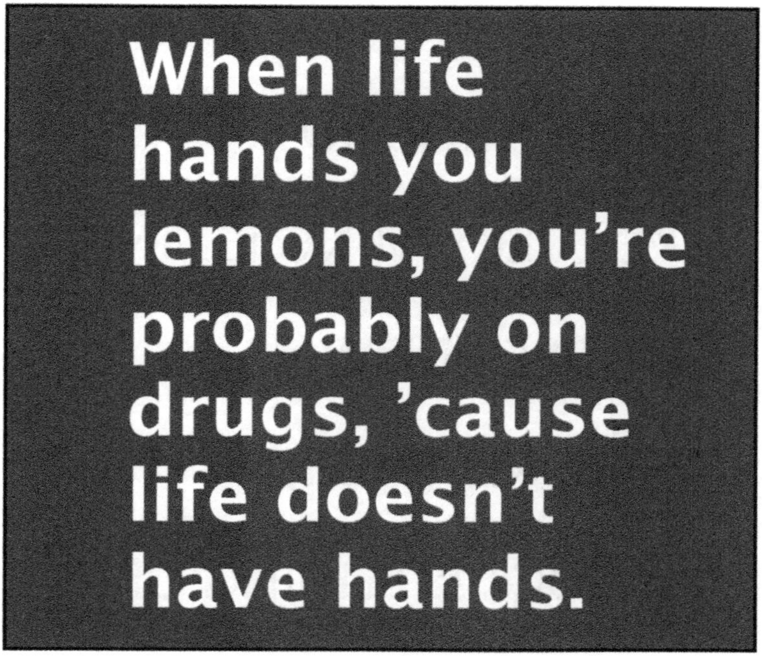

> When life hands you lemons, you're probably on drugs, 'cause life doesn't have hands.

FIGURE 17 This meme critiques the proverb *When life hands you lemons, make lemonade.*

the result is even stranger. If I tell you, *There's something fishy up your sleeve*,[11] metaphorically I might mean that you are hiding (have 'up your sleeve', via UNDERSTANDING IS SEEING) something suspicious ('fishy', via SUSPICIOUS IS STINKY), or, conceivably, I might mean that there are actual fish entrails in the sleeve of your shirt. Hopefully, the intended meaning would be apparent from the context.

Metonymy

Frequently, metaphors are ambiguous when they combine with metonymies. A *metonymy* occurs when a word's meaning is extended to a related meaning. For example, when I say *Buses are on strike today*, I actually mean that the drivers of the buses are on strike. Vehicles are not allowed to go on strike. I'm using the word *buses* metonymically, in order

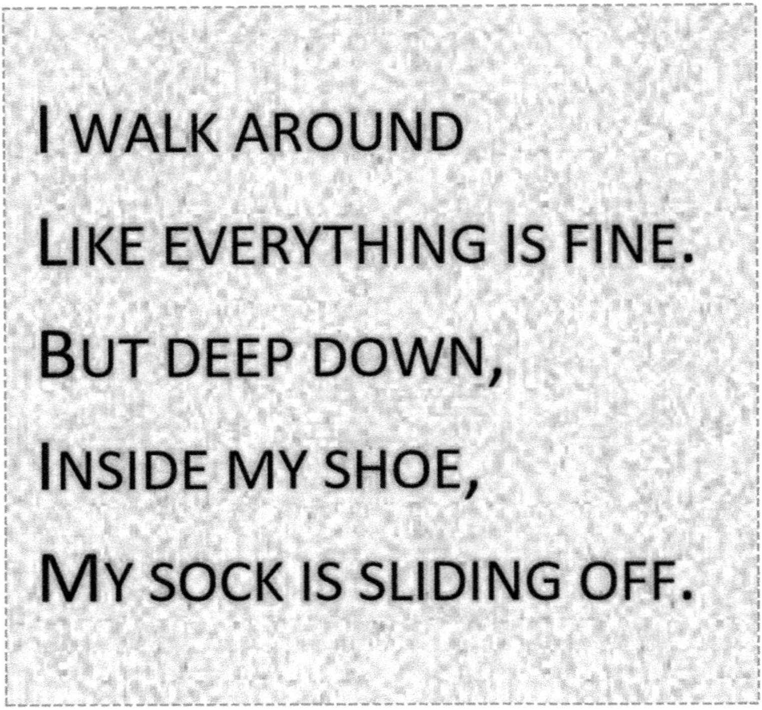

> I WALK AROUND
>
> LIKE EVERYTHING IS FINE.
>
> BUT DEEP DOWN,
>
> INSIDE MY SHOE,
>
> MY SOCK IS SLIDING OFF.

FIGURE 18 Cues such as the textured background encourage readers to first interpret this meme metaphorically.

to refer to the related concept 'bus drivers'. Similarly, when I say, *Let's get a platter to share*, I mean we should share the food that comes on the platter, not break the platter and divide the pieces. In fact, we will probably eat the food but give the platter back. I'm saying *platter* but I mean 'the food on the platter'. There are many types of metonymies, though an inventory of these types is outside the scope of this book. General overviews of metonymies are included in Lakoff and Johnson's *Metaphors We Live By* and Kövecses' *Metaphor: A Practical Introduction*, among others.

For the purposes of this book, we can think of metonymy as a shortcut that allows us to say *buses* instead of *bus drivers* or *platter* instead of *food on a platter*. Metonymy is a simpler process than metaphor in many ways, but like metaphor, it causes one word to have more than one meaning. For example, *platter* literally refers to a serving dish but metonymically refers to food, and *buses* literally refers to vehicles but metonymically refers to drivers. Since metonymy, like metaphor, creates multiple meanings, it can lead to ambiguity. If I hear that a friend 'had to pay for a platter in a restaurant', for example, I might not know whether the friend paid to eat the food on the platter, or broke a literal platter and had to pay for it.

When metaphors and metonymies combine, they can create even more confusion than either alone. This is apparent in news headlines such as *Red Tape Holding Up Bridges*. Here, *red tape* stands metonymically for regulations because regulatory documents were once bound with red tape. The intended metaphoric meaning of *holding up* involves ACHIEVING A PURPOSE IS REACHING A DESTINATION, in which hindering the accomplishment of goals, such as planning and building bridges, is understood as delaying progress towards a destination (*holding up* the forward movement). Together, the metaphor and metonymy permit a literal reading that red-coloured tape is the only thing that's keeping the bridges from falling apart.

Another headline *Local High School Dropouts Cut in Half* combines metonymy and metaphor, in that *dropouts* stands metonymically for the rate of dropouts. Although *cut in half* was doubtless intended to express QUANTITY IS SIZE, it can be read as indicating literal dismemberment of the students who dropped out. Presumably, they were dismembered as punishment for their failure to graduate.

English footballer Dalian Atkinson made the following ambiguous statement:

If I was still at Ipswich, I wouldn't be where I am today.

Atkinson wasn't speculating about still being physically located 'at Ipswich'. Rather, he intended *at Ipswich* to mean 'playing for the Ipswich Town club'. Playing for the club required Atkinson's physical presence in Ipswich, so the concepts are related, which allows the latter to metonymically stand for the former.

In the second clause, Atkinson's being 'where he is today' metaphorically represents the successful stage of his life he was enjoying when he made the statement (LIFE IS A JOURNEY). Both the metonymy and the metaphor are ambiguous with a literal reading, which produces the banal literal interpretation that if Atkinson was in one place (Ipswich) he wouldn't be in another place (where he is today).

Even one metonymy alone can be ambiguous between a metonymic and non-metonymic reading. I initially misunderstood the headline

Actresses' lines decrease with age, study claims and thought it meant that actresses used so much Botox and other treatments that their faces had fewer lines as they got older.[12] The headline appeared next to the face shot of a well-preserved older actress, which probably encouraged my misguided reading. Of course, the intended meaning involves the metonymically extended sense of *lines*, indicating the speech segments assigned to particular actors, which would traditionally be written in lines of text. Actresses are apparently given less to say as they get older.

Literal meanings that detract from the metaphor

Sometimes we can eventually figure out that a statement is intended as metaphoric, but the target and source domains are so similar that it takes us a while to notice the metaphor. This can lead to confusion in the seconds before the metaphor is processed. When a reporter describes country music singer Glen Campbell as *fiddling with a guitar*,[13] this might come across as odd, because a fiddle is an instrument similar to a guitar. Likewise, the news headline *Wind, solar to eclipse coal in 20 years* may prompt a reader to think of a literal solar eclipse, rather than the intended metaphoric 'eclipse' in which renewable energy sources 'block out' the significance of coal via IMPORTANCE IS SIZE and UNDERSTANDING IS SEEING.[14] Similarly, it may sound strange to celebrate *kicking off the hockey season*.[15] Even though the metaphor *kicking off* allows any kind of event to be understood as a football game (GENERIC IS SPECIFIC), it's confusing in this case because it describes a team sport that resembles football in several ways but lacks actual kicking.

When only part of a metaphoric sentence is ambiguous, the rest of the sentence makes it clear that a metaphor is intended. This doesn't necessarily prevent readers from accessing the non-metaphoric interpretation of the sentence, however.

> But just how big it (the new courthouse) would be … and where it would go … remain up in the air.[16]

If it weren't for the first part of the sentence, this example could be ambiguous. By the time readers reach the phrase *up in the air* and UNCERTAINTY IS VERTICALITY is evoked, readers can already tell that the sentence is about

UNCERTAINTY, not literally about VERTICALITY. The clause *where it would go is up in the air* could mean either 'it's uncertain where it would be built' or 'it will be built up in the air'. Nevertheless, the idea of a 'floating building' may never occur to many readers because the phrase *how big it would be* rules out the non-metaphoric meaning even before the metaphor is evoked.

If the disambiguating context comes at the end, a metaphoric expression will be more ambiguous.

> New statistics (suggest) that obesity is reversing decades of steady expansion in Americans' life spans ...[17]

Obesity is a condition that makes people larger. For a reader who hasn't yet reached the words *life spans*, the 'expansion' might seem literal. It doesn't make sense that a condition of increased size could reverse an expansion in size. This confusion would be brief, however, because the phrase *in Americans' life spans* disambiguates the expression and indicates that the expansion is metaphoric via QUANTITY IS SIZE.

A reader of the following passage about microbreweries might be excused for imagining a massive explosion of beer, until the second sentence disambiguates the meaning (QUANTITY IS SIZE):

> There has been a literal explosion of craft breweries in the Northwest during the past five years. Competition for shelf space and tap handles is fierce.[18]

The ambiguity is worsened by the addition of *literal*, which misleads the reader into thinking that the 'explosion' is, in fact, literal. Instead, the author apparently intended *literal* to be understood in its more recent sense, meaning 'astounding'.

In the following headline, the 'planting' probably seems non-metaphoric until the preposition phrase *of doubt* indicates it should be understood metaphorically (IDEOLOGIES ARE ORGANISMS):

> Organic produce purists planting seeds of doubt about food certification.[19]

Finally, in this passage from a novel, the first non-metaphoric clause makes the second clause likely to be read as literal, until the rest of the passage makes the metaphoric meaning clear:

As Morio backed out of the driveway, I ran over everything I'd seen the night before, in as much detail as I could.[20]

The phrasal verb *run over* is often used to describe a driving accident. The first clause about driving (... *backed out of the driveway*) might make the 'driving mishap' meaning of *run over* come to mind before the metaphoric meaning 'methodically recall' (from THINKING IS MOVING).

Idioms are phrases with fixed meanings, so we might expect that they would be less prone to ambiguity than other expressions. However, even in metaphoric idioms, the non-metaphoric meanings of words can interfere. Here, a sports reporter describes a crew team's performance:

The stroke rate was high, but the boat was spinning its wheels.[21]

The idiom *spinning its wheels* 'accomplishing nothing' is based on the source-domain scenario of a wheeled vehicle that's stuck in mud, sand, or snow (LIFE IS A JOURNEY). Since a boat is itself a vehicle, readers will be prompted to consider the literal 'vehicle' reading of *spinning its wheels*. This doesn't work well for a boat, which has no wheels, so readers who are misled by the clause's ambiguity will arrive at a self-contradictory interpretation.

Idiom choice can lead to even more unfortunate results, as in the following complaint:

These haemorrhoids are a real pain in the neck.[22]

The idiom *pain in the neck* uses a type of physical pain to describe an annoying circumstance (THE MIND IS A BODY). When applied to a physical discomfort located in a part of the body that is not the neck, the idiom draws attention to the contrast between the neck and the body part in question, which in this case sounds embarrassing or humorous.

Sometimes literal meanings not only distract readers, but also downplay the significance of metaphoric statements. When readers are made to think about the non-metaphoric meaning of an expression, this can detract from the power of the metaphor. When a British reporter remarks, *Here we are in the Holy Land of Israel – a mecca for tourists*,[23] the literal meaning of *mecca* designating a Muslim holy site springs to mind. The metaphoric sense of *mecca*, meaning a 'popular destination' sought with a religious-like fervour, is suppressed by the reference to an actual holy site. When the 'tourist destination' meaning is finally accessed, it makes the reporter's choice of words seem like a superficial way to present the Holy Land – which is, after all, better known for its religious significance than its tourism potential.

The metaphoric meaning in the following passage likewise devalues the target domain by its close proximity to a similar source domain:

> She (the Virgin Mary) entered upon the slow crucifixion of seeing her son take the lonely, sad and inevitable road to his cross.[24]

Mary's suffering in watching Jesus's crucifixion is compared to the pain of the crucifixion itself. Since it is presumably worse to be crucified than to watch it happen to someone else, this comparison fails to impress us with the enormity of Mary's pain.

In the 'mecca' and 'crucifixion' examples, the target-domain meaning is sabotaged by its similarity to the source-domain meaning. When the non-metaphoric meaning and the metaphoric meaning of a word are starkly opposed or contradictory, this also detracts from the intended metaphoric meaning. If I suggest, *We need to sit down and walk through some things*,[25] you may notice the contradiction between *sit* and *walk*. Literal walking is impossible while seated (even though metaphoric ambulation is possible via THINKING IS MOVING) so my word choice may distract you from my intended message.

The choice of words is even worse in the statement that US civil rights heroine Rosa Parks *stood up for what she believed*,[26] because Parks protested racial segregation on buses specifically by refusing to stand up for a white passenger. Even though you can metaphorically 'stand up for' a belief (THE MIND IS A BODY, in which moral character is physical posture), this metaphor sounds inappropriate when applied to someone who protested by remaining seated.

The contradiction between metaphoric and non-metaphoric meanings is equally obvious in the following image metaphor from radio personality Rush Limbaugh:

> Brilliant sunshine rained down on Fort Collins.

Although the trajectories of many substances can be described as 'raining', the image metaphor doesn't work well for sunshine, since it's most likely to be sunny when it isn't raining.

Metaphoric and literal meanings that are opposites are nearly as confusing as ones that are overly similar. Although eventually readers will figure out that the sun can indeed metaphorically rain, for example, the apparent contradiction between the source and target domains may slow readers down almost as much as ambiguity between the domains.

Tautologies

Even if a metaphoric meaning is obvious and unambiguous, the metaphor will lack explanatory power if its source and target domains are too similar. Metaphors with overly similar domains are not normally called mixed, but they are considered *tautological*, meaning that they compare something to itself.

The lamp just sat there, like an inanimate object.[27]

Since a lamp is literally inanimate, a comparison between lamps and inanimate objects is tautological and meaningless. Without the *like-*construction (i.e. simile) to signal a possible attempt at metaphor, the sentence would probably not even be suggestive of metaphor, as in *The lamp, an inanimate object, just sat there*. A different subject could save the sentence, as in *Grandpa just sat there, like an inanimate object*. The motionlessness of an animate being, such as Grandpa, can be meaningfully compared to the stillness of a non-living object, via image metaphor.

A meaningful metaphor not only needs distinct source and target domains, but also needs the relevant portions of each domain to be different. For example, it's sensible to compare the motion of human beings to the movement of hummingbirds via an image metaphor because humans and hummingbirds move in fundamentally different ways. When these types of motion are compared in former US President Ronald Reagan's autobiography, the image metaphor is not tautological:

He and Meiklejohn circled me like a pair of hummingbirds ...[28]

However, not everything about human beings and hummingbirds is different. The following example is tautological because it compares something that humans and hummingbirds have in common. That is, both humans and hummingbirds may be strangers to each other.

John and Mary had never met. They were like two hummingbirds who had also never met.[29]

Human beings can be compared to trees, as in *Theseus grew up tall and strong, like a tree rooted in rich earth.*[30] Trees can grow taller and sturdier than any human, so comparing a human to a tree can suggest that the human is unusually tall and strong. However, if a particular human and a particular tree are of the same height, then the metaphorical comparison is tautological and useless, as in *He was as tall as a 6'3" tree.*[31] Both this sentence and the 'hummingbirds' example above are supposedly from high school students' essays. I suspect, or at least I hope, that they were actually invented as a joke.

In sum, when literal and metaphoric references to the same domain are unambiguous but in close proximity, the literal use may weaken the metaphoric one, such as when the Virgin Mary viewing her son's crucifixion is itself described as a 'crucifixion'. When the source and target domains are actually the same domain, metaphor is impossible, such as when a lamp is compared to an inanimate object. When the two domains are different but the part that's compared is the same, the metaphor conveys no new information, such as when a 6'3" man is compared to a 6'3" tree.

There is one way that activating a literal reading of a word or phrase can actually enhance its metaphoric interpretation. This strategy is similar to the 'crucifixion' example, in that it juxtaposes source- and target-domain meanings of a word or phrase, but with one important difference. If the source- and target-domain meanings are contrastive, rather than analogous, the contrast actually adds force to the metaphoric meaning. When the poet Dylan Thomas writes *light breaks where no sun shines*, the absence of literal sunlight makes the metaphoric light (hope) all the more astonishing (via HAPPINESS IS BRIGHTNESS).[32] When a novelist writes *And yet ... the sun might shine, but it did not shine in her life*, this involves the same metaphor as the Dylan Thomas line (HAPPINESS IS BRIGHTNESS) and has a similar effect.[33] Even though the weather is literally bright and sunny, the character does not feel the metaphoric light of HAPPINESS. The character's metaphoric 'darkness' is more surprising because the day is literally bright.

To consider a less poetic example, radio personality Jack Fleming describes meeting Frank Sinatra at a recording studio:

'I was surprised to find he was a short man', Fleming said of the 5-foot-8 Sinatra. 'But larger than life.'[34]

Sinatra's 'big' personality and reputation are even more striking in consideration of his small physical stature (IMPORTANCE IS SIZE). Happiness is less surprising on a sunny day, 'crucifying' anguish is less shocking when compared to a literal crucifixion, and the tourist appeal of a 'mecca' is less dramatic when it's an actual sacred site. On the other hand, happiness without sunshine is more striking than happiness on a sunny day, and a man's greatness is more surprising if he is short. Literal references to source domains usually weaken nearby metaphoric references to the domains, but have the opposite effect when the literal references contrast with the metaphoric ones.

In general, metaphor works best when the source and target domains are separate, distinct, and recognizable. Total ambiguity between the domains is confusing. Temporary ambiguity is distracting. And too much similarity between the domains makes a metaphor tautological and meaningless. Exceptions to these trends, such as in the Frank Sinatra quotation above, seem to be few and far between.

Humorous ambiguity

Ambiguity between metaphoric and literal interpretations can be irritating, but intentional ambiguity of this kind can also be humorous:

> I didn't like my beard at first, but then it grew on me.

Here, the idiom *it grew on me* involves IMPORTANCE IS SIZE and uses a now-rare sense of *on* indicating affectedness, in order to indicate that the subject (here, the beard) became more important and positive for its owner. Beards actually grow, so literal and metaphoric growth could happen at the same time.

The familiar metaphor UNDERSTANDING IS SEEING underlies the following joke:

> I stayed up all night to see where the sun went. Then it dawned on me.

If you're trying to figure out where a light source has gone, and then it appears, you are both literally and metaphorically 'enlightened'.

An almost identical joke uses THE MIND IS A BODY:

I wondered why the baseball was getting bigger. Then it hit me!

Here, again, the speaker simultaneously experiences a mental realization and a physical effect. In this case, the realization is conceptualized as a physical impact rather than a visual stimulus. The final joke I will mention is in slightly poor 'taste':

> The soldier who survived mustard gas and pepper spray is now a seasoned veteran.

This joke makes use of both metaphoric and non-metaphoric puns. The names of condiments, *mustard* and *pepper*, are also the names of weapons that use chemicals that are similar to the spices in the condiments of the same names. The word *seasoned* is metaphoric. The seasoning of food improves it and prepares it for its purpose. Via GENERIC IS SPECIFIC, *seasoned* can describe any other kind of preparedness, including military experience. The non-metaphoric and metaphoric puns both involve dual meanings related to food preparation and military combat, reinforcing the overall ambiguity. The joke's potential humour relies on this ambiguity between a serious interpretation related to the brutality of war and a frivolous interpretation involving condiment use.

Some humorous uses of ambiguity may be too lengthy or complex to be considered jokes, but involve metaphoric word play similar to the above examples. When your life is on the 'wrong track', you can 'turn yourself around' and choose another 'direction', via ACHIEVING A PURPOSE IS REACHING A DESTINATION. The pseudo-inspirational billboard in Figure 19 plays with this metaphoric meaning.

The hokey pokey is a dance for children that involves turning around in circles. The billboard message might mean that the addict 'turned around' and chose a life 'direction' leading away from addiction, or could

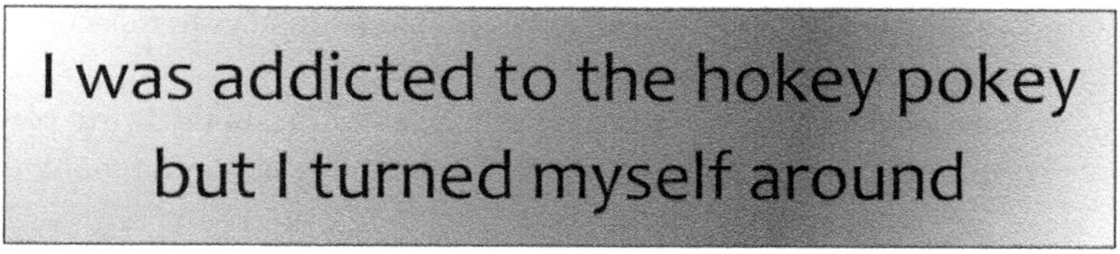

> I was addicted to the hokey pokey but I turned myself around

FIGURE 19 This message of hope appeared on a billboard, photographs of which were circulated online.

mean that the addict continued 'turning around' as part of his ongoing hokey pokey addiction. The unlikely scenario of an addiction to the hokey pokey, which is not normally a serious interest for adults, allows the ambiguity to work.

Source and target meanings can also be forced into ambiguity through the careful choice of words with multiple unrelated (homonymous) meanings, as in the following advice from actor George Jessel (emphasis in the original):

> If you haven't struck oil in the first three minutes, *stop boring!*

Jessel sets up a context where conversational success (a special case of ACHIEVING A PURPOSE) is metaphorically described as drilling for oil (a special case of ACQUIRING A DESIRED OBJECT). The failure to be interesting and the failure to find oil through unsuccessful drilling can both be described with the word *boring*. Jessel's advice therefore works on two levels. He advises that you should give up boring for oil, metaphorically meaning you should abandon the conversation. He also advises you to literally stop being boring.

The winning entry to a purple prose competition, written by Mike Pedersen of North Berwick, Maine, uses repetition to make readers consider a literal reading where they otherwise wouldn't have experienced ambiguity. This passage relies on repeated non-metaphoric references to the colour blue, so that when this colour is finally used as a source domain it seems banal:

> As his small boat scudded before a brisk breeze under a sapphire sky dappled with cerulean clouds with indigo bases, through cobalt seas that deepened to navy nearer the boat and faded to azure at the horizon, Ian was at a loss as to why he felt blue.[35]

In a different context, *Ian was at a loss as to why he felt blue* wouldn't sound strange or ambiguous. Only the repeated references to this colour make readers think about the literal meaning of *blue*.

Serious works of prose can also get away with subtle word play involving ambiguity. The following example is from a nonfiction book:

> Octopuses have reached their long arms into all of the world's oceans and most of its seas.[36]

The passage uses CONTROL IS REACH to describe how octopuses have 'extended' their territory. Of course, octopuses are famous for their long, sinuous arms. Most readers probably begin reading the sentence thinking that it describes octopuses literally extending their arms. When readers reach *the world's oceans*, they have to revise their reading of the sentence and interpret it metaphorically. This can be awkward for a reader, so most authors use this kind of strategy sparingly.

Allegory

Most of the humour based on ambiguity between source- and target-domain interpretations is unsophisticated. Many examples could be called puns, as in the 'beard' joke or the 'seasoned veteran' joke. It may be surprising, then, that this kind of ambiguity is also the basis of a subtle literary device. This section can offer only a brief introduction to this literary strategy, but it's worth being aware that ambiguous metaphoric language isn't just an error or a game. Some of the most famous poetry and literature of all time relies on ambiguity between metaphoric and literal readings.

When a lengthy text or speech is technically ambiguous but designed to be interpreted metaphorically, this is called *allegory*.[37] In allegorical texts, ambiguity adds subtlety. Allegorical texts don't throw the metaphor in the reader's face. The reader has to figure out the metaphoric meaning, which can make the reader more engaged in the text. More than this, allegory allows a writer to leave the metaphoric interpretation open, so that multiple readings of the text are possible. This openness can make the reader think about all the possible target-domain meanings of the text.

For example, poet Emily Dickinson's 'Over the fence' describes a little girl's longing to pick the strawberries that grow on the other side of a fence. Although the poem never names a metaphoric target domain, it's generally agreed that the poem metaphorically describes a grown woman who has a forbidden desire that is probably more complex than eating strawberries. Whereas the little girl is worried that God will be angry if she climbs the fence and stains her apron, the woman is presumably afraid that God will condemn her for 'staining' herself with sinful behaviour (MORALITY IS PURITY).

Although 'Over the fence' involves MORALITY IS PURITY, the most important metaphor in the poem is LIFE IS A JOURNEY. According to the structure of this metaphor, the little girl's yearning to climb a fence and eat strawberries corresponds to a woman's desire to achieve some forbidden LIFE goal. But what is this illicit desire? What goal in LIFE could be as delicious yet forbidden as the fenced-off field with the luscious strawberries? We don't know the answer because Dickinson never overtly mentions the woman or her desires. In theory, the poem could be nothing more than a simple narrative about a little girl.

The intentional ambiguity of 'Over the fence' makes us think about its possible readings. That is, the poem invites us to consider all the pleasurable life activities that were forbidden to women in nineteenth-century America. The poem could be about the stigma of female authorship, forbidden love, or countless other topics. Its meaning will probably forever remain a mystery.

Robert Frost's famous 1916 poem 'The Road Not Taken' is also allegorical. The poem begins, 'Two roads diverged in a yellow wood' and goes on to describe a traveller's anguish over having to choose one road in preference to the other. Throughout the poem, Frost never explicitly mentions the target domain of LIFE, so a purely literal reading of the poem is possible. The poem is technically ambiguous. However, most readers automatically assume that the poem metaphorically describes the choice of one life path over another, via LIFE IS A JOURNEY. Whereas Dickinson's allegory makes the reader brainstorm multiple interpretations, Frost's allegory seems to be intended to make us think about the metaphor itself. The LIFE IS A JOURNEY reading of the poem is so natural and automatic that most readers discount a literal reading right away, despite the poem's ambiguity.

But it's possible that these readers of 'The Road Not Taken' have been deceived. Frost described the work as a 'tricky poem'.[38] At one point, he claimed that the poem was about his friend Edward Thomas, 'who when they walked together always castigated himself for not having taken another path than the one they took'.[39] To Frost's disappointment, not even Thomas interpreted the poem as about himself and his walks. Thomas was apparently unashamed by his failure, writing 'I doubt if you can get anybody to see the fun of the thing without showing them and advising them which kind of laugh they are to turn on'.[40]

Thomas seems to have been right. Generations of readers of 'The Road Not Taken' have effortlessly, perhaps even unconsciously, accessed the domain of LIFE via the familiar metaphor LIFE IS A JOURNEY. Frost may have intended to draw attention to the ease of this metaphoric interpretation, and the power of the metaphor to obscure the literal meaning of the poem. Frost must have had some hidden intention with the poem, for he wrote that 'I bet not half a dozen people can tell who was hit and where he was hit by my Road Not Taken'.[41] Of the millions of people who have read this poem, it is indeed likely that fewer than six have immediately understood Frost's intention.

Perhaps, Frost's poem was meant as a comment on the automatic, instantaneous processing of metaphor. If so, he was ahead of his time. It's only in the past few decades that academics have begun to study the automaticity and naturalness of metaphoric interpretations. Of course, there's no way of knowing whether 'The Road Not Taken' was intended this way. Since the poem is ambiguous, its meaning will remain open to interpretation.

Whether or not 'The Road Not Taken' is a subtle joke, as Frost told his friend Thomas, we've seen that ambiguity does allow for the creation of jokes. Most of these are simple puns in which a metaphoric interpretation is encouraged but then negated. This process is not unlike the one readers go through when reading Frost's 'The Road Not Taken', which leads readers to first interpret the poem metaphorically and only then possibly question whether the metaphor was intended. Frost's poem suggests that the humorous and allegorical uses of ambiguous metaphoric language may be more related than they first appear.

Blending metaphoric and literal meanings

Some metaphoric passages don't force us to choose between a literal and a metaphoric reading. Instead, they make us consider both readings and then ask us to put these meanings together into something entirely new. This is called *blending* between the source and target domains.[42]

The blending of source and target domains can fulfil numerous purposes, from the silly to the serious. The internet meme in Figure 20 is on the playful side of the spectrum.

Glow sticks light up when you snap and shake them. The author of the 'glow sticks' meme suggests that people's intelligence, which is

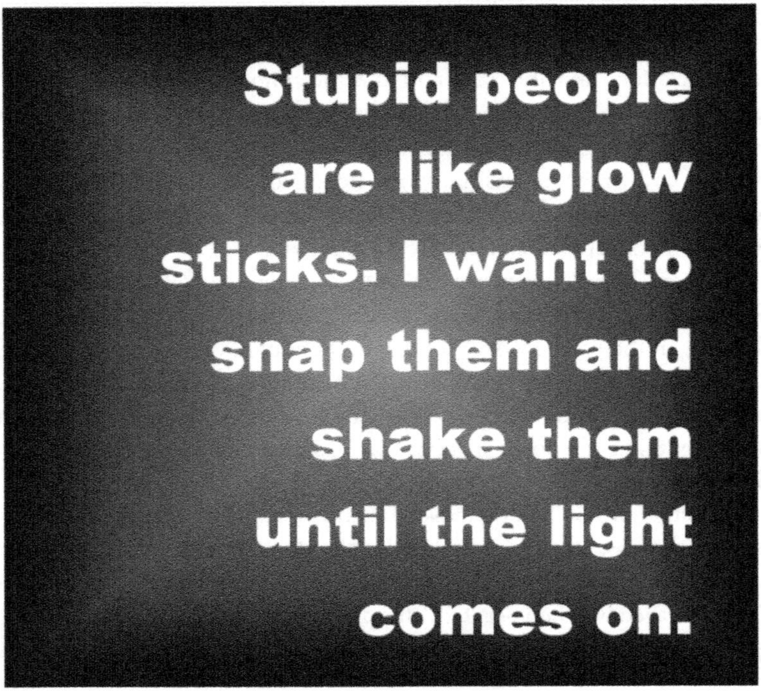

> **Stupid people are like glow sticks. I want to snap them and shake them until the light comes on.**

FIGURE 20 Glow sticks are activated by shaking, but human comprehension is not.

metaphorically the light they emit via UNDERSTANDING IS SEEING, can also be activated by snapping and shaking. Unfortunately, though it might be satisfying to shake someone who's annoying you, it won't make the person actually become 'brighter'. Humans never emit light, nor gain intelligence, no matter how much you shake them.

This example is blended, rather than strictly ambiguous, because it includes some information that can only be interpreted literally and some that only makes sense metaphorically. The suggested violence is literal (the author wants to physically shake the people's physical bodies), but it's predicted to have a metaphoric effect (it makes a metaphoric light come on, so the people stop being stupid). The example only makes sense when these two types of information are put together, which produces the novel idea that shaking people will make them smarter.

Some expressions that would never normally be ambiguous, such as the idiom *bite one's head off* 'severely criticize', can be forced into ambiguity via blending, in order to create humour. This occurs in the cartoon depicting a praying mantis in Figure 21.

Humans criticize each other (the metaphoric meaning of *bite one's head off*), whereas non-human animals literally bite each other's heads off. The idiom is only ambiguous when human and animal traits are blended, such as when an animal is given the ability to speak. The choice of a praying mantis adds to the double meaning because female mantises literally eat their mates and human wives stereotypically complain when their husbands are late (metaphorically 'biting their heads off'). This

FIGURE 21 Talking mantises might bite each other's heads off either literally or figuratively.

example artificially brings together the source and target meanings of a metaphor by creating a blended fantasy world in which mantises are able to talk, be married, and drink beer.

Blending has more serious uses, however. Since blended expressions draw on our knowledge of both the source and target domains of a metaphor, they can sound original and profound, as in this Buddhist advice:

> Holding on to anger is like grasping a hot coal with the intent of throwing it at someone else. You are the one who gets burned.

When we are angry, we may literally throw things with the intent of hurting someone. We may also 'throw' angry remarks around, via ARGUMENT IS PHYSICAL COMBAT, and our anger may be 'burning' via ANGER IS HEAT. Of course, if we were to grab an actual burning coal, it would sear our hands before we could throw it. The Buddhist advice blends literal 'throwing' and 'holding on' with metaphoric 'burning'. In the metaphor, the angry person will physically hold the hot coal, but will be emotionally 'damaged'. Like the 'glow sticks' example, the non-metaphorical action is expected to lead to a metaphoric result.

The following quotation from Ingrid Bergman uses the same strategy as the 'glow sticks' and 'burning coal' examples, but does so more subtly:

> Old age is like climbing a mountain. You climb from ledge to ledge. The higher you get, the more tired and breathless you become – but your views become more extensive.

Here, Bergman elegantly integrates LIFE IS A JOURNEY, UNDERSTANDING IS SEEING, and the real-world knowledge that older people more easily become tired and breathless. As you JOURNEY (i.e. LIVE your life), you can SEE more of the landscape around you (i.e. you UNDERSTAND more about life), but you also age and become more tired and out of breath. The passage is clever in that both climbing a mountain and ageing make you tired and breathless. The metaphors ring true because they include inferences that are valid in both the source and target domains. Not only does the passage seamlessly combine two metaphors, but it also includes details about ageing and physical exertion that make perfect sense in both the source and target domains of LIFE IS A JOURNEY.

Zeugma

Although two domains can sometimes be blended, this must be done with care, as in the Bergman example. It's easy to blend domains in ways that don't work. This is apparent in the phenomenon called *zeugma*, a literary term related to the Greek word for 'yoke'. Zeugma 'yokes together' two incompatible meanings of a word and forces them to be understood simultaneously in a way that doesn't make sense. The type of zeugma that is relevant here requires that a word be understood both metaphorically and non-metaphorically, as in *He fished for compliments and trout*.

Zeugma is immediately obvious to language users. We like to know what a word means in context, which is why we often find ambiguity irritating or funny. Zeugma tends to elicit even stronger reactions than ambiguity. Not only does it make us question whether a word is metaphoric or not, but it makes the question impossible to resolve, because it requires that the same word simultaneously have both meanings.

The sentence *He fished for compliments and trout* involves zeugma because it indicates that the word *fished* should be understood both metaphorically and literally. If you 'fish for compliments', the fishing is metaphoric, via ACHIEVING A PURPOSE IS ACQUIRING A DESIRED OBJECT. If you 'fish for trout', on the other hand, the fishing is literal. If you fish for both at once, then the verb *fish* has to simultaneously have two meanings. The zeugma in the sentence makes it sound strange or funny.

It's not difficult to come up with new examples of zeugma (there are long lists of these online, for the true aficionados). Many of these closely resemble the 'fishing' sentence above. In *She opened her mind and her wallet*, the verb *opened* has to indicate both literal and metaphoric 'opening'. If you open your mind, you metaphorically allow ideas to enter it, via COMMUNICATING IS OBJECT TRANSFER. If you open your wallet, you literally cause your wallet to be open. Technically, opening a wallet is metonymic in this sentence, since it stands for the act of giving money. Regardless, opening a wallet is not the same as opening a mind. Both can't be accomplished as part of the same act of 'opening'.

Usually, zeugma affects only a single word, such as *fished* or *opened*. Any additional relevant words help disambiguate the meaning. The sentence *He fished for compliments by frequently mentioning his snazzy outfit* makes it clear that the 'fishing' is metaphorical. *He fished for compliments and trout by frequently mentioning his snazzy outfit* is nonsense, not zeugma. The extra phrase *by frequently mentioning his snazzy outfit* makes it clear that the sentence is about metaphoric 'fishing' not literal fishing, and the zeugma disappears.

Zeugma is so conspicuous that it is used as a linguistic test for whether words have multiple distinct meanings. For example, if we want to test whether the sense of *have* in *have a house* is the same as the sense of *have* in *have a dog*, we can coordinate the two, as in *He had a nice house and a cute little dog*. This sentence sounds fine, so these meanings of *have* appear to be the same. If we want to test these senses against the meaning of *have* in *have a grudge*, we can coordinate this sense too: *He had a nice house, a small dog, and a grudge against society*. If this sentence sounds odd or funny to you (as it does to me), then it can be judged to demonstrate zeugma and involve more than one sense of *have*. In fact, the sense of *have* as in *have a grudge* is metaphoric because a grudge is an attribute of a person, not a possession, so it can be 'had' ('possessed') only in a metaphoric sense via ATTRIBUTES ARE POSSESSIONS.

Metaphoric zeugma rarely occurs by accident. It's usually used to create a humorous effect, as in:

The farmers grew potatoes, radishes and bored.

In literature, zeugma tends to be subtler, but still has humorous overtones, as when Charles Dickens writes:

Mr. Pickwick ... took his hat and his leave ...[43]

Here, the physical and metaphorical 'taking' are juxtaposed (ACHIEVING A PURPOSE IS ACQUIRING A DESIRED OBJECT). Similarly, in the title of the comedic novel *Tea and Trouble Brewing*, the 'brewing' is both literal and metaphorical (IDEAS ARE OBJECTS, so causing trouble can be understood as 'making' trouble).[44]

The humour is darker in *Star Trek: The Next Generation* when Commander Riker tells an alien representative:

'You are free to execute your laws, and your citizens, as you see fit.'

Although Riker's comment is cynical, it's far from the darkest use of zeugma in the English language. This award might have to go to the following passage from Robert Bloch's classic horror novel *Psycho*:

It was the knife that, a moment later, cut off her scream. And her head.⁴⁵

All of these examples are typical of zeugma, in that they conjoin two arguments, such as *laws* and *citizens*, with the conjunction *and*. Occasionally, the two arguments are juxtaposed in different ways. For example, when the characters in a novel contemplate leaving their hiding place as an army approaches, the narrator reports their failure to flee using two senses of *run out*, the first of which involves TIME IS A RESOURCE:

Time ran out. We didn't.⁴⁶

The subjects *time* and *we* necessitate the metaphoric and literal senses of *run out*, respectively. In the second sentence, the verb *did* refers back to the verb phrase *ran out*, which relates the two subjects and allows zeugma to occur without the use of *and*. Like the Star Trek and *Psycho* quotations, however, the passage sounds ironic or darkly humorous.

The zeugma in the subtitle of the 1970 pulp erotic novel *Nympho Librarian* is unusual in that it doesn't directly name the object of the literal sense of verb phrase *took off*:

The prim miss took off more than her mask of respectability behind the stacks ... with any man who asked⁴⁷

The text doesn't directly state what else the librarian 'took off' besides the 'mask' that metaphorically hid her promiscuity via UNDERSTANDING IS SEEING. Any confusion, however, would soon be dissipated by the cover image, which depicts a near-nude librarian straddling a male library visitor – still helplessly clutching his library book – which makes it obvious that she took off her clothes.

Zeugma can seem less glaring when the two senses are compared, rather than directly conjoined. This is usually accomplished with *as ... as*, like in *as black as* in the following:

(He) stood just inside the fall of the light, meticulously dressed, eyes as black as his heart.⁴⁸

The effects of zeugma are also softened by the use of a *like*-construction (i.e. by simile). This draws attention to the metaphor and shows that the juxtaposition of two meanings is intentional. The actress Zsa Zsa Gabor comments:

> Husbands are like fires. They go out when unattended.

The physical motion sense of *go out* is evoked alongside the metaphoric 'extinguish' sense (EXISTING IS BEING PHYSICALLY AT THIS LOCATION). Gabor's remark relies on the fact that we have many other conceptual metaphors involving fires, such as PASSION IS FIRE. Gabor's initial comparison of husbands and fires might lead us to expect a more romantic metaphor involving passion or even anger. In Gabor's second sentence, the relatively prosaic comparison is unexpected and perhaps funny.

English poet Edward Young uses a *like*-construction to express a gloomier sentiment:

> Like our shadows, our wishes lengthen as our sun declines.

The double meaning of *lengthen* (the physical sense applicable to shadows, and the metaphoric sense referring to an 'increase' in intensity via QUANTITY IS SIZE) is reinforced by another metaphor, A LIFETIME IS A DAY, in which old age is understood as evening. Shadows literally lengthen near sunset, which adds a ring of truth to the poignant observation that our wishes (and our regrets) become more intense as death approaches.

Graceful uses of zeugma, such as Young's nostalgic sentiment, are rare. The widespread unacceptability of zeugma supports the generalization that metaphors work best when the source and target domains are distinct. Zeugma is the ultimate infraction of this advice, in that it requires words to simultaneously have source- and target-domain meanings. The discomfort that most people have with zeugma suggests that the less extreme infractions, described throughout the chapter, might also be expected to bother or distract some readers.

This chapter finishes our survey of the ways that metaphors can mix. However, all along we've left out one crucial ingredient from the metaphor mix. That is, we haven't discussed metaphoric idioms. Idioms were saved for last because they are a complicating factor all their own, which can be better appreciated after considering the behaviour of non-idiomatic metaphors.

Let's now add this factor into consideration and see the mixes that can result.

Notes

1. *The British National Corpus*, version 3, BNC XML Edition. Distributed by Oxford University Computing Services on behalf of the BNC Consortium, 2007. Available online: http://www.natcorp.ox.ac.uk/ (accessed 7 October 2017).
2. Semino, 'A Corpus-Based Study of "Mixed Metaphor"'. Scott, 'Mixed Metaphors'. Carlton, 'My Favorite Mixed Metaphors'.
3. Grace Gagliano and Sara Kennedy, 'Much of the Gulf Dodged the Oil But Not Its Taint', *Bradenton Herald*, 29 July 2010. Available online: http://www.sacbee.com/latest-news/article2572971.html (Accessed 10 April 2018).
4. Green Mill Restaurant and Bar. Paper menu.
5. Yael Chanoff, 'Project Censored: The Expanding Police State Tops the Annual List of Stories Underreported by the Mainstream Media', *Boulder Weekly*, 11 October 2012. Available online: http://www.boulderweekly.com/news/project-censored/ (accessed 11 December 2016).
6. Several metaphors may be involved here: ACHIEVING A PURPOSE IS REACHING A DESTINATION, in which 'sinking' is understood as the failure to achieve; and a special case of GOODNESS IS VERTICALITY, in which you stay 'up' by staying afloat.
7. Redcliffe KiteFest, Facebook event, 2016.
8. Scott, 'Mixed Metaphors'.
9. Camilla Läckberg, *The Ice Princess*, trans. Steven T. Murray (New York: Harper Collins, 2003), 214.
10. *Watercolor Artist*, February 2016, 60.
11. *The British National Corpus*.
12. BBC News, 'Actresses' Lines 'Decrease with Age', Study Claims', May 2016. Available online: http://www.bbc.com/news/entertainment-arts-36195979 (accessed 13 December 2016).
13. *Fresh Independence*, '"I Was a Stoner & He Was the Cowboy" – Songwriter Jimmy Webb Remembers Glen Campbell', 30 November 2015. Available online: http://freshindependence.com/friends-for-life/ (accessed 11 December 2016).
14. Brisbane City Cat, On-screen public announcement, 31 July 2012. In the intended compound metaphor, one bright object (renewable energy)

increases in size relative to another (coal), eventually blocking the light (renown) of the smaller object.

15 Scott, 'Mixed Metaphors'.
16 Saul Hubbard *The Register-Guard*, 'Courthouse Size Would Double', 25 May 2015.
17 Melissa Healy. 'Will Obesity Reverse the Life-Span Gains Made over Decades of Health Triumphs?' *Los Angeles Times*, 4 April 2016. Available online: http://www.latimes.com/science/sciencenow/la-sci-sn-obesity-will-reverse-lifespan-20160403-story.html (accessed 16 March 2018).
18 Kevin Gifford, 'Let's Talk Saturation: Is There Such a Thing as Too Many Breweries?', *Source Weekly*, 1 March 2017. Available online: http://www.bendsource.com/bend/lets-talk-saturation/Content?oid=2893289 (accessed 14 March 2017).
19 Stephanie Strom, 'Organic Produce Purists Planting Seeds of Doubt about Food Certification', *The Register-Guard*, 16 November 2016.
20 Yasmine Galenorn, *Demon Mistress* (New York: Berkley, 2005).
21 Andrea Jensen, Nicole Weymouth and Beth Sebern, 'Women's Crew Claims First Season Victories', *The Tech* 115, no. 19 (21 April 1995). Available online: http://tech.mit.edu/V115/N19/wcrew.19s.html (accessed 11 December 2016).
22 Carlton, 'My Favorite Mixed Metaphors'.
23 Hofstadter and Moser, 'To Err Is Human'. Scott, 'Mixed Metaphors'.
24 *The British National Corpus.*
25 Scott, 'Mixed Metaphors'.
26 Library of Congress, 'Rosa Parks Was Arrested for Civil Disobedience December 1, 1955', *America's Story,* 2017. Available online: http://www.americaslibrary.gov/jb/modern/jb_modern_parks_1.html (accessed 23 May 2017).
27 Jeff Wysaski, 'Really Bad Analogies Written by High School Students', *Pleated Jeans*, 12 October 2012. Available online: http://pleated-jeans.com/2012/10/12/analogies-written-by-high-school-students/ (accessed 11 December 2016).
28 Ronald Reagan, *An American Life* (New York: Simon and Schuster, 1990), 80.
29 Wysaski, 'Really Bad Analogies'.
30 Michael Foss, *Gods and Heroes: The Story of Greek Mythology* (London: Michael O'Mara Books, 2014).
31 Wysaski, 'Really Bad Analogies'.

32 Walford Davies and Ralph Maud, eds. *The Collected Poems of Dylan Thomas* (London: Dent, 1988) 24.

33 Jean Bow, *Jane's Journey* (Leicester: The Book Guild Ltd., 1991).

34 *The Register-Guard*, 'KWAX Nostalgic: Jack Fleming Ends More than 30 Years at Eugene Radio Station', 21 April 2016.

35 *Fosters.com*, 'North Berwick Writer Wins Contest's Purple Prose Category', 1 August 2011. Available online: http://www.fosters.com/article/20110801/gjcommunity_01/110729486 (accessed 11 December 2016).

36 Katherine Harmon Courage, *Octopus! The Most Mysterious Creature in the Sea* (New York: Penguin Group, 2013), 13.

37 Brooke-Rose 1958. Stockwell, 'The Metaphorics of Literary Reading'. Peter Crisp, 'Allegory: Conceptual Metaphor in History', *Language and Literature* 10, no. 5 (2001): 5–19. Peter Crisp, John Heywood, and Gerard J. Steen, 'Metaphor Identification and Analysis, Classification and Quantification', *Language and Literature* 11, no. 1 (2002): 55–69. Pragglejaz Group, 2007.

38 William H. Pritchard, *Frost: A Literary Life Reconsidered* (Oxford: Oxford University Press, 1984), 128.

39 Pritchard, *Frost: A Literary Life Reconsidered*, 128.

40 Pritchard, *Frost: A Literary Life Reconsidered*, 128.

41 William H. Pritchard, *Shelf Life: Literary Essays and Reviews* (Amherst, MA: University of Massachusetts Press, 2003), 7.

42 To some extent, all metaphors put together aspects of the source and target into something new, so many researchers treat all metaphors as blends and consider the unidirectional metaphors discussed elsewhere in this book as a special kind of blend. See Gilles Fauconnier, *Mental Spaces* (New York: Cambridge University Press, 1994). Joseph E. Grady, Todd Oakley, and Seana Coulson, 'Blending and Metaphor', in *Metaphor in Cognitive Linguistics*, ed. Gerard J. Steen and Raymond W.Gibbs Jr (Amsterdam and Philadelphia: John Benjamins, 1999). However, only metaphors that mingle source- and target-domain information in a non-unidirectional way are here termed 'blends'.

43 Charles Dickens, *The Posthumous Papers of the Pickwick Club* (London: Chapman & Hall, 1827).

44 Dorcas Smucker, *Tea and Trouble Brewing* (Intercourse, PA: Good Books, 2012).

45 Robert Bloch, *Psycho* (New York: Simon & Schuster, 1959).

46 Naomi Novik, *Uprooted* (New York: Del Rey, 2016), 162.

47 Les Tucker, *Nympho Librarian* (New York: Bee-line Press, 1970).

48 Nicole Margot Spencer, *The Lady in the Locket* (Lincoln, NE: iUniverse, 2005), 76.

Further Reading on Blending

Coulson, Seana. *Semantic Leaps: Frame-Shifting and Conceptual Blending in Meaning Construction*. New York and Cambridge: Cambridge University Press, 2001.

▌Dancygier, Barbara. 'What Can Blending Do for You?' *Language and Literature* 15, no. 1 (2006): 5–15.

Fauconnier, Gilles. *Mental Spaces*, 1985. Reprint. Cambridge: Cambridge University Press, 1994.

▌Fauconnier, Gilles. *Mappings in Thought and Language*. Cambridge: Cambridge University Press, 1997.

Fauconnier, Gilles and Mark Turner. 'Blending as a Central Process of Grammar'. In *Conceptual Structure, Discourse, and Language*, edited by A. Goldberg, 113–30. Stanford, CA: CSLI, 1996.

Fauconnier, Gilles and Mark Turner. 'Conceptual Integration Networks'. *Cognitive Science* 22, no. 2 (1998a): 133–87.

Fauconnier, Gilles and Mark Turner. 'Principles of Conceptual Integration'. In *Discourse and Cognition: Bridging the Gap*, edited by Jean-Pierre Koenig, 269–83. Stanford, CA: CSLI, 1998b.

▌Fauconnier, Gilles and Mark Turner. *The Way We Think. Conceptual Blending and the Mind's Hidden Complexities*. New York: Basic Books, 2002.

Grady, Joseph, Todd Oakley and Seana Coulson. 'Conceptual Blending and Metaphor'. In *Metaphor in Cognitive Linguistics*, edited by Gerard Steen and Raymond W. Gibbs Jr, 100–24. Amsterdam and Philadelphia: John Benjamins, 1999.

Turner, Mark, and Gilles Fauconnier. 'Conceptual Integration and Formal Expression'. *Metaphor and Symbolic Activity* 10, no. 3 (1995): 183–203.

Turner, Mark, and Gilles Fauconnier. 'A Mechanism of Creativity'. *Poetics Today* 20, no. 3 (1999): 397–418.

▌Turner, Mark. *Cognitive Dimensions of Social Science*. Oxford: Oxford University Press, 2001.

6 MALAPHORS AND OTHER 'DUCKS OUT OF WATER'

Many mixed metaphors are actually combinations of metaphoric idioms.[1] For instance, every single mixed metaphor in *The Complete Idiot's Guide to Grammar and Style* involves idioms, as in *That wet blanket is a loose cannon* and *A rolling stone gathers no bird in the hand*. Expressions such as *wet blanket, loose cannon, rolling stone,* and *bird in the hand* are considered idioms because they are fixed expressions with meanings that we have to learn separately, even if we know all the words they include. Someone who knows the meanings of *wet* and *blanket*, for example, still has to learn that *wet blanket* refers to a person who's no fun, rather than a blanket that's literally wet. Many idioms, including *wet blanket*, have meanings that involve conceptual metaphors, which makes them specifically metaphoric idioms.[2]

Why do writing guides such as *The Complete Idiot's Guide to Grammar and Style* choose metaphoric idioms to illustrate the concept of mixed metaphor? Metaphors can be mixed in a variety of ways without the need for idioms, as we've seen throughout this book. Nonetheless, metaphoric idioms seem particularly easy to mix because their metaphoric meanings aren't apparent unless we know the idioms' historical origins. For example, wet blankets were traditionally used to put out fires. Because PASSION is metaphorically HEAT, a metaphoric 'wet blanket' is someone who stifles the enthusiasm ('puts out the fire') of others. Only this historical link to firefighting connects *wet blanket* 'person who spoils others' fun' to the metaphor PASSION IS HEAT. For speakers who lack this historical knowledge, *wet blanket* is a dead metaphor, and the idiom directly means 'person who spoils others' fun' without any metaphoric connection.

Similarly, a loose cannon on a ship would roll around and risk damaging its own vessel, which is why a human 'loose cannon' is considered to metaphorically shoot off an unpredictable barrage of rhetoric via ARGUMENT IS PHYSICAL COMBAT. However, for speakers who don't think of a ship when they use the idiom *loose cannon*, the idiom is a dead metaphor that simply means 'unpredictably destructive person'.

A speaker who is aware of the metaphoric meaning of *wet blanket* will probably take care to combine this phrase with compatible metaphoric language, as in *He was a wet blanket who extinguished any spark of humour*. On the other hand, a speaker who doesn't know that a *wet blanket* is a fire-fighting tool is unlikely to select compatible metaphors. This kind of speaker might produce an idiom combination such as *He was a wet blanket and a loose cannon* with the intended meaning 'he was unpredictably destructive and no fun'. Of course, nothing can simultaneously be a blanket and a cannon. Even someone who is unfamiliar with the metaphoric origins of the idioms may recognize that a blanket and a cannon are two different things and therefore may consider the metaphor mixed.

Although *that wet blanket is a loose cannon* was presumably invented by the author of *The Complete Idiot's Guide to Grammar and Style*, equally bizarre idiom combinations are produced in real life. Some of the oddest idiom combinations are attributed to politicians, who either are particularly prone to produce them or are especially likely to be quoted if they do. UK Labour Secretary Ernest Bevin provided a classic example in 1948, when he issued the following warning:

> When you open that Pandora's box, you will find it full of Trojan horses!

The Labour Secretary seems to have had a general sense of the idioms' metaphoric meanings because he chose two idioms that involve the metaphor UNDERSTANDING IS SEEING, in which sudden knowledge is understood as sudden visibility. Both Pandora's box and the Trojan horse are containers that open and reveal dangerous contents (evil demons and enemy warriors, respectively). The concepts can therefore metaphorically describe unpleasant discoveries. In addition, both idioms have mythological origins. One refers to the opening of Pandora's box, which contained all the evils of the world, and the other is based on the wooden horse full of warriors that the Greeks supposedly used to win the Trojan War. Although *Pandora's box* and *Trojan horse* are similar idiomatic noun phrases with similar metaphoric meanings, the Trojan horse was never inside Pandora's box, so the metaphors don't make sense together.

The same politician Bevin produced a second scintillating example when he issued another warning:

> If you let that sort of thing go on, your bread and butter will be cut out right from under your feet.

Back when the expression *one's bread and butter* became an idiom, bread and butter were the staple foods of many people's diets. Metaphorically, they represented one's main form of income (via WEALTH IS FOOD). The idiom *bread and butter* retains this metaphoric meaning, even though bread and butter have arguably lost their importance now that much of the English-speaking population avoids carbs, fat, or gluten.

The idiom *cut out from under one's feet*, on the other hand, involves ASSISTANCE IS SUPPORT, in which the sudden cessation of an essential resource is understood as the abrupt loss of physical support. Since one's main form of income is always an essential resource, Bevin's idioms work well together on the target-domain level and describe the sudden loss of one's main form of income. The problem, as usual, is that the source-domain meanings of the two idioms are inconsistent. Even people who eat bread and butter do not stand on top of it, and therefore would not be worried about it being cut out from under their feet.

In 2010, before he became Prime Minister of Australia, Opposition Leader Tony Abbott mixed two idioms in reference to the Labor government:

> There's a lot of dirty water to flow under the bridge – they're throwing the kitchen sink at us.

The idiom *water under the bridge* involves TIME IS A MOVING OBJECT, according to which events 'flow by' into the past. Here, the *water* is *dirty*, which tells us that the events in question were nasty (MORALITY IS PURITY). The idiom *throwing the kitchen sink at us* uses ARGUMENT IS PHYSICAL COMBAT, by which an uncalled-for verbal attack is understood as a large unwieldy, and inappropriate weapon (the kitchen sink).

Two issues make the idioms likely to be interpreted as a mixed metaphor. First, many readers will attempt to combine the metaphors because they seem at first glance to be related. Both idioms' literal meanings involve water, which flows out of sinks and under bridges. Second, kitchen sinks and bridges don't usually have much to do with each other, so readers will quickly discover that it's hard to put the two source domains together in any meaningful way. Abbott's expression might therefore suggest the unusual scenario in which a sink with broken plumbing is spouting dirty water that then flows under a bridge.

It may be easier to form a mental image for the following example, a news headline. It describes a news corporation chief's visit to a rival news corporation headquarters:

> Michelle Guthrie enters the News Corp lion's den and circles the elephant in the room.[3]

The author of the headline may have thought she was clever to combine idioms about lions and elephants, which are both African animals. It may have been cleverer, though, to consider the structure of the two metaphoric idioms. A lion's den is a physically dangerous place, so a metaphoric 'lion's den' is a socially or intellectually threatening location (THE MIND IS A BODY). The *elephant in the room* idiom involves IMPORTANCE IS SIZE and UNDERSTANDING IS SEEING. The elephant is a big, visible animal that metaphorically represents an important topic that everybody knows about but nobody mentions. From one perspective, this idiom shouldn't work, because the source domain is unfamiliar. None of us have entered a room and discovered an elephant, or attended a party where a huge elephant took up most of the space. On the other hand, we've all seen pictures of elephants, and we've all been in crowded rooms, so it's easy to imagine how awful it would be to be in a small, crowded space with an elephant. Also, now that the idiom is so well established, anyone who has heard it once has imagined the elephant, which makes it easier to do the next time.

The 'elephant' idiom still doesn't combine well with other metaphors. This is especially true in cases such as the above example, in which the metaphors are obviously contradictory. In the 'lion' metaphor, the NewsCorp headquarters is a den, whereas in the 'elephant' metaphor, it is a room. Any readers who notice that a lion's den can't be a room are likely to perceive the metaphors as mixed. There's an additional logical flaw to the metaphors, in that lions would surely attack an elephant that was in their den. Even if humans managed to ignore the elephant, hungry lions would notice potential prey. The lions might even choose to attack the elephant instead of Guthrie, which would make the lion's den actually safer than usual.

A superficial similarity between idioms, such as the 'lion' and 'elephant' metaphors, encourages the metaphors to combine, but does nothing to help them do so in a meaningful way. Some authors seem to assume that any commonality between two idioms makes them compatible. These authors then produce metaphors that readers will put together and often will perceive as mixed.

As another example, the following news headline from 2016 mixes two ship-related idioms:

Grim future with loose cannon Trump at the helm.[4]

A loose cannon rolls around a ship and shoots unpredictably. Here, the newly elected US President is metaphorically steering a ship into the future (LIFE IS A JOURNEY). The oddity in this passage is that the loose cannon is also the ship's helmsman. Both cannons and helmsmen are found on ships, but this doesn't make them equivalent or interchangeable.

Some pairs of metaphoric idioms, like other metaphor combinations, lead to source domains that are improbable rather than impossible. The idiom *on the fence* 'undecided' frequently participates in combinations of this kind. If you are balanced on a literal fence, you can jump down on either side and go in either direction. If you're metaphorically 'on a fence', then you're free to choose either of two life options, via LIFE IS A JOURNEY. The idiom also implies that the choice is not easily reversible. It's a lot of work to change your mind and climb over a fence again to go the other way.

Anyone who was on the fence about voting for Trump was pushed firmly into his corner by the behaviour exhibited by his opponents.[5]

If you 'go into someone's corner', you agree with and assist that person. The idiom is based on boxing, in which each opponent fights from a particular corner. Of course, a real-world boxing ring doesn't have fences that you can balance on, so the idioms don't make sense if they're put together.

The next misuse of *on the fence* is attributed to Sir Joh Bjelke-Petersen when he was the Premier of Queensland, Australia:

> You can't sit on a fence, a barbed wire fence at that, and have one ear to the ground.⁶

This idiom combination is especially delightful because it's negated. That is, the scenario is described as something you can't do. It's completely true that you can't literally sit on a barbed wire fence and also have your ear on the ground. Of course, the Premier meant that you can't be indecisive (LIFE IS A JOURNEY) in a painful situation such as sitting on barbed wire (THE MIND IS A BODY) and still have a good idea of what's happening (UNDERSTANDING IS HEARING). The source domain, however, is so obviously impossible that we don't really need to be warned about it.

Metaphoric idioms, like other metaphors, are more likely to combine if they're similar. They are then likely to appear mixed if they don't combine well. This is apparent in the 'Pandora's box', 'elephant in the room', and 'on the fence' examples above. In idioms, as in non-idiomatic expressions, metaphors that are very different are less likely to combine and therefore less likely to cause problems. The idioms in the following expression (from Montana State Senator Chuck Swysgood, R-Dillon) sound regional and rural, but they may seem less confused than the previous examples, because the idioms are more dissimilar:

> I'm going to be like a burr under a saddle blanket because I want to know exactly what kind of a pig in a poke we bought here.

The 'burr' idiom involves THE MIND IS A BODY and the 'pig in a poke' draws on UNDERSTANDING IS SEEING. Of course, burrs don't buy pigs. Despite this potential issue, the two idioms' literal meanings have so little in common that some readers won't even attempt to understand them together, in which case the metaphors won't mix.

All the above quotations from politicians convey emotional agitation, outrage, and suppressed anger. Mixed metaphors in idioms, like other mixed metaphors, suggest a lack of emotional control. As you might have guessed from the above examples, politicians generally use them when complaining about their political opponents. The mixed metaphors certainly communicate the politicians' sense of outrage, but they also suggest confusion and ignorance, which may not be to the politicians' advantage.

Of course, politicians are not the only people who combine metaphoric idioms in nonsensical ways. Constantine Kortesis, the president of a consulting company, uses three idioms and a metaphoric use of *worship* when he describes his experience at his former company:

> While I was still at EDS, I encountered many loyalists who continued to 'drink the Kool-Aid' in worship of the top bananas who were literally selling us down the river.

Bananas, of course, are not usually worshipped with Kool-Aid rituals, nor are they capable of selling human slaves. Kortesis's criticism is as emotionally charged and confused as any of the politicians' quotations. Like the politicians, the company president uses idioms with mixed metaphors to denigrate his competitors. Perhaps, the only difference between business executives and politicians is that the politicians receive more attention from the press, so their mixed metaphors are more often recorded.

After politicians and businesspeople, sportspeople seem to be the most frequent perpetrators of mixed metaphors involving idioms. Here, Seahawks athletic director Eric Nelson describes the disappointing end to a losing season.

> 'Obviously, it's been a difficult two days for us', Nelson said. 'We kind of saw the writing on the wall Friday night. It's just apples versus oranges, and it's not a level playing field by any means.'⁷

As in many mixed metaphors, the coach's string of three idioms reflects emotional distress. There is no easy way to put together Nelson's metaphoric idioms, which actually saves them from being even more confusing. Nevertheless, the number of unrelated idioms seems unwarranted. Idioms draw attention to themselves, so if they're not used with discretion, even a few can seem excessive.

Mixed metaphors in idioms, like other mixed metaphors, can express ignorance and lack of control. They also resemble other mixed metaphors in that they can be mixed in various ways. For instance, the last chapter looked at examples where the metaphoric meaning was at odds with the literal meaning. Idioms can have this problem, too. An announcer for the 2012 London Olympics said that swimmer *Ryan Lochte is in the gravy now*, meaning that he was likely to win gold. The idiom *in the gravy* reflects GOODNESS IS FAT, in which over-the-top luxury is understood as the final, excessive, fatty addition to a meal. It sounds odd in this context because a swimmer could potentially compete in actual gravy, though this would be a strange Olympic event. Idioms with this problem seem to be relatively rare.

What are malaphors?

Some might excuse the mixed metaphors in idioms as mere 'slips of the tongue', but most of these mixes are not speech errors in the traditional linguistic sense. Genuine speech errors in idioms usually take the form of *malaphors*,[8] called 'idiom blends' by linguists, in which one or more words from one idiom are replaced by words from another idiom.[9] Sometimes this results in a mixed metaphor, and sometimes it does not. Although the term *malaphor* derives from *malapropism* and *metaphor*,[10] not all malaphors are metaphors. Similarly, not all malaphors are malapropisms (speech errors that replace one word with a similar-sounding one), in that the replacement word in the idiom often does not sound like the original word.

When one or both of the idioms in a malaphor are metaphoric, the malaphor is indeed often a mixed metaphor. This is easy to see in the popular malaphor *wake up and smell the music*, which combines *wake up and smell the coffee* 'pay attention to what's going on' and *face the music* 'suffer the consequences'. The source-domain meanings of the two idioms are technically incompatible because music is heard, not smelled. As in most mixed metaphors, the target-domain meaning of the idiom combination is fine. It's perfectly possible to simultaneously become aware of what's going on and suffer the consequences for your actions. Only the source domains of the metaphors clash. As a side note, though *wake up and smell the music* may have started life as a speech error, some speakers have adopted it as an idiom, and now use it intentionally. It has even inspired the title of a music-themed radio show and several music events.

The exclamation *he's got a lot of balls in the fire!* is another mixed-metaphor malaphor. This malaphor was presumably intended to mean something like 'he's busy and audacious', based on its component idioms *he's got a lot of balls* 'he's audacious' and *he's got a lot of irons in the fire* 'he's busy'.[11] In the malaphor, however, the source-domain scenario goes beyond 'audacious' and isn't a normal way of keeping 'busy'. This outlandish source domain qualifies the malaphor as a mixed metaphor.

Many malaphors are non-metaphoric and therefore never involve mixed metaphors. A popular non-metaphoric malaphor is *Does the Pope shit in the woods?* This expression is a blend of *Is the Pope Catholic?* meaning 'Yes, of course' and *Does a bear shit in the woods?* meaning 'Yes, of course'. These idioms are not metaphoric and instead play with the usual structure of the question–answer exchange. Instead of directly answering 'yes' to a question that clearly deserves a 'yes' response, speakers can answer with one of these idiomatic questions that also have an obvious 'yes' answer. Of course, the Pope is an elderly man with access to good lavatory facilities, so the malaphor differs from both of the blended idioms in that it has a 'no' answer. This reversal makes the malaphor potentially humorous.

Like other slips of the tongue, malaphors can reveal sentiments that the speaker didn't intend to share, such as when a member of the US men's 4×100 Olympic team said, *We can still hang our heads high*, replacing hold in *hold one's head high* 'be proud' with *hang* from *hang one's head* 'be ashamed'. The Olympian wanted to say that their team could take pride in their performance despite failing to win, but his disappointment showed in his accidental use of *hang* instead of *hold*. Again, no metaphor is involved in this example. Both 'hanging one's head' and 'holding it high' are metonymic. These are bodily postures that tend to accompany particular emotional states, so they can stand for those emotions metonymically (see Chapter 5 or the appendix for a definition of metonymy).

Usually, metaphoric idioms produce mixed-metaphor malaphors, and non-metaphoric idioms result in non-metaphoric malaphors. However, this is not necessarily the case. For example, some metaphoric malaphors make sense and therefore avoid the status of mixed metaphors according to the criteria listed in Chapter 1. In the malaphor *he's like a duck out of water*, *duck* is substituted for *fish* in the idiom *fish out of water* 'person in an unaccustomed context'.[12] Here, *duck* probably was taken from the idiom *water off a duck's back*. Of course, *duck* is not a good replacement for *fish*, because ducks can breathe, walk, and even fly when they're out of the water (Figure 22). The malaphor cannot mean that a person is in an unfamiliar and uncomfortable context, because ducks spend a lot of time out of the water. It might mean that the subject has lost one of his options (swimming) but still has others (walking and flying). For speakers who can make sense of the changed malaphor, it's still a metaphor, but it's not a mixed metaphor.

In most malaphors, one word comes from a different idiom. This is the case in the 'duck out of water' malaphor and can also be seen in *keep a stiff upper chin* 'be brave and don't show your emotions'. This malaphor is identical to the standard idiom *keep a stiff upper lip*, except that the word *chin* replaces *lip*. The changed word can be attributed to the idiom *keep your chin up*, which also means 'be brave and don't show your emotions'. Just as a fish and a duck are both animals, a chin and a lip are both body parts, which may have encouraged the speech error.

In some malaphors, the replaced word comes from the speaker's mental associations rather than from another idiom, as in *it'll be a cold day in January when that happens!*[13] Here, *January* replaces *hell*. This error replaces the contextually surprising word *hell* (where there are no cold days) with a more contextually obvious one, *January* (when there are many cold days). Unfortunately, this replacement undermines the basis of the idiom's meaning, which derives from the unlikelihood of a cold day in hell. In *it's like locking the barn door after the nuts have bolted*, where *nuts* replaces *horse*, the erroneous word *nuts* seems to have been

FIGURE 22 'Ducks out of water' seem fine.

prompted by the meaning of *bolted* 'attached with bolts' as opposed to the relevant meaning of *bolted* 'ran off'.[14]

Finally, the malaphor *you could have knocked me over with a fender* appears to be a genuine malapropism, in that the similar sounds in *feather* and *fender* seem to encourage the speech error.[15] As in the previous examples, however, the erroneous word is also semantically related to other words in the idiom. Fenders of motor vehicles can easily knock people over. The expression *knocked me over* may have led the speaker of this sentence to think of the word *fender* instead of the similar-sounding word *feather*. In all three of the previous malaphors, then, the inaccurate word (*January, nuts,* or *fender*) is inspired by other words in the same idiom, rather than coming from a different idiom.

Two psychologists at the University of Illinois, J. Cooper Cutting and Kathryn Bock, studied speech errors in idioms in a series of experiments.[16] Participants in these studies read two idioms in quick succession and then were asked to recall one of the idioms. The experimenters hoped that the participants would confuse the two idioms and produce malaphors (or 'idiom blends', in their terminology). These errors could then be studied to discover more about how idioms work. The studies were successful in that participants blended together idioms with similar syntax, such as *flip your lid* 'be angry' (ANGER IS THE HEAT OF FLUID IN A CONTAINER) and *hold your tongue* 'be quiet' (metonymic), producing malaphors such as *hold your lid* (Figure 23).

Participants were even more prone to blending idioms that had both similar syntax and meaning, as in *kick the bucket* 'die' and *meet one's maker* 'die', which led them to produce malaphors such as *kick the maker* and *kick the bucket maker*. This tendency showed that speakers are aware of the syntax of idioms, even when the syntax doesn't seem very important to the idiom's meaning, as in *kick the bucket* 'die'. When people 'kick the bucket', they're not causing a change to anyone or anything other than themselves, so the transitive syntax of the idiom doesn't make much sense. Nevertheless, Cutting and Bock's experiments showed that speakers were aware of the transitive syntax of the idiom because they were more likely to blend it with idioms that had similar syntax. The studies also help explain why malaphors such as *keep a stiff upper chin*, which combine idioms with similar meanings and similar syntax, are so widespread.

The malaphors produced in Cutting and Bock's experiments were true speech errors. When participants produced a malaphor, they

FIGURE 23 This man needs to 'hold his lid'.

usually knew they'd made a mistake. When the study was over, and the participants left the laboratory and went on with their lives, they didn't continue saying *kick the maker* to mean 'die' as if this were a real idiom. Rather, the participants had been temporarily confused into making one-off mistakes. This is not the case for the quotes from politicians at the start of this chapter, for example. These quotes don't blend together idioms, but instead combine whole idioms in ways that are at odds with the idioms' underlying metaphors. These combinations cannot be attributed to speech errors. Rather, they usually result from the speakers' unfamiliarity with the idioms' metaphoric meanings.

Malaphors, like most speech errors, can become part of the language if they are repeated often enough. For example, some speakers recurrently (and to their minds, correctly) use the expression *keep a stiff upper chin* because when they first heard this malaphor they accepted it as a correct usage. For these speakers, *keep a stiff upper chin* 'be brave and don't show your emotions' is a single idiom rather than a blend. Idioms with similar syntax and meaning are not only produced more frequently, as shown by Cutting and Bock's studies, but also more often become established as new 'real' idioms. This helps explain why *keep a stiff upper chin* has become a genuine idiom for some people, since the idioms *keep a stiff upper lip* and *keep your chin up* have similar forms and almost identical meanings.

Folk etymologies

Once a malaphor has been reanalysed as a single idiom, it may evolve and change independently of the original idioms. Sometimes, the new idiom is even reinterpreted so that it makes more sense. This has apparently happened in the case of *green behind the ears* 'inexperienced', which began as a blend of *wet behind the ears* 'inexperienced' and *green* 'inexperienced'. 'Grammar girl' Fogarty explains the probable origins of these two idioms:

> The most common explanation for why 'wet behind the ears' means young is that new babies are born covered in fluid, so they're wet, and behind the ears is one of the last places that dries if they aren't wiped off … There are a few reasons 'green' can mean young and inexperienced – branches are green before they harden into brown wood, and apparently horns can also be green in young animals, thus the word 'greenhorn'.[17]

According to Fogarty, *green behind the ears* is understood by corn farmers as referring to unripe ears of corn. If this is true, then the farmers have not only reanalysed the malaphor as a single idiom, but also invented a new reason for it to mean 'inexperienced'. This creative explanation is a *folk etymology*, a fictional history for a word or phrase. Folk etymologies usually occur when the original motivation for an expression is lost. This is the case for *wet behind the ears*, which few present-day speakers would connect to fluid-covered infants. A folk etymology involving ears of corn might make more sense to some speakers.

Interestingly, the folk etymology for *green behind the ears* removes the mixed metaphor from the idiom. The source-domain scenario of a person with green colouration behind the ears is an unfamiliar one, so the original malaphor is a mixed metaphor according to the criteria listed in Chapter 1. On the other hand, there's nothing odd or unfamiliar about finding green colour on a corn plant, so the reanalysed idiom is not a mixed metaphor. Folk etymologies are attempts to make sense of expressions such as idioms, and in this case the folk etymology seems to have succeeded.

As a side note, if you see a connection between 'ears' of corn and human or animal ears, this too is a folk etymology. Historically, these two senses of *ear* are unrelated. The 'corn' sense of *ear* comes from Old English *éare*, which refers to a stage of corn growth and has nothing to do with the ears on human beings or animals.

Although *green behind the ears* began as a blend of two idioms, folk etymologies affect single idioms, too. A well-known example is *toe the line*, which has been reinterpreted as *tow the line* for many speakers. The older version describes the practice of drawing a line in the sand to establish a boundary, which people could then challenge by inching their toes over the line. The folk etymologized meaning is instead based on the idea of a group of people working in unison to tow a rope.

A single speaker can create a folk etymology, if the speaker misidentifies the origin of an idiom. The speaker of *he was watching me like I was a hawk* presumably didn't know much about hawks, but thought they might be dangerous.[18] For this speaker, the idiom was based on the need to closely monitor hawks. Of course, the original idiom *to watch like a hawk* 'to watch very carefully' is based on hawks' alertness and visual acuity, but a speaker who didn't know this might imagine a different basis for the idiom. This would be especially likely if the speaker had heard the variant *he was watching me like a hawk*, which is syntactically ambiguous – that is, the sentence may be read as comparing the person who is watched (*me*), rather than the watcher (*he*), to a hawk. This ambiguity would make it easier for a speaker to invent a new interpretation for the idiom.

When idioms are reanalysed according to folk etymologies, sometimes their form changes to match the new meaning. For some speakers, the idiom *to be on tenterhooks* 'to experience painful suspense or impatience' has become *to be on tender hooks*, in which *tender* emphasizes the painful nature of the suspense or impatience. The reanalysed idiom still doesn't make sense unless you know its actual etymology described in Chapter 2, since it's unclear why hooks would be 'tender', but the folk etymologized version apparently makes more sense for some speakers. The idiom *the whole kit and caboodle* 'the entire set' has led to *the whole shittin' caboodle* because the adjective *shittin'* is more comprehensible to some people than the reference to a 'kit'.[19] Similarly, *a wolf in sheep's clothing* 'person who hides malicious intent' has become *a wolf in cheap clothing* 'person who hides malicious intent and dresses poorly' for some speakers, who presumably are more familiar with cheap clothing than sheep's clothing.[20]

Although only a minority of English speakers ever talk about 'tender hooks' or 'wolves in cheap clothing', other folk etymologized idioms, such as *tow the line*, are extremely widespread. It's not always obvious when a word or phrase has been affected by a folk etymology, so it's often necessary to check a reference such as the *Oxford English Dictionary* if you're curious about the earliest forms and meanings of a word or idiom.

In sum, malaphors are speech errors that generally affect only one or two words in an idiom. Sometimes, malaphors result in mixed metaphors, as in *wake up and smell the music*, but many malaphors are entirely non-metaphoric and therefore involve no mixing, as in *you could have knocked me over with a fender* or *Does the Pope shit in the woods?* When malaphors are repeated often enough, they can become genuine single idioms like *green behind the ears* or *keep a stiff upper chin*. Sometimes, along the way, speakers invent folk etymologies for the idioms in an attempt to make them more meaningful.

Although most malaphors are speech errors, most mixed metaphors are not. Uses of idioms such as the 'wet blanket' and 'Pandora's box' examples given earlier are cases in point. These quotations clearly aren't malaphors, because they combine entire idioms rather than replacing one or two words in a single idiom. Slips of the tongue generally affect a few words, not entire clauses such as *When you open that Pandora's box*. Mixed metaphors like these are better characterized as 'slips of the mind'. Malaphors are the only speech errors that can lead to mixed metaphors, so if a mixed metaphor involves more than two or three words out of place, it's apparent that it's not a malaphor and therefore isn't a speech error.

Conversely, malaphors result in mixed metaphors *only* through speech errors or intentional language play, never through accidental mixed metaphors like the 'Pandora's box' example. When malaphors are created on purpose, speakers always know that the malaphors are technically incorrect, because they replace part of one idiom with part of another, or swap one word with a related word. Since malaphors are inherently erroneous, the mixed metaphors that sometimes accompany them are either by-products of speech errors or part of intentional language play aimed at creating humour or other effects. No malaphor can mix metaphors using otherwise 'correct' English, since malaphors are always non-standard English.

We've already seen a number of accidental malaphors, so let's look now at why speakers might create mixed-metaphor malaphors on purpose.

Intentional mixed-metaphor malaphors

Like other mixed metaphors, mixed-metaphor malaphors can be used for humour, language play, or to express emotional intensity. Speakers often create mixed-metaphor malaphors for their own amusement, as in *you can't make an omelette without skinning a cat*, which replaces the words *breaking some eggs* with the phrase *skinning a cat* from another idiom,[21] or *a loose tongue spoils the broth*, which swaps *too many cooks* with *a loose tongue* from another idiom.[22]

Along similar lines, inserting two words from the idiom *to beat a dead horse* into *don't look a gift horse in the mouth* results in the grotesque advice *don't beat a dead horse in the mouth*.[23] A playful malaphor, *you can take that to the bank and smoke it*, adds part of the idiom *you can put that in your pipe and smoke it* to the idiom *you can take that to the bank*. Both idioms mean roughly 'That's what I think, and I'm right. So there'! The malaphor seems to also mean 'that's what I think, and I'm right' but also conjures up the image of smoking a dubious substance inside a bank.

In the 1940 Disney film, the puppet Pinocchio falls in with a bad crowd and starts gambling and playing pool. His 'conscience' Jiminy Cricket reproves him, *You buttered your bread. Now sleep in it!* apparently inserting the words *bread* and *butter* from *to know which side your bread is buttered on* into the idiom *You made your bed, now sleep in it!*, with the intended meaning of the latter idiom. I've also heard the more grotesque combination, *You opened that can of worms, now lie in it!* in which 'opening a can of worms' means irreversibly initiating a complicated situation and the command *lie in it!* derives from a variant of *You made your bed, now sleep in it!*

One clever malaphor combines two idioms that both involve the conceptual metaphor LIFE IS A JOURNEY. The consistent use of LIFE IS A JOURNEY in both idioms has doubtless made the idiom combination more popular. It's the only malaphor that I've heard repeatedly in daily life: *Let's burn that bridge when we come to it*, meaning 'We'll deal with that issue in an irrevocable manner when it arises'. Of course, this expression combines *we'll cross that bridge when we come to it* 'We'll deal with that issue when it arises' and *to burn one's bridges* 'to make irrevocable decisions'.

The metaphors in *to see the carrot at the end of the tunnel* are more varied, consisting of HAPPINESS IS BRIGHTNESS, LIFE IS A JOURNEY, and ACHIEVING A PURPOSE IS ACQUIRING A DESIRED OBJECT.[24] The 'carrot' malaphor includes the idiom *to see the light at the end of the tunnel*, which involves HAPPINESS IS BRIGHTNESS and LIFE IS A JOURNEY. These metaphors allow the light up ahead to stand for future happiness. In the other component idiom in the malaphor, *the carrot or the stick* 'reward or punishment', the carrot represents a desired goal via ACHIEVING A PURPOSE IS ACQUIRING A DESIRED OBJECT.

Despite the oddity of the 'carrot' malaphor, however, its three component metaphors frequently combine without problems. We can 'reach for a bright future' just as we can try to grasp a shiny object (HAPPINESS IS BRIGHTNESS and ACHIEVING A PURPOSE IS ACQUIRING A DESIRED OBJECT), and we can 'go hunting for a job' just as we can go looking for food (LIFE IS A JOURNEY and ACHIEVING A PURPOSE IS ACQUIRING A DESIRED OBJECT). In this specific case, however, it's hard to think of a reason why a carrot would be hanging at the end of a tunnel, so the malaphor is mixed.

Carefully chosen mixed-metaphor malaphors can result in memorable commentaries that are as humorous as they are brutal. These include Ann Richards's description of George H. W. Bush as *born with a silver foot in his mouth*, a combination discussed in the introduction to this book. Both idioms in the malaphor are derogatory and target potential weaknesses for Bush, namely, his privileged upbringing and frequent verbal blunders. Idioms, as fixed expressions, are remembered as units and are more likely to be recalled word for word than other expressions. Mixed metaphors also tend to be memorable. For both of these reasons, a mixed-metaphor malaphor can make an insult unforgettable.

An Australian journalist tried to duplicate the efficaciousness of Richards's insult with the headline *Tony shoots fish in barrel, avoids foot*, describing the error-prone Australian Prime Minister Tony Abbott's cautious performance at a debate. By answering easy questions, Abbott managed to avoid *shooting himself in the foot* 'saying something to his own disadvantage' via ARGUMENT IS PHYSICAL COMBAT. He was only able to do so by *shooting fish in a barrel* 'doing something easy' (GENERIC IS SPECIFIC). Incidentally, a *MythBusters* episode 'tested' this idiom and found that fish in a barrel are in fact easy to shoot. Even if you don't hit any fish, the shockwave from the gunshot ruptures their blood vessels and they all die.

The news headline *Tony shoots fish in barrel, avoids foot* uses zeugma (see Chapter 5) to coordinate the uses of *shoot* as found in the two different idioms. The combination works fairly well on the literal level, because if you are shooting into a barrel, you probably will miss your own foot. Figuratively, it also makes sense that by answering only easy questions you will avoid a damaging mistake. The idiom combination therefore is comprehensible even though the two idioms draw on different metaphors.

For an idiomatic insult that you can use more often, try wishing an untalented musician, *Have a nice day job*, as you walk out, combining *Have a nice day* and *Don't quit your day job*. You could also refer to your classiest business outfit as your *no sweat suit*, blending *no sweat* 'easy' and *sweat suit* 'workout wear', with the meaning that you can get anything done when you're wearing that suit.[25] However, since novel uses of idioms are so memorable, they quickly become cliché, so you want to save your best ones for a special occasion.

Extended idioms

Perhaps, the most creative way to use metaphoric idioms is by extending the metaphors that they're based on. Not everyone recognizes the metaphoric underpinnings of idioms, so playing with their metaphoric structures shows that you not only are familiar with these structures but understand them well enough to manipulate them. The metaphors that underlie idioms can be extended in ways that are entirely consistent with their conceptual structure, such as when a newspaper is described as *still toeing a line that was trampled on ages ago*.[26] A line in the sand that's frequently crossed might, indeed, be eventually wiped out.

The extended metaphors in idioms are usually more blatant. For instance, tennis player Andy Roddick doesn't strive for subtlety when he describes losing to his long-term rival:

> I threw the kitchen sink at him, but he went into the bathroom and got his tub.[27]

In a brawl, tearing up the kitchen sink and throwing it at your opponent is a dramatic move that will probably end the fight. Roddick creatively suggests that an even larger plumbing fixture could also be hurled at an opponent. Since tennis and other SPORTS are metaphorically conceptualized as BATTLES, playing an intense game is understood as attacking with dangerous weapons. The extended metaphor in Roddick's idiom indicates that he played a winning game, but his opponent improbably performed even better.

CBS TV personality Dan Rather extends the idiom *until the cows came home* 'for a long time' (GENERIC IS SPECIFIC) in a similar way when he describes a delayed election result:

> They counted the votes until the cows had literally gone to sleep!

If it takes ages for the cows to come home, it takes even longer for them to come home, settle down for the night, and go to sleep.

A similar, but more esoteric, example comes from the title of Samuel Beckett's absurdist play *Waiting for Godot*. This title has led to an idiom in which *waiting for Godot* designates any long period of waiting for something that never comes. Here, the Republicans are not only waiting for Godot, but waiting for him to bring beer:

> Waiting for 'the establishment' to save the party from Trump's hostile takeover is like waiting for Godot to bring the beer to the party.[28]

The passage also seems to play on the two senses of *party*, 'political group' and 'festive celebration'.

Novel extensions to idioms typically take one aspect of an idiom (such as waiting for Godot, or the cows coming home) and replace it with something more extreme (such as waiting for Godot to bring beer, or the cows going to sleep). The next extension follows the same pattern, but is more complex.

> If presidential candidates once promised the sun, moon and stars, this time around they're promising multiple galaxies, plus the turtles all the way down.[29]

Here, 'promising the moon' is replaced by 'promising multiple galaxies', following the same pattern of exaggeration as the previous examples. It adds in 'turtles all the way down', from a mythological model of the universe in which the world is supported by a giant turtle (Figure 24). This turtle is on top of another one, and so on, 'all the way down' (whatever that means).

Not only the politicians are promising much more than the 'sun, moon and stars', they are promising people exaggerated amounts of whatever they believe in. If constituents believe in the solar system, they're promised multiple galaxies. If they believe the world rests on a giant turtle, then they're promised the world, the turtle, and turtles all the way down. Whatever you want, they're prepared to promise that you'll get it.

Metaphor extension in idioms can be more complex than just replacing *kitchen sink* with the stronger term *bathroom tub* or *come home* with *gone to sleep*. Metaphoric idioms, like other metaphors, can be extended in a variety of ways. As a simple example, the idiom *let the genie out of the bottle* can be extended to include multiple genies (Figure 25). Each of the genies metaphorically represents a separate problem.

> 'The world has failed to put the nuclear genie back in the bottle,' Dr. Gubrud said. 'And new genies are now getting loose.'[30]

Almost the same extension occurs in the following example, in which the 'ducks' in the idiom *to get all one's ducks in a row* represent preparations before marriage:

> The vast majority of never-married millennials still say they aspire to get hitched someday. They just want to get their ducks in a row first – and my, are those ducks multiplying. A survey from last fall found that young Americans believe they should wait to marry until they have a stable job, have reduced their debt levels or accumulated savings, have a college degree, have successfully cohabited with their future spouse, have had previous serious relationships and even own their home.[31]

FIGURE 24 The Earth is carried by a giant turtle. Underneath that, it's turtles all the way down.

The 'ducks' in this passage are prerequisites to marriage. Some of these are listed: having a stable job, reducing debt levels, and so on. The 'ducks' are not only hard to line up, but are 'multiplying'. Apparently while the ducks are waiting to be shot, they are laying eggs and raising new ducks, making it increasingly harder to line them all up. It's a bit odd that the

FIGURE 25 The nuclear genie is here to stay – and he brought friends.

ducks are breeding while the hunter waits to kill them – but then, freeing genies from bottles isn't an everyday experience, either.

When idioms are metaphorically extended in novel ways, audiences seem to be more forgiving of source-domain oddities than they are for similar issues in non-idiomatic metaphors. Perhaps, this is because idioms have fixed meanings, so the metaphors that underlie them are less active for readers. In Müller's terms, the metaphors are less 'awake'.[32] Another possibility is that readers recognize that it is harder to manipulate idioms, because they are fixed expressions, so they are willing to accept creative idioms even if they're a bit strange. Whatever the reason, extended idioms such as those included here are rarely criticized or considered mixed. If anything, they're praised as clever and original.

In the following example, the author's self-description comes across as witty yet self-deprecating, thanks to her creative extension of the idiom *to lose one's marbles* 'to go crazy' (THE MIND IS A CONTAINER). Like the ducks in the previous example, the marbles here are doing something that's more complicated than in the conventional version of the idiom.

> I have a fabulous support network here – people who want to help me through this and make sure I don't completely lose my marbles. I am sure I have lost a few. They are rolling around on the floor, and I'll find them when I am packing up to leave.[33]

Usually, lost marbles bounce away in all directions and are gone, which metaphorically means that someone's mental faculties will never again be coherent. However, the speaker of the above passage hopes to keep most of the marbles and find the others someday, even though the original idiom doesn't provide for this possibility.

So far, we've looked at examples that exaggerated the original idiom (waiting for Godot's beer instead of waiting for Godot), made it more specific (losing marbles temporarily as opposed to losing them forever), or increased a quantity in the original idiom (many genies instead of one genie). The metaphors in idioms can be extended even more creatively. The next example differs considerably from its originating idiom *you've made your bed, now sleep in it,* meaning 'you've caused a situation, now you have to live with it'.

> Cruz brilliantly made his bed, and Trump leapt into it when Cruz wasn't looking.[34]

According to this passage, Ted Cruz set everything up so he would be the US Republican Presidential nominee in 2016, but didn't get to enjoy the outcome of his work. Instead, Donald Trump took advantage of Cruz's preparations to further his own campaign and set himself up as the nominee. Usually, the 'bed' in this idiom represents an unpleasant situation of one's own making. Here, Cruz has actually done a good job with the bed. But just when he's made it perfect and he's ready to enjoy it, Trump jumps in and gets to benefit instead. In the original idiom, this never happens. The whole point of the idiom is that you're supposed to deal with the situations you're responsible for. The novel usage subverts the intent of the original idiom by adding a second participant who steals the bed, which emphasizes the unfairness of Trump benefitting from Cruz's work.

The next example also reverses an idiom's usual meaning. Coincidentally, it also describes Trump's presidential campaign:

> Journalists are accustomed to covering candidates who may be apples and oranges, but at least are still both fruits. In Trump ... we have not fruit but rancid meat.[35]

If the idiom *comparing apples to oranges* is extended to encompass rancid meat, then apples and oranges don't seem so different after all. Since rotten meat is messy and disgusting, the extension criticizes the quality of Trump as a candidate via MORALITY IS PURITY.

One of the most frequently extended idioms is *the carrot or the stick* 'reward or punishment'. This idiom can take many forms. We can say *let's try the carrot instead of the stick* or *he alternated using the carrot and the stick*, along with many other possibilities. The following example describes a preference for greenhouse gas reduction incentives over emissions penalties:

> At a time when carrots are having a meaningful impact on Oregon's greenhouse emissions, the Legislature shouldn't be giving us all the stick.[36]

Apparently, *the carrot* and *the stick* don't even have to be in the same clause for the idiom to work.

The next example describes a new invention, the Textalyzer, as the 'stick' that allows the police to enforce a law against texting while driving. It is apparently being introduced to supplement an ad campaign encouraging drivers to obey the texting law.

> Winston said the new campaign could be a kind of carrot to encourage better behaviour by drivers, but he added that a stick was also needed.

… 'Right now, we have a reed, not a stick,' Winston said, adding that the Textalyzer would 'make enforcement that much more credible'.[37]

Since the idiom *the carrot or the stick* is normally so flexible, the only real novelty in this usage is the criticism that the police force has a 'reed' rather than a 'stick'. That is, the current tools for enforcement don't function to punish lawbreakers, in the same way that whipping a donkey with a reed wouldn't make it move. This is similar to the examples with exaggeration, like the 'kitchen sink' quotation. The difference is that a 'reed' is a flimsier tool than a 'stick', whereas a 'bathtub' is a more serious weapon than the 'kitchen sink'.

I came across an even more complicated extended metaphor in the British National Corpus text collection:

You're sometimes so busy looking at the wood that you don't smell the trees are rotten.

This expression twists around the idiom *not to see the forest for the trees* 'to ignore the overall issue in favour of the details' and suggests not only that the major issue (the 'wood') is distracting from the details (the 'trees'), but also that there is a serious problem with the trees themselves. Calling the trees *rotten* brings in MORALITY IS PURITY and suggests that the problem with the details is specifically moral corruption. The modified idiom therefore means that someone is concentrating on the overall situation and ignoring the problem of underlying immorality.

Noun-swapped idioms

If you're looking for an easy way to creatively use an idiom, it's possible to take an idiom with two nouns and swap them around. We've seen that you can exchange the nouns *forest* and *trees* in *not to see the forest for the trees* and say that someone *doesn't see the trees for the forest* 'ignores the details in favour of the overall issue', as in the 'rotten trees' idiom described above. This noun-swapping may be the simplest and most frequent way that people manipulate the metaphoric structure of idioms for rhetorical effect. A famous example is *to snatch defeat from the jaws of victory* 'to improbably lose when success seemed certain', which of course derives from the idiom *to snatch victory from the jaws of defeat* 'to improbably win when failure seemed certain' (ACHIEVING A PURPOSE IS ACQUIRING A DESIRED OBJECT). Even though noun-swapped idioms are less logical than the original idioms, they seem to be easily understood and even admired by listeners.

I've also heard the noun-swapped idiom *the storm before the calm* 'the frantic activity before a peaceful time', based on *the calm before the storm* 'the peaceful time before a period of frantic activity'. Again, the new idiom makes less sense, in that storms are often preceded by a calm front of warm air, but calm weather is not necessarily preceded by a storm.

Noun-swapped idioms are easy to make. When someone is less organized than they appear, you can suggest there is *a madness to their method*. When they reject the bad with the good, you can say they've *thrown the bath water out with the baby*. On the other hand, you should never pay attention to anyone who complains about your idioms, because you don't want to *feed the hand that bites you*.

To summarize, metaphors are often captured and preserved in idioms.[38] When a metaphoric idiom has been around for a while, speakers may continue to use it even though they're no longer aware of the metaphor. These speakers will likely combine the idiom with different, incompatible metaphors, which often results in mixing. As we've seen, the mixed metaphors in writing guides are usually combinations of metaphoric idioms, such as *that wet blanket is a loose cannon*.

In most respects, mixed metaphors in idioms resemble other mixed metaphors. They generally combine two contradictory source domains or involve ambiguity between the source and target domains. They can sound confused, angry, or out of control, and are often used in criticisms or insults. Sometimes, they are employed creatively for humour, exaggeration, or emphasis. When they occur, for whatever reason, they're unlikely to be forgotten. They will stick in your memory like a burr under a saddle blanket.

Notes

1   Müller, *Metaphors Dead and Alive*. Karen Sullivan, 'Lexical Filledness and Metaphor in Idioms', in *Collocations and Idioms 1: Papers from the First Nordic Conference on Syntactic Freezes*, ed. Marja Nenonen, Sinikka Niemi, and Jussi Niemi (Joensuu, Finland: Joensuu University Press, 2007).

2   Geoffrey Nunberg, Ivan A. Sag, and Thomas Wasow, 'Idioms', *Language* 70, no. 3 (1994): 491–538. Sullivan, 'Lexical Filledness and Metaphor in Idioms'.

3   Amanda Meade, 'Michelle Guthrie enters the News Corp lion's den and circles the elephant in the room', *The Guardian. Australian media: The Weekly Beast*, 29 July 2016. Available online: https://www.theguardian.com/media/2016/jul/29/michelle-guthrie-enters-the-news-corp-lions-den-and-circles-the-elephant-in-the-room (accessed 16 March 2018).

4   Greg Smart, 'Grim Future with Loose Cannon Trump at the helm', *Dubbo Photo News*, 31 January 2016. Available online: dubbophotonews.com.au/news/dubbo-weekenderolumnists-opinion/item/4170-grim-future-with-loose-cannon-trump-at-the-helm (accessed 25 January 2017).

5   Carl Falsgraf, 'Protesters' Actions Likely Backfired', *The Register-Guard*, 10 May 2016.

6   Sir Joh Bjelke-Petersen.

7   Matt Tait, 'Seabury's Football Team Done for the Season', *Lawrence Journal-World*, 22 September 2009.

8   Lawrence Harrison, 'Searching for "Malaphors"', *The Washington Post*, 6 August 1976. Hofstadter and Moser, 'To Err Is Human', 196. Miss Celania, 'Malaphors', *Neatorama*, 5 May 2017. Available online: http://www.neatorama.com/2017/05/05/Malaphors/ (accessed 27 November 2017).

9   J. Cooper Cutting and Kathryn Bock, 'That's the Way the Cookie Bounces: Syntactic and Semantic Components of Experimentally Elicited Idiom Blends', *Memory and Cognition* 25, no. 1 (1997): 57–71.

10 Harrison, 'Searching for "Malaphors"'.

11 Don Bender, *Mixed Metaphor Madness Volume 1: Real Sayings by Real People from Real Meetings*, Kindle edition (Amazon Digital Services LLC, 2012).

12 Carlton, 'My Favorite Mixed Metaphors'.

13 Scott, 'Mixed Metaphors'.

14 Scott, 'Mixed Metaphors'.

15 Scott, 'Mixed Metaphors'.

16 Cutting and Bock, 'That's the Way the Cookie Bounces'.

17 Mignon Fogarty, 'Mixed Metaphors', *QuickAndDirtyTips.com*, 6 December 2008. Available online: http://www.quickanddirtytips.com/education/grammar/mixed-metaphors?page=all (accessed 13 December 2016).

18 Scott, 'Mixed Metaphors'.

19 Bender, *Mixed Metaphor Madness*.

20 Carlton, 'My Favorite Mixed Metaphors'.

21 Mollusque, 'Well-Mixed Metaphors', *Wordnik*, 26 April 2008. Available online: https://www.wordnik.com/lists/well-mixed-metaphors (accessed 11 December 2016).

22 Scott, 'Mixed Metaphors'.

23 Mollusque, 'Well-Mixed Metaphors'.

24 Alyssa Severin, personal communication. Attributed to Kate Burridge.

25 Mollusque, 'Well-Mixed Metaphors'.

26 Josh Lambert, 'I Swear', *The New York Times Book Review*, 2 October 2016, BR17.

27 Piers Newbery, 'Federer Fights Back to Retain Title', *BBC Sport*, 4 July 2004. Available online: http://news.bbc.co.uk/sport2/hi/tennis/3865037.stm (accessed 13 December 2016).

28 Jonah Goldberg, 'Just the Ticket to Defeat Trump', *The Register-Guard*, 24 February 2016. Available online: http://www.latimes.com/nation/la-oe-0223-goldberg-trump-despair-20160223-column.html (accessed 16 March 2018).

29 Catherine Rampell, 'More Fantasy than Reality in Political Promises', *The Register-Guard*, 2 March 2016, A7.

30 William J. Broad and David E. Sanger, 'Race Escalates for Latest Class of Nuclear Arms', *The New York Times*, 17 April 2016, A1.

31 Catherine Rampell, 'Marriage Sits on a Lonely Pedestal', *The Register-Guard*, 21 April 2016, A9.

32 Müller, *Metaphors Dead and Alive*.

33 Catherine Neilan, 'Flat Out at Work', *Financial Times Magazine*, 6/7 May 2006, 7.

34 Jonah Goldberg, 'Like Him or Not – and Many Don't – Cruz Is the GOP's Best Hope', *The Register-Guard*, 13 March 2016, G3.

35 Liz Spayd, 'Here's the Truth about "False Balance"', *The New York Times*, 11 September 2016, SR12.

36 Chris McCabe, 'Carbon-reduction Bill Is Wrong Path for Oregon', *The Register-Guard*, 10 February 2016. Available online: http://projects.registerguard.com/rg/opinion/34027301-78/carbon-reduction-bill-is-wrong-path-for-oregon.html.csp (accessed 26 December 2016).

37 *The Register-Guard*, 'Driving: Privacy Concerns Make Legislation an Uphill Battle', 28 April 2016, A7.

38 Nunberg et al., 'Idioms'. Sullivan, 'Lexical Filledness and Metaphor in Idioms'.

Further Reading on Idioms

¶ Billig, Michael and Katie MacMillan. 'Metaphor, Idiom and Ideology: The Search for "No Smoking Guns" across Time'. *Discourse and Society* 16, no. 4 (2005): 459–80.

Cacciari, Christina, Raymond W.Gibbs Jr, and Albert Katz, eds. *Figurative Language and Thought*. Oxford: Oxford University Press, 1997.

Clausner, Tim and William Croft. 'Productivity and Schematicity in Metaphors'. *Cognitive Science* 21 (1997): 247–82.

Jr. Gibbs, Raymond W. Psycholinguistic Studies on the Conceptual Basis of Idiomaticity'. *Cognitive Linguistics* 1, no. 4 (1990): 417–51.

Jr. Gibbs, Raymond W. Josephine M. Bogdanovich, Jeffrey R. Sykes, and Dale J. Barr. 'Metaphor in Idiom Comprehension'. *Journal of Memory and Language* 37 (1997): 141–54.

Kay, Paul and Charles Fillmore. 'Grammatical Constructions and Linguistic Generalizations: The What's X Doing Y? Construction'. *Language* 75, no. 1 (1999): 1–33.

¶ Kövecses, Zoltán and Péter Szabcó. 'Idioms: A View from Cognitive Semantics'. *Applied Linguistics* 17, no. 3 (1996): 326–55.

Nunberg, Geoffrey, Ivan A. Sag, and Thomas Wasow. 'Idioms'. *Language* 70, no. 3 (1994): 491–538.

¶ Sullivan, Karen. 'Lexical Filledness and Metaphor in Idioms'. In *Collocations and Idioms 1: Papers from the First Nordic Conference on Syntactic Freezes*, edited by Marja Nenonen, Sinikka Niemi, and Jussi Niemi, 330–41. Joensuu, Finland: Joensuu University Press, 2007.

7 WHY WE NEED MULTIPLE METAPHORS

When I asked a friend what she learned about metaphors in school, the only thing she remembered was 'not to use mixed metaphors'. Secondary schools don't explain the role of metaphor in abstract reasoning or teach kids how to design effective metaphors. They bombard kids with cautions such as 'Warning! Don't mix metaphors',[1] but often teach nothing else about metaphors at all. Students are taught to avoid mixed metaphors before they even know what metaphor is, just like in some schools they are taught abstinence without learning about sex. But is an 'abstinence-only' approach to mixed metaphor workable? Should we use only one metaphor at a time or no metaphors at all, in order to prevent any chance of mixing?

If we never used multiple metaphors, our cognition would be impaired and our ability to use language would suffer. Even in everyday situations, we sometimes require more than one metaphor. Once we begin philosophizing about the human condition or theorizing about the quantum world, we need a multitude of metaphors. Although mixed metaphors can be a problem, avoiding multiple metaphors would be devastating.

Fortunately, there are a number of ways we can use more than one metaphor without mixing them. We've seen throughout this book that metaphors can be kept from combining, which keeps them from mixing. This doesn't mean restricting ourselves to one metaphor per paragraph, as one writing guide suggested, but it does mean keeping metaphors sufficiently far apart and adequately differentiated, as discussed in Chapters 3 and 4. When it's clear that two metaphors should be understood separately, rather than together, we can benefit from both metaphors without any confusion or mixing.

Although separated and differentiated metaphors don't mix, they only allow us to make use of the metaphors sequentially, rather than together. For instance, the sentence *John was feeling down but he staggered forward with his life* uses one metaphor (HAPPY IS UP) in its first clause and a different metaphor (LIFE IS A JOURNEY) in its second clause. This allows us to think about John's situation first in terms of one concrete source domain (UP) and then in terms of another one (A JOURNEY). The two metaphors are distinct and separated by a clause boundary, so their source domains are unlikely to combine or interact. This prevents mixing. Unfortunately, it also prevents any of the new cognitive connections that might have resulted from combining the metaphors. Metaphor combinations produce structures that aren't found in either of their component metaphors, so it's sometimes necessary to let metaphors combine.

The above sentence can be compared with one where the metaphors are allowed to integrate, such as *John staggered up out of his depression*. Here, HAPPY IS UP and LIFE IS A JOURNEY are mingled together, creating a compound metaphor that could be labelled ACHIEVING A HAPPIER LIFE IS JOURNEYING UPWARDS. The metaphors combine, but they don't mix, because there is no incompatibility between them. It's perfectly possible to move forward and upward at the same time, so the source domains of UP and JOURNEY combine seamlessly.

The compound metaphor offers inferences that aren't found in either HAPPY IS UP or LIFE IS A JOURNEY alone. For example, moving upwards is effortful, so we know that John is working hard to be happier. When one direction on a slope leads upwards, we know that the opposite direction leads downwards, so we can reason that if John turns around and goes back, he'll become more depressed. Each of these new inferences is potentially useful in reasoning and communication, so it's sometimes worthwhile to combine these metaphors.

Whether metaphors are strung together like separate beads on a string, or kneaded together into a compound, it's important that we can use more than one of them. This chapter discusses first why it's so crucial that we use multiple metaphors, even if they're not combined (as in *John was feeling down but he staggered forward with his life*), and second why it's even more valuable to combine metaphors in ways that work (as in *John staggered up out of his depression*).

Multiple metaphors in life, literature, and the sciences

Some of the fundamental issues that arise in daily life require multiple metaphors, such as when we reason about time and scheduling. Remember the two conflicting metaphors in the 'trains' example in Chapter 3:

> We've seen this train coming. We've tried every alternative and put every engine on the track, but none of them run.

The trains in the second sentence represent the tomato farmers' attempts at problem-solving via LIFE IS A JOURNEY, whereas the oncoming train represents a crisis via TIME IS A MOVING OBJECT. Although in this example the two metaphors contradict each other, this isn't always the case. We frequently use these metaphors in close proximity without any confusion.

For example, we think of ourselves as 'moving through' time via LIFE IS A JOURNEY when we 'race through' work in order to 'get to' the weekend. We think of time as 'moving towards' us via TIME IS A MOVING OBJECT when the weekend 'rushes by' and we don't know 'where it went'.[2] We can even use both metaphors in one sentence, such as when we 'race through an assignment because the deadline is quickly approaching'. Here, the two metaphors are useful because LIFE IS A JOURNEY emphasizes our intentional effort to 'move forward' and TIME IS A MOVING OBJECT expresses our helplessness to slow the deadline's 'approach'. As long as we don't encourage the metaphors to combine (by making them both involve 'trains', for example), we can benefit from both. We wouldn't want to abandon the cognitive benefits of one of these metaphors just because we're afraid of mixing.

We need the advantages of multiple metaphors even more when we think about weightier concerns, such as love or death. Scientific research, philosophy, and literature on these topics is often thick with metaphor combinations. For example, the 'Tomorrow, and tomorrow, and tomorrow' soliloquy in Shakespeare's *Macbeth* is packed with metaphors. The passage describes LIFE as a JOURNEY, a SPEECH, a CANDLE, a SHADOW, an ACTOR, and a STORY:

> Tomorrow, and tomorrow, and tomorrow,
> Creeps in this petty pace from day to day,
> To the last syllable of recorded time;
> And all our yesterdays have lighted fools
> The way to dusty death. Out, out, brief candle!
> Life's but a walking shadow, a poor player,
> That struts and frets his hour upon the stage,
> And then is heard no more. It is a tale
> Told by an idiot, full of sound and fury,
> Signifying nothing.

The metaphors in this passage do not seem mixed, but rather offer a string of different possible perspectives on LIFE.[3] Macbeth seems to be intentionally trying out these various metaphors, hoping that one will help him view his life in a more positive light. Unfortunately, none of them works.

Macbeth was on the right track, though, because metaphors do help us cope with life's mysteries, and different metaphors can help us in different ways. For example, ageing comes as a surprise to each of us. When I first started finding grey hairs on my head, I thought it was house paint. I knew objectively about ageing, but I subconsciously didn't expect it to happen to me. We also know that all humans die, but it's a struggle for most of us to come to terms with our own deaths. Clever thinkers can help us reason about ageing, death, and other life experiences by presenting these metaphorically, often with multiple metaphors that let us understand these concepts in an entirely new way.

Shakespeare, the perennial master of metaphor, describes OLD AGE with three different metaphors in Sonnet 73.

> That time of year thou may'st in me behold
> When yellow leaves, or none, or few, do hang
> Upon those boughs which shake against the cold,
> Bare ruin'd choirs, where late the sweet birds sang.
> In me thou see'st the twilight of such day,
> As after sunset fadeth in the west,
> Which by-and-by black night doth take away,
> Death's second self, that seals up all in rest.
> In me thou see'st the glowing of such fire
> That on the ashes of his youth doth lie,

As the death-bed whereon it must expire
Consum'd with that which it was nourish'd by.
    This thou perceivest, which makes thy love more strong,
    To love that well which thou must leave ere long.

The first stanza represents old age as autumn via A LIFETIME IS A YEAR, the second depicts it as twilight via A LIFETIME IS A DAY, and the third describes it as the ashes of a fire via A LIFETIME IS A FIRE. Years, days, and fires are natural cycles of light and heat that can be savoured as they are ending, so all three metaphors reinforce the inference that love in old age should be appreciated because it will soon be gone. If these metaphors weren't separated into different stanzas, they might mix, particularly because they are so similar. However, the metaphors are neatly divided so that readers won't put them together. Instead, each new metaphor in the string reinforces the inferences of the previous one. All the metaphors entail that human life is just one of many fleeting pleasures, such as firelight, sunlight, and summer. They suggest that the end of human life is as natural as any of these.

If Shakespeare had chosen only one metaphor, it would not have established this broad category of natural light/heat cycles to which a LIFETIME metaphorically belongs. Shakespeare needed to include multiple metaphors to demonstrate that these cycles are normal and common in nature, and should be expected and appreciated in our own lives.

Although Shakespeare's metaphoric passages are noteworthy for their beauty and creativity, the number of metaphors they contain is not particularly unusual. It's typical for poems, literature, or philosophical writing to combine numerous metaphors. On questions relating to the human condition, no single metaphor has all the answers.

In the sciences, multiple metaphors are needed at least as much as in literature and philosophy. Many scientific theories rely on multiple metaphors because these theories attempt to explain phenomena that are too complex for one metaphor alone.

Think back to your secondary school years. More than likely, your chemistry teacher showed you a model of a water molecule. You couldn't look at a real molecule, because they are too small and don't reflect light in a way we can see. You probably looked at coloured balls attached by sticks. Maybe you were lucky enough to have one of those playsets where you can build molecules out of wooden balls that fit on little poles. If your class didn't use the ball-and-stick model of molecules, you may have been shown molecules made out of coloured bubbles stuck together. The 'ball-and-stick' and 'bubble' models of molecular structure look something like the images in Figure 26 for a water molecule.

In both models, atoms are conceptualized as physical objects that attach together to form molecules. The molecules' chemical bonds are represented as physical connections, and the different structures of the oxygen and hydrogen atoms are indicated by their colours and sizes. That is, the two hydrogens are of the same size and colour, whereas the one oxygen is larger and has a different colour. Both models are special cases of the basic metaphor IDEAS ARE OBJECTS, which allows us to think about a wide range of concepts, in fields from chemistry to philosophy, as physical objects we can see and touch. Sometimes, this metaphoric process is called *reification*, meaning 'to make into a thing'.

Why are there different ways of representing molecules? Why not just choose one and use it consistently? Both metaphoric models are still used because each offers advantages that the other lacks. In the ball-and-stick model, for example, the length of the sticks represents the characteristic distance between the atoms in this kind of hydrogen-oxygen bond. This isn't visible in the bubble model. On the other hand, the bubble model shows that the distance between bonded atoms is typically less than the distance between unbonded atoms. The bubbles look squished together because their centres are closer to each other than they would be to atoms of a different molecule, such as another water molecule bouncing around nearby. Apparently, the relative distances in the bubble model are consistent with scientific findings. Although beginning students are usually taught either the ball-and-stick model or the bubble model, more advanced students know both models and can choose whichever

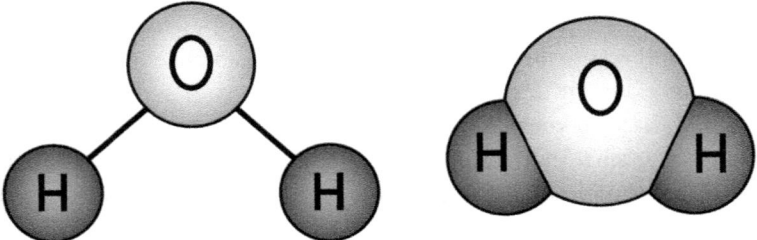

FIGURE 26 Molecules are often represented as balls on sticks (left) or as attached bubbles (right).

one is most useful at the moment. These and other models of molecules are explored in more detail in *Making Truth: Metaphor in Science* by chemistry professor Theodore Brown.

The familiar example of molecular models shows that there is rarely one perfect metaphor for the things we cannot see or touch. Usually, we just have to choose the best metaphor for whatever we're trying to do. When no single metaphor is good enough, we may have to switch back and forth between two different metaphors in order to enjoy the cognitive advantages of both.

Electricity is another concept that is best modelled by multiple metaphors. It's usually explained either as flowing water or as a crowd of hurrying, excited people. The next passages illustrate these two models, respectively.

> Electricity moves through wires like water moves through a hose.[4]

> Hordes of excited electrons are speeding through gates and causing other hordes of electrons to get excited ... in a ceaseless, frantic relay race.[5]

Conceptualizing electricity as water provides a system of correlations between water height and pressure differences that can be applied to reasoning about combinations of batteries. Thinking of electricity as a crowd of people, on the other hand, allows the inference that some people will get in the way of others, which improves reasoning about parallel resistors.[6] Studies show that when subjects are taught either the WATER metaphor or the CROWD metaphor for electricity, this affects their performance on tests about electricity. Students taught the WATER metaphor do better on questions about batteries, which can be thought of as reservoirs of liquid. Those taught the CROWD metaphor perform better on questions about resistors because these can be conceptualized as 'gates' through which crowds move.[7] Of course, students who are taught both the WATER and CROWD metaphors can solve both types of problems.

In fact, as you become more expert in a technical area, you tend to use more metaphors. Studies have found that the use of multiple metaphors correlates with technical expertise in a field.[8] An expert electrician, for example, may use several metaphors in quick succession to explain electricity, describing it as *a water reservoir and pipes ... many small billiard balls ... a field*, whereas a novice may use only one metaphor.[9] This is because each metaphor offers ways of thinking about the target domain that are useful in different contexts. Experts become more comfortable with multiple metaphors so that they can choose the most effective metaphor in any given situation.

One reason that experts can pick and choose parts of multiple metaphors is because they don't confuse the metaphors with reality itself. The more we know about a topic, the less we tend to believe that the relevant metaphors are real. Some students might think that electrons literally 'crowd' through a resister or 'flow' through a wire, but expert electricians know that these are just approximations of electrical phenomena. This understanding is what allows good electricians to rapidly recognize which model is most appropriate at a given moment and to quickly switch between models without confusion or mixing.

Sometimes, though, almost no one is expert enough on a topic to distinguish metaphor and reality. For example, nobody completely understands the nature of light and matter, which share some of the characteristics of particles and some of the behaviours of waves. Of course, light and matter are not literally either waves like ocean surf or particles like sand. Physicists describe them as both because certain behaviours of light and matter are most easily understood in terms of waves and others are better represented in terms of particles. Because we know relatively little about light and matter, it is easy to see the 'particle/wave duality' as a paradox. If we instead think of waves and particles as metaphoric models of light and matter, then the inconsistencies between the two models aren't surprising. The models are just two imperfect metaphors for a phenomenon we don't completely understand.

Presenting metaphors as alternatives

Whether we're navigating our daily lives or studying quantum physics, we frequently need multiple metaphors. Experts in a particular area become skilled at keeping the relevant metaphors separate. However, not everyone is an expert, and even experts can mix metaphors, so expertise is not a complete solution to the issue of combining multiple metaphors. We've seen some strategies that help prevent mixing, such as keeping metaphors in separate sentences. These strategies work because they discourage readers from putting the metaphors together and using them as part of the same reasoning process. When two metaphors are very different and separated by several sentences, they won't mix, but they also might not help us solve a problem that requires both metaphors at once.

There are two main ways to use two metaphors simultaneously without any chance of mixing. First, the metaphors can be presented as structures to be compared, rather than structures to be fitted together. Second, the metaphors can be selected and shaped so that they fit together without contradictions, as in the sentence *John staggered up out of his depression* mentioned earlier. Let's begin with the first of these two strategies. How do we convince readers to compare two metaphors rather than combining them? We can't just instruct readers not to put the metaphors together. As soon as readers consider combining the metaphors, it's too late. They've already done it. For example, try to understand the following sentence without mingling the metaphors:

That pig is fishing for compliments.

Were you able to understand the metaphoric meaning of the sentence (namely, that someone is selfish and wants to be complimented)? Could you do this without imagining, even briefly, a pig with a fishing rod? If you were able to keep the two metaphors separate, then you're unusual. Most people cannot refrain from combining metaphors. If you tell readers not to mix two metaphors, they'll realize that mixing is possible and they'll have to try it out.

A more subtle and effective way to keep two metaphors separate is to present them as alternatives. For example, you can introduce one metaphor, then disagree with it, and suggest a replacement metaphor, via a process that the linguist and computer scientist John Barnden terms 'corrective juxtaposition'.[10] The 'correction' from one metaphor to another allows us to reason about the two metaphors without putting them together, which prevents mixing. Barnden offers the following example:

Libraries aren't like supermarkets, they are magical places where dreams begin.[11]

This sentence suggests that libraries shouldn't be considered utilitarian facilities like supermarkets (GENERIC IS SPECIFIC), but rather imagined as the starting point for magical adventures (LIFE IS A JOURNEY). Most relevantly for the current discussion, no reader of the sentence would be tempted to put the metaphors together and imagine a magical supermarket. The 'correction' keeps the metaphors neatly separated.

There are more subtle ways than outright 'correction' to present metaphors as alternatives. For example, Lebanese Canadian educator Najwa Zebian replaces one version of LIFE IS A JOURNEY with an alternative one when he offers the following advice:

> These mountains that you are carrying, you were only supposed to climb.

The problems in our lives can be understood as two kinds of physical objects via LIFE IS A JOURNEY. They can be physical burdens that we carry on our life JOURNEYS, or they can be physical barriers that we have to overcome in order to continue those JOURNEYS. If these metaphors were presented as applying simultaneously to the same life problem, as in *He has climbed and carried that mountain for too long*, we'd recognize that we can't climb something that we're carrying, and the metaphors would be contradictory. Zebian's advice introduces both of these possibilities, yet no reader would be tempted to imagine simultaneously climbing and carrying a mountain. Even if we were to put the metaphors together, we would think about a JOURNEY that potentially involves both burdens and barriers, and would imagine a choice between carrying and climbing an obstacle.

Zebian's strategy is also effective because it allows us to compare the usefulness of the metaphors for thinking about life's problems. According to Zebian, we make life harder for ourselves in two ways. First, we 'pick up' heavy burdens rather than just 'climbing over' them. That is, we deal with difficult situations in a way that's more difficult than necessary. Second, we 'carry' our burdens along with us on our JOURNEY instead of leaving them behind. That is, we deal with our difficulties continuously rather than confronting them once and moving on. The 'climbing' metaphor seems preferable to the 'carrying' metaphor in both respects.

The only unrealistic aspect of the sentence is the impossible scenario of carrying a mountain, which no human can do. This contributes to Zebian's point in two ways. First, it emphasizes the undesirability of the carrying option as compared to the climbing option. Second, the impossibility of the scenario accentuates the absurdity of the choice to 'carry' life's problems. Unrealistic source-domain scenarios are often employed to ridicule poor choices or bad ideas, as we'll see in the next chapter.

Whereas Zebian uses two metaphors to reason about LIFE, the cartoon in Figure 27 employs two different metaphors to describe happiness. These metaphors are also presented as alternatives and do not mix.

Metaphorically, there are a couple of ways to 'obtain' happiness via ACHIEVING A PURPOSE IS ACQUIRING A DESIRED OBJECT. You could 'go looking' for it, you could be 'given' it, or you could 'create' it. Normally, only one of these ways of ACQUIRING A DESIRED OBJECT will be used at a time. The sentence *I found this happiness and made it myself* doesn't make sense, because you can't find and make the same object. The below cartoon overcomes this limitation by 'correcting' the metaphor used by the speaker on the left, in which happiness is found, with the other speaker's metaphor, in which happiness is created. Creating an object often involves more planning and effort than finding one, and relies less on luck, so the cartoon suggests that being happy is a matter of effort rather than luck. The metaphors don't mix because they describe the

FIGURE 27 These two characters have different metaphors for happiness.

different experiences of two separate people attempting to 'create' or 'find' their own happiness.

The examples we've seen so far have presented two metaphors as alternative ways of thinking about life and happiness, and have gently advised readers that one of these alternatives is healthier than the other. Some authors are blunter. In the following example, comedian Minnie Pearl surprises us by replacing an expected source domain with a different one.

> Getting married is a lot like getting into a tub of hot water. After you get used to it, it ain't so hot.

Like Zsa Zsa Gabor's cynical comment on husbands in Chapter 5, Pearl's quotation plays with our expectation that metaphoric language about something 'hot' will describe the joys of wedded life via PASSION IS HEAT. It's therefore startling and funny when Pearl describes a different interpretation, in which married life rapidly loses its intensity in the same way that we quickly get used to the intensity of a hot bath (GENERIC IS SPECIFIC). If PASSION IS HEAT is involved in Pearl's comment at all, the diminishing intensity of the heat is understood specifically as diminishing passion. There is no question of mixing our default interpretation (that marriage is passionate) and Pearl's intended one (that marriage quickly loses intensity) because the quotation's second sentence makes it clear which metaphor she favours.

The following quotation from a newspaper columnist also shows a definite preference for one option, being 'at the table' to bargain, rather than being 'on the table' as a meal.

> The lobbyists for big business explained at the time that if you're not at the table, you're on the menu. That proved to be prescient for all of the small business owners … who were chewed up because they were too small to get a seat.[12]

The two metaphors apply to different groups of people. The small business owners are 'chewed up' and presumably eaten. Those who were 'big' enough to sit at the table were apparently spared this fate (IMPORTANCE IS SIZE) and were instead allowed to negotiate.

The authors of the LIFE, 'happiness', 'hot bath', and 'table' examples show a clear predilection for one of the two described options. Zebian recommends that we think of difficulties as obstacles, not burdens. The cartoon suggests that happiness is made, not found. Pearl opines that marriages lose their intensity. The newspaper columnist suggests it's better to be a diner than a meal. However, an author can present two metaphors as alternatives without recommending one over the other, as in the following lines from 'The Evidence' by Erica Jong:

> I'm not sure at all
> If love is a salve
> Or just
> A deeper kind of wound
> I do not think it matters.[13]

In these lines, Jong puzzles over what element from A BODY should metaphorically represent love in THE MIND domain. Does love heal the wounds caused by life experiences or does it cause even more pain? Like the authors of the previous examples, Jong not only keeps the metaphors separate, but encourages the reader to compare the two metaphors in an interesting way.

The final line of the excerpt concludes that the choice between a 'salve' and a 'wound' isn't important because the consequences of the metaphors are the same. This baffling comment forces the reader to speculate what a salve and a wound have in common. At first, it might appear that a salve and a wound have opposite effects, in that a wound causes pain and a salve helps soothe it, so Jong's poem presents an interesting riddle. The reader may conclude, for example, that both a salve and a deeper wound make you forget the previous injuries that life has given you, either by healing them or by distracting you with a worse pain.

The 'salve' example, like the previous ones, compares two metaphors. It differs from the other passages in that it doesn't finish the comparison by concluding that one of the metaphors is better than the other. This impartiality doesn't diminish the effectiveness of the strategy. By merely suggesting that the metaphors can be compared, Jong forestalls any risk of mixing.

Another way to keep two metaphors separate is to show that the metaphors apply to different target domains. For example, poet Maya Angelou's two metaphors in the following passage don't mix because one describes resentment and one applies to anger.

> Bitterness is like cancer. It eats upon the host. But anger is like fire. It burns all clean.

According to Angelou, anger is a healthier reaction to adversity than bitterness. Like a cancer that slowly kills the body, bitterness gradually destroys the mind (THE MIND IS A BODY). Anger, on the other hand, burns up the harmful feelings that fuel it, leaving nothing behind (ANGER IS HEAT). The metaphors don't mix because they describe different emotional reactions. Note that this passage also demonstrates that *bitterness* 'resentment' is a dead metaphor for Angelou. If she had perceived it as a living metaphor that actively compared resentment to a particular taste sensation via THE MIND IS A BODY, she might have rejected it as incompatible with the 'cancer' metaphor.

Sometimes, we don't get to choose the metaphor that applies to our life situation, according to actress Joan Crawford:

> Love is a fire. But whether it's going to warm your hearth, or burn down your house, you never can tell.

In both metaphors, humans are metaphorically houses, which can be heated by a fire but can also be destroyed by it. Usually love is pleasantly warm, via PASSION IS HEAT. But love can also be a dangerous fire that 'burns down your house', meaning that it ravages your mind (THE MIND IS A PHYSICAL STRUCTURE). Crawford suggests that you don't know beforehand which metaphor will be applicable.

Crawford's quotation, like the others in this section, presents two metaphors as alternatives. It's possible to describe two simultaneously occurring qualities using two different metaphors, though it seems to require skill to keep the qualities and metaphors distinct. For example, *The New York Times* columnist Anna Quindlen writes:

> I remember adolescence, the years of having the impulse control of a mousetrap, of being as private as a safe-deposit box.

Adolescents are compared to mousetraps (which snap if they are so much as touched, which metaphorically describes how teenagers respond impulsively to any provocation, via ARGUMENT IS PHYSICAL COMBAT) and safe-deposit boxes (which let nothing out, much as teenagers tell nothing to anyone, via COMMUNICATING IS OBJECT TRANSFER). Yet we would never, on reading this passage, imagine some kind of hybrid mousetrap/safe-deposit box, which snaps shut and then locks up its contents like a safe. Readers are instructed to understand the teenager's impulsive reactions in terms of the mousetrap's sensitivity, and to think of the teenager's secretiveness in terms of the security of the safe-deposit box. The two metaphors describe these different aspects of teenage behaviour, as specified by *impulse control* and *private*. Since the metaphors describe unrelated teenage traits, the reader won't attempt to put the metaphors together and the metaphors won't mix.

In sum, mixed metaphors can be avoided if we either present them as alternative ways to understand the same concept, as in Zebian's two versions of LIFE IS A JOURNEY, or make it clear how each metaphor should be applied to the target domain, as in the 'mousetrap' and 'safe-deposit box' metaphors. These strategies appear to override all the other factors that encourage metaphors to combine, including proximity and similarity. Why, then, aren't these strategies more frequent?

First, these methods require finesse. If an author simply tells readers to keep two metaphors separate, the reader won't be able to comply. The metaphors have to be presented in such a way that the reader will not even consider combining them. Second, it's not always possible or practical to explain exactly how each metaphor should apply to the target domain.

For example, imagine that Robert Frost's poem *The Road Not Taken* (discussed in Chapter 5) had explained exactly how it should evoke LIFE IS A JOURNEY. *Two roads diverged in a yellow wood*, Frost writes. These roads represent life choices via LIFE IS A JOURNEY. But if Frost had written *Two roads, each a possible life plan, diverged in the yellow wood of my life*, the line would never have become famous. Although explaining the structure of a metaphor prevents confusion and mixing, it's usually more effective and efficient to let readers figure it out themselves.

Metaphors that combine well

When writers and speakers design metaphors that fit together perfectly, they don't have to keep their metaphors separate or present them as alternatives. Not all metaphor combinations result in mixing. For example, we saw in Chapter 2 that all compound metaphors are combinations of simpler metaphors such as primary metaphors. We wouldn't have some of our most frequent metaphors, such as COMMUNICATING IS OBJECT TRANSFER, if we couldn't build more complex metaphors out of simpler ones.

Even though we use compound metaphors all the time, it can be surprisingly hard to invent new metaphor combinations that avoid mixing. When an author achieves this, it can give us a whole new way of thinking about the world. Here's another example by Frost, the title of one of his poems:

Happiness makes up in height what it lacks in length.

Frost suggests that the happy stretches of our lives are not long (LIFE IS A JOURNEY). Nevertheless, happiness is worthwhile because it makes us feel 'high' (HAPPINESS IS VERTICALITY). Physical objects normally have both height and length, so there is no contradiction between these concepts. For instance, a wall tapestry can be literally high and narrow, so there's no reason a metaphoric 'object' such as happiness can't also be high but not long. The metaphors combine, but they do so flawlessly, without contradictions.

The following example from Albert Einstein also elegantly combines two metaphors:

Life is like riding a bicycle. To keep your balance you must keep moving.

Bicycling involves both balancing and moving forward, and a bicycle stays upright only if it's moving. Crucially, the first sentence of the quotation mentions bicycling, so we know that this is the metaphor's source domain. Without this sentence, we might not even think about riding a bicycle and might not understand the metaphor. To demonstrate, consider the sentence *To keep your balance in life, you must keep moving.* This is less effective than the original quotation, because the source domain isn't consistent with our life experience. When we're walking or driving, for example, we can easily stop without falling over.

The explicit mention of bicycling keeps the metaphors LIFE IS A JOURNEY (in which progress towards life goals is understood as forward motion) and THE MIND IS A BODY (in which mental or emotional 'stability' is understood as physical stability) from mixing. The two metaphors fit together once we think of bicycling, and the resultant metaphor combination suggests that our lives are mentally and emotionally stable as long as we keep working towards our life goals.

I've noticed a popular saying that is similar to Einstein's quotation. It may be more memorable than Einstein's example because it involves sharks rather than bicycles.

We're like sharks. We die if we stop moving.

Many species of sharks can breathe only when they swim, so they have to keep swimming their whole lives without stopping. This information about sharks makes it possible to fit together LIFE IS A JOURNEY and EXPERIENCING A NEGATIVE STATE IS EXPERIENCING HARM, with the resultant inference that if we ever stop trying to achieve our goals, the result will be so damaging that we might as well be dead. This saying tends to be repeated by ambitious high-energy people who think that others should be the same. Again, the metaphors make sense together only when they're specifically about sharks. The sentence *In life, we die if we stop moving* corresponds poorly to our everyday experience as humans and doesn't provide the inferences generated by the 'sharks' example.

Another popular metaphor combination is found in the following American proverb.

There may be snow on the roof but there's a fire in the furnace!

In case you're not familiar with this proverb, it can be used to describe a sexually active (or otherwise passionate) old person. The 'snow' is the person's white hair (an image metaphor), whereas the 'fire' is the passion in the person's heart (PASSION IS FIRE). Human bodies metaphorically 'contain' emotions such as passion (THE MIND IS A BODY). In this example, the person's BODY is specifically a house. In cold climates, houses are often white on top but toasty inside. This fact about the world makes the 'snow' image metaphor and PASSION IS FIRE work together gracefully. If there were no containers that were white on top and warm inside, we would search our memories in vain for a way to make the metaphors fit, and the metaphors might come across as mixed. In fact, I've found it difficult to explain this proverb to my students in Queensland, Australia, because many of them have never seen snow and their houses don't require furnaces.

The following passage by humourist Henry Wheeler Shaw is more complex than the 'bicycle' and 'shark' examples. Like these, however, it begins by introducing the context in which the metaphor combination makes sense:

> Life is a grindstone, and whether it grinds a man down or polishes him up depends on what he is made of.

Although literal grinding and polishing can both be accomplished by the same grindstone, the 'grinding' and 'polishing' of human character involve two distinct metaphors. When an object is ground down, it becomes smaller and probably shorter. Metaphorically, if an experience 'grinds you down', it makes you feel unimportant (IMPORTANCE IS SIZE), and probably miserable (HAPPINESS IS VERTICALITY) and worthless (STATUS IS VERTICALITY). On the other hand, if you become 'polished', you are improved to the point of 'brilliance' via GOODNESS IS LIGHT. According to this metaphor, improving a skill is understood as polishing an object. Usually this improvement is accomplished through a repeated action, such as practising a martial art or playing a musical instrument, because physical polishing itself is repetitive. In the above passage, the 'polishing' is the result of repeated life experiences.

Shaw's 'grindstone' passage brings together all these metaphors and makes readers consider how life experiences make people either 'shrink' or 'shine' depending on their characters – that is, depending on what they are 'made of'. The metaphor combination is particularly effective since different materials are milled or polished at different rates depending on their hardness. These properties of different materials metaphorically represent people's inherent mental 'toughness'.

The German author Jean Paul Richter also specifies the context in which his metaphor combination makes sense, but he avoids an obvious preamble such as *life is a grindstone*:

> The more sand has escaped from the hourglass of our life, the clearer we should see through it.

This combination of TIME IS A RESOURCE (in which the RESOURCE is sand) and UNDERSTANDING IS SEEING works only in the context of an hourglass. The sand in an hourglass descends from the upper bulb and leaves it transparent. Over our lives, as the bulb metaphorically empties, we can see deeper into it than we could before and can metaphorically understand events in our past that didn't make sense at the time. In other contexts, however, we don't necessarily see better when we have fewer resources. Having less money doesn't help us see better, for example (unless we spent the money on glasses). The combination of TIME IS A

RESOURCE and UNDERSTANDING IS SEEING works only in this specific context.

I've always liked the following metaphor combination, which I first encountered in the lyrics of 'Heavyweight Champion of the World' by Reverend and The Makers (2006). It's also attributed to Jim Whittaker, who became the first American to climb Mt Everest in 1963.

If you're not living on the edge, you're taking up too much space.

Living 'on the edge' means taking risks. According to LIFE IS A JOURNEY, living your life in a daring way is metaphorically travelling in dangerous areas, such as balancing along a cliff edge. 'Taking up space', that is, using more space than you really need, metaphorically refers to acting more important than you are, via IMPORTANCE IS SIZE.

When these two metaphors are put together, they produce the strange scenario in which crowds of people are trying to travel along a narrow ledge. This scenario metaphorically represents people living their lives in a world with limited resources. Those who hog the middle of the ledge are wasting space, whereas those who risk themselves by staying close to the edge help everyone by making room for others.

Sometimes this metaphor combination is understood as saying that only risk-takers are important, but that's not strictly correct. If we assume that all the people on the ledge are of the same size, they're all equally important. The ones on the edge are simply using fewer resources. A more apt metaphor might present the risk-takers as contributing more to society, rather than consuming less. In fact, innovative, daring people possibly use more resources than average, but they also give more back to society than the average citizen. Still, this flaw in the metaphor can be forgiven because the source domain naturally produces the inference that risk-takers benefit everyone, just as the self-sacrificing travellers on the cliff risk themselves to keep everyone else safe.

Early American politician Horace Mann combined two metaphors to create a novel source domain explaining his reasons for supporting universal public education:

> Ignorance breeds monsters to fill up the vacancies of the soul that are unoccupied by the verities of knowledge.

An 'empty' mind, Mann suggests, is a 'breeding ground' for monstrous beliefs. The metaphor combination includes a special case of IDEOLOGIES

ARE ORGANISMS, in which the organisms are specifically monsters. It isn't clear whether the 'verities of knowledge' are living beings, too, or merely inanimate objects (IDEAS ARE OBJECTS). Because the monsters are necessarily alive, however, they can reproduce, making it possible for their CAUSATION to be understood as PROCREATION. In this special case of CAUSATION IS PROCREATION, ignorance is the 'mother' of monstrous ideas (Figure 28).

Even though most of us have never seen any monsters, we can imagine that they might infest empty spaces. Maybe, when we were kids, we

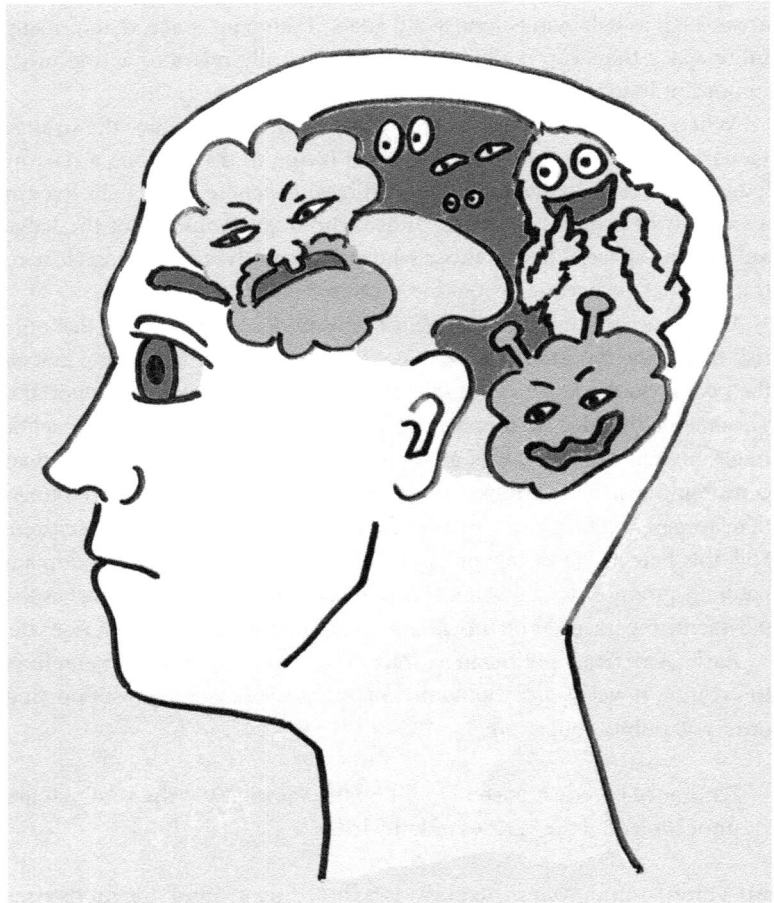

FIGURE 28 Empty minds fill up with monsters.

worried about monsters under the bed or in the closet. We can think of monsters multiplying in hiding, like rats breeding in the walls of a house or raccoons raising noisy families under the floorboards. One way to prevent infestations of vermin is to fill the spaces they might inhabit. We can eradicate rats and raccoons by filling the walls with insulation or filling the space under the house with concrete, for example. Infestations might also be prevented by introducing more desirable inhabitants such as cats or dogs. We can therefore imagine that monsters, like other vermin, might be eradicated if their breeding space is filled with something else – in this case, with 'the verities of knowledge'.

American author Henry David Thoreau wrote what is perhaps an even more innovative metaphor combination in a private letter:

> New ideas come into this world somewhat like falling meteors, with a flash and an explosion, and perhaps somebody's castle-roof perforated.

In UNDERSTANDING IS SEEING, new ideas are often described as sources of light, such as light bulbs or meteors. The novel aspect of this metaphor is that the ideas might cause damage, as falling meteorites occasionally do. The meteoric ideas in this metaphor 'damage' theories ('castles') via THEORIES ARE BUILDINGS. Crucially, the meteorites don't hit a random roof. They specifically break through the roof of a castle, which suggests that they are damaging grand, elaborate theories. Without the specific source domain of falling meteorites, however, UNDERSTANDING IS SEEING and THEORIES ARE BUILDINGS would probably mix instead of fitting together so well.

In sum, multiple metaphors are indispensable for reasoning about concepts that cannot be seen or touched, such as electricity. They are also integral to some of the cleverest, most insightful and most famous writing in the English language. If the entire human race suddenly decided to avoid multiple metaphors, human culture would deteriorate and scientific progress would cease. A better way to avoid mixed metaphors is to identify what makes metaphor combinations seem mixed, so that we can either keep our metaphors from combining or else productively combine metaphors in exactly the way we intend.

In addition to overviewing the benefits of multiple metaphors, the current chapter has introduced two new strategies for preventing mixed metaphors: (1) presenting metaphors as alternatives and (2) carefully fitting metaphors together in ways that avoid mixing. Alongside the methods introduced in previous chapters, such as distancing and distinctness, these techniques should allow us to avoid mixed metaphors without sacrificing the benefits of multiple metaphors.

Sometimes, though, an author will deliberately throw all these strategies out the window. In the next chapter, we'll see how authors sometimes mix metaphors intentionally and how this can communicate extreme exuberance, anger, or astonishment.

Notes

1. Horsfield, *Creative Writing*, 125.
2. Lakoff and Johnson, *Metaphors We Live By*. Lera Boroditsky, 'Metaphoric Structuring: Understanding Time through Spatial Metaphors', *Cognition*, 75, no. 1 (2000): 1–28.
3. Eve Sweetser and Karen Sullivan, 'Minimalist Metaphors', *English Text Construction* 5, no. 2 (2012), 153–173.
4. Field Enterprises Educational Corp., *Childcraft: The How and Why Library, Volume 7* (Chicago, IL: World Book, Inc., 1976), 201.
5. Marks, Laura U. *Sensuous Theory and Multisensory Media* (Minneapolis, MN: University of Minnesota Press 2002), 172.
6. Dedre Gentner and Donald R. Gentner, 'Flowing Waters and Teeming Crowds', in *Mental Models*, ed. Dedre Gentner and Albert L. Stevens (Hillsdale, NJ: Erlbaum Associates, 1983), 99–129.
7. Gentner and Gentner, 'Flowing Waters and Teeming Crowds', 99–129.
8. Tarciso A. Borges, 'Mental Models of Electricity', *International Journal of Science Education* 21, no. 1, (1999): 95–117. Andrea A diSessa, 'Phenomenology and the Evolution of Intuition', in *Mental Models*, ed. Dedre Gentner and Albert L. Stevens (Hillsdale, NJ: Erlbaum Associates, 1983).
9. Borges, 'Mental Models of Electricity', 108–09.
10. Barnden, 'Communicating Flexibly with Metaphor', 444; the corrections discussed here are specifically Barnden's 'Type C' (452).
11. Barnden 'Communicating Flexibly with Metaphor', 452.
12. Jonah Goldberg, 'What to Make of the Plutocrats in Trump's Midst', *National Review*, 16 December. 2016. Available online: https://www.nationalreview.com/2016/12/donald-trump-wealthy-cabinet-historical-lessons/ (accessed 19 March 2018).
13. Erica Jong, *Becoming Light: Poems New and Selected* (New York: Harper Collins, 1991).

Further Reading on Metaphors in Mathematics and the Sciences

▌ Brown, Theodore L. *Making Truth: Metaphor in Science*. Urbana and Chicago, IL: University of Illinois Press, 2003.

Hallyn, F., ed. *Metaphor and Analogy in the Sciences*. Dordrecht: Kluwer, 2000.

▌ Lakoff, George and Rafael Nuñez. *Where Mathematics Comes From: How the Embodied Mind Brings Mathematics into Being*. New York: Basic Books, 2000.

▌ Larson, Brendon. *Metaphors for Environmental Sustainability: Redefining Our Relationship with Nature*. New Haven: Yale University Press, 2014.

Lakoff, George and Rafael Núñez. 'The Metaphorical Structure of Mathematics: Sketching Out Cognitive Foundations for a Mind-Based Mathematics'. In *Mathematical Reasoning: Analogies, Metaphors, and Images*, edited by Lyn D. English, 21–89. Hillsdale, NJ: Erlbaum, 1997.

Lakoff, George and Rafael Núñez. 'Conceptual Metaphor in Mathematics'. In *Discourse and Cognition: Bridging the Gap*, edited by Jean-Pierre König. Stanford, CA: CSLI, 1998.

Núñez, Rafael. 'Conceptual Metaphor, Human Cognition, and the Nature of Mathematics'. In *Cambridge Handbook of Metaphor and Thought*, edited by Raymond W. Gibbs Jr, 339–62. Cambridge, MA: Cambridge University Press, 2008.

Nuñez, Rafael and George Lakoff. 'The Cognitive Foundations of Mathematics: The Role of Conceptual Metaphor'. In *Handbook of Mathematical Cognition*, edited by Jamie I. D. Campbell, 109–24. New York: Psychology Press, 2005.

Further Reading on Metaphors in Literature

Freeman, Donald C. '"Catch[ing] the Nearest Way": *Macbeth* and Cognitive Metaphor'. *Journal of Pragmatics* 24, no. 6 (1995): 689–708.

Freeman, Donald C. '"The Rack Dislimns": Schema and Metaphorical Pattern in *Antony and Cleopatra*'. *Poetics Today* 20 (1999): 443–60.

Freeman, Margaret H. 'Momentary Stays, Exploding Forces: A Cognitive Linguistic Approach to the Poetics of Emily Dickinson and Robert Frost'. *Journal of English Linguistics* 30, no. 1 (2002): 73–90.

Freeman, Margaret H. 'The Poem as Complex Blend: Conceptual Mappings of Metaphor in Sylvia Plath's "The Applicant"'. *Language and Literature* 14, no. 1 (2005): 25–44.

Hiraga, Masako K. *Metaphor and Iconicity: A Cognitive Approach to Analyzing Text*. Basingstoke and New York: Palgrave Macmillan, 2005.

▌ Lakoff, George and Mark Turner. *More than Cool Reason*. Chicago, IL: The University of Chicago Press, 1989.

Mahlberg, Michaela. 'Corpus Stylistics: Bridging the Gap between Linguistic and Literary Studies'. In *Text, Discourse and Corpora*, edited by Michael Hoey, Michaela Mahlberg, Michael Stubbs, and Wolfgang Teubert, 219–46. London: Continuum, 2007.

Pasanek, Brad. *Metaphors of Mind: An Eighteenth-Century Dictionary*. Baltimore, MD: Johns Hopkins University Press, 2015.

Semino, Elena and Jonathan Culpeper, eds. *Cognitive Stylistics: Language and Cognition in Text Analysis*. Amsterdam and Philadelphia, PA: John Benjamins, 2002.

Stockwell, Peter. *Cognitive Poetics: An Introduction*. London and New York: Routledge, 2002.

Stockwell, Peter. 2012. *Texture: A Cognitive Aesthetics of Reading*. Edinburgh: Edinburgh University Press.

Sweetser, Eve and Karen Sullivan. 'Minimalist Metaphors'. *English Text Construction* 5, no. 2 (2012), 153–73.

Turner, Mark. *The Literary Mind*. New York: Oxford University Press, 1996.

Turner, Mark. *Reading Minds: The Study of English in the Age of Cognitive Science*. Princeton: Princeton University Press, 1991.

8 MIXING METAPHORS FOR FUN AND PROFIT

We've seen that multiple metaphors are essential in the sciences, literature, and everyday reasoning about abstract concepts. Usually, these metaphors seem most effective if they're not mixed, whether mixing is avoided by presenting the metaphors as alternatives, designing them to be completely compatible, or using any of the strategies described in the previous chapters. Unless we're being funny or trying to win a bad-writing competition, mixed metaphors don't seem particularly useful.

Is there ever a place for mixed metaphors outside of jokes and bad writing? We've seen that mixed metaphors give the impression of ignorance and lack of control (Chapter 1), which aren't usually qualities that we want to convey. Indeed, there isn't much point in sounding ignorant unless we're writing dialogue for a fictional character that we want to portray as stupid or bumbling. On the other hand, seeming out of control can be useful in a number of situations.

Out-of-control writing can convey the enormity of an emotional state such as love, anger, or outrage; the intensity of a physical experience, such as pain; or the chaos of a situation, such as a storm. Since mixed metaphors are normally associated with a lack of control, they can convey the impression that the writing has escaped the author's supervision and is running wild.

Expressing emotional intensity

Mixed metaphors can communicate emotional exuberance, as in author Toni Morrison's description of love:

That magic axe that chops away the world in one blow … it leaps over anything, takes the biggest chair, the largest slice, rules the ground wherever it walks … People with no imagination feed it with sex – the clown of love.

Morrison's metaphors sound almost breathless, as if she is at risk of being overwhelmed by the momentousness of her topic and needs every metaphor at her disposal to describe it. This rhetorical strategy effectively conveys the author's strong sentiments. The metaphors cannot, of course, be put together coherently – a magic axe cannot leap, sit, rule, or consume clowns. (The magic axe separates the lovers from the world via EMOTIONAL INTIMACY IS PHYSICAL PROXIMITY. The next metaphors personify love as a powerful egotistical human. It's also suggested that love can be fed and made to grow larger via IMPORTANCE IS SIZE. Finally, sex is personified as a clown that's compared unfavourably to love.) Since the metaphors are blatantly incompatible, if we try to combine them, they will seem mixed. This doesn't bother Morrison, however, because the mixing accentuates the emotional intensity of the passage.

Mixed metaphors excel at expressing out-of-control negative emotions, such as anger. This is one reason that they are so frequent in politicians' speeches. In modern Anglo cultures, politicians are expected to appear angry a lot of time, as they attack their rivals and opposing viewpoints. Most of the examples from politicians in this book are accusatory outbursts, including the UK representative's accusation that an opponent 'produced the rabbit, the temporary provisions Bill, as her fig leaf to cover her major U-turn'. Most of these mixes seem unintentional. If any were calculated to communicate outrage, this intention was lost in the actual anger of the politicians' delivery.

As we saw in the introduction, however, mixed metaphors are not limited to expressing anger. They can communicate a range of overwhelming feelings or situations. Uncontrollable leg pain was described as 'wearing burning barbed wire pantyhose', for example. Barbed wire pantyhose doesn't exist, and if it did, it couldn't burn. Instead of being incomprehensible or distracting, however, the strangeness of this source domain conveys the sufferer's lack of control over the horrible pain of the leg condition.

Mixed metaphors can effectively describe out-of-control natural phenomena, such as the D. H. Lawrence quotation in Chapter 1 that describes wild weather conditions in which 'ragged fumes of light' terrify the 'liquid-brilliant' moon. Liquids can't be terrified, and light can't be both a ragged fabric and a fuming gas, but here these metaphors add drama. The confusing, clashing metaphors convey the wildness of the storm.

Confusion, chaos, and strangeness are all associated with mixed metaphors. They can evoke emotional intensity or other extreme experiences. The odd, otherworldly element of mixed metaphors can be useful, too – for describing the surreal, the strange, and the shocking.

Expressing oddity with peculiar source domains

Unfamiliar metaphors are certain to be noticed. Some authors use this to their advantage. For example, you've probably never considered that you might have to eat a frog (Figure 29). The idea might make you feel a bit sick. American author Mark Twain uses this icky sensation to make the following advice more memorable:

FIGURE 29 Many frog species are threatened and some are poisonous, so it's not recommended to eat wild frogs.

If it's your job to eat a frog, it's best to do it first thing in the morning. And if it's your job to eat two frogs, it's best to eat the biggest one first.

If you have to do something that gives you a yucky feeling, Twain suggests it's best to get it over with. The horrible sensation of frog-swallowing figuratively represents the disagreeableness of whatever it is you need to get done, whether it's breaking bad news to someone, cleaning the toilet, or editing spreadsheets for eight hours. Eating frogs is a specific case of an unpleasant task via GENERIC IS SPECIFIC, so it can describe any kind of unappealing activity.[1] Since frog consumption is shocking and gross, it works perfectly to communicate the distaste of doing anything disagreeable. In fact, Twain's comparison was so effective that it's become a modern-day proverb in parts of the United States and has inspired a motivational book, *Eat That Frog!*[2]

Though eating frogs is strange, this source domain is not the result of compounding, since it involves only the structure GENERIC IS SPECIFIC. When weird source domains arise by accident, they're usually the result of unintentionally combining two contradictory metaphors, such as the 'lamp by a seesaw' example in Chapter 3. However, when source domains are strange by design, they more often involve novel special cases of a single source domain, as in the 'frogs' example, the metaphor about 'hyenas' on the *Colbert Report*, and the bad-writing contest winner about 'wind turbines'. Though these examples are not compound metaphors, they are nevertheless considered 'mixed' both in popular culture and in the definition codified in Chapter 1.[3]

It's easier to design a mixed metaphor that is not a compound, since you don't have to deal with the complication of fitting multiple metaphors together. You also have a better chance of getting readers to understand the metaphor in the way that you want. When you use two metaphors rather than one, it's always possible that readers won't put the metaphors together and they won't mix (see Chapters 3 and 4). It's much easier for readers to observe that it's abnormal to eat frogs than it is for them to recognize that it's weird to put a lamp by a seesaw, or even to hang a hat on gruel, to mention some of the mixed metaphors from earlier chapters.

Whether or not a mixed metaphor is a compound, if its source domain is sufficiently surreal, it can be used to emphasize oddity or unpleasantness. This example describes having to keep working long after you're ready to stop:

> (Acting) is a little like wrestling a gorilla. You don't quit when you're tired, you quit when the gorilla is tired.

Actor Robert Strauss describes the mental and emotional challenge of an acting career as a specific, unusual type of physical exertion: gorilla wrestling. This novel variation of THE MIND IS A BODY offers two advantages. First, it implies that acting is a challenge that you have to continue long after you want to quit, just as an angry gorilla is unlikely to stop fighting just because you want it to. This makes gorilla wrestling different than other physical activities, such as running or lifting weights, which can be stopped at any time. Second, the challenge of gorilla wrestling conveys Strauss's opinion that acting takes an unusual dedication that many people don't experience in their everyday lives. Again, the metaphor is not a compound. It is instead a novel special case of THE MIND IS A BODY that the author has designed specifically to be unusual.

The literary critic Cyril Connolly uses an extended metaphor to describe the horrors of another career path:

> The artist of to-day … walks at first with his companions, till one day he falls through a hole in the brambles, and from that moment is following the dark rapids of an underground river which may sometimes flow so near the surface that the laughing picnic parties are heard above.

In the real world, few people fall in pits and spend the rest of their lives wandering underground. Yet for Connolly, this solitary journey (LIFE IS A JOURNEY) in darkness (HAPPINESS IS BRIGHTNESS) below the earth (HAPPINESS IS VERTICALITY) perfectly represents the gloomy adventures of the artistic life. Strauss and Connolly both seem to be stressing the oddity and difficulty of the career choices they describe.

Strauss and Connolly don't need to make a special effort to tell us that their source domains are unusual, since they give us detailed descriptions that let us figure this out for ourselves. For writers and speakers who do want to show exactly how their novel source domains differ from more conventional variants, however, it's easy to directly compare the two using a structure like this: TARGET DOMAIN *isn't (just/merely) (like)* CONVENTIONAL SOURCE DOMAIN, *it's (like)* NOVEL SOURCE DOMAIN, as in *Acting isn't just like wrestling, it's like wrestling a gorilla*. Metaphor researcher John Barnden discusses a number of examples that follow this pattern, including the following:[4]

> The Jerusalem Post ... states that maintaining the delicate economic equilibrium isn't merely like walking a tightrope, it's like walking an invisible one.

Whereas 'walking a tightrope' metaphorically represents attempting a difficult task (LIFE IS A JOURNEY), the unlikely scenario of 'walking an invisible tightrope' represents an impossibly difficult task (LIFE IS A JOURNEY) with no way of knowing the path to success, since the tightrope can't be seen (UNDERSTANDING IS SEEING). By introducing the more familiar scenario first, the author makes it easier for the audience to imagine the less familiar scenario. In addition, when a novel source domain is particularly strange, as in the case of walking an invisible tightrope, the sentence structure accentuates the domain's oddity by directly contrasting it with a more normal variant. The format is therefore a simple but effective way to introduce an unrealistic source domain.

Although improbable source domains can express extremes of difficulty and unpleasantness, as in the 'gorilla', 'pit', and 'tightrope' passages, this doesn't seem to be their usual purpose. More often, novel source domains are used to underscore the absurdity of an idea, usually one that the author disagrees with. In this example, Clarence Manion, Dean of the Notre Dame Law School, criticizes a view that he attributes to most other people:

> The average man ... regards government as a sort of great milk cow, with its head in the clouds eating air, and growing a full teat for everybody on earth.

In other words, Manion thinks that people are stupid and expect unreasonable amounts of government benefits (MONEY IS FOOD). The salient point, though, is that the 'cow' is 'eating air' – that is, the money is coming from nowhere. This in itself is impossible, but the bizarre image of a giant magical cow functions to communicate Manion's disdain of government-issued benefits and those who expect them.

In the following example, a news writer criticizes the behaviour of the minor candidates in the 2016 US Republican primary, who were focused on discrediting each other instead of challenging the frontrunners Trump and Cruz:

> (The candidates) seem to have formed themselves into a circular firing squad and are busy spraying each other with gunfire.[5]

A circular firing squad serves no purpose other than creating an unnecessary bloodbath (ARGUMENT IS PHYSICAL COMBAT). Still, the concept effectively conveys the author's disgust over the candidates' counterproductive attacks.

Exaggerated, unusual source domains are effective for deriding any idea that an author finds idiotic or impossible. Here, management consultant Peter Drucker colourfully expresses his disdain for attempting to guess what the future will bring:

> Trying to predict the future is like trying to drive down a country road at night with no lights while looking out the back window.

Of course, the scenario Drucker describes would kill anyone who tried it.

Drucker's passage is interesting because it brings together UNDERSTANDING IS SEEING and LIFE IS A JOURNEY in a way that is usually impossible in English. According to English speakers' version of LIFE IS A JOURNEY, we 'move ahead' blindly. That is, we know what's behind us, but don't know what lies ahead, because we remember the past but not the future. In UNDERSTANDING IS SEEING, this equates to looking backward but not forward. When we put the metaphors together, we are moving forward but aren't able to look in front of us, only behind us. This is normally a flaw in the metaphor, because it diverges from normal everyday experience and makes the metaphor less useful for thinking about time.

Not all language communities model time this way. The traditional view of time among Aymara speakers, in the Andes, is that we are metaphorically standing still, facing the past (UNDERSTANDING IS SEEING).[6] This view of time makes more sense, insofar as future events are behind us and therefore invisible (unknown), whereas past events are in front of us and can be seen (remembered).

Drucker combines LIFE IS A JOURNEY and UNDERSTANDING IS SEEING in a way that fixes the usual problem with this combination in English. However, he has to create a strange source domain in order to do it.

Nobody would actually drive down a dangerous road while looking out the back window. Nevertheless, this scenario works well for Drucker because it conveys the futility and danger of fortune-telling.

When a source domain becomes *too* outrageous and surreal, it loses its power to convince. However, it can still be funny. Cartoonist Matt Groening doesn't seem to be making a serious point when he bemoans the horrors of romance in the following passage from *The Big Book of Hell*:

> Love is a snowmobile racing across the tundra and then suddenly it flips over, pinning you underneath. At night, the ice weasels come.

Love is often conceptualized as travelling in a vehicle via LOVE IS A JOURNEY, a special case of LIFE IS A JOURNEY. In this metaphor, the lovers are travelling together in a car, boat, or other mode of transport (which brings in EMOTIONAL INTIMACY IS PHYSICAL PROXIMITY). LOVE IS A JOURNEY is the basis of common expressions such as *their marriage is on the rocks, they hit a dead end*, and so forth.

Even though lovers rarely make their metaphoric journey in a snowmobile, most readers will be prepared to accept this variation. They probably expect that it will produce some new way of understanding LOVE. Groening disappoints this expectation and instead describes the surreal horrors of the snowmobile trip, which serves no purpose other than to suggest that love can be awful.

The meme in Figure 30, which recently appeared on my Facebook feed, is similar to the Groening quotation but simpler. Here, the mental anguish of dealing with petty teenage problems is understood in terms of the physical suffering of chicken-inflicted injuries (THE MIND IS A BODY). As is often the case for humorous examples of this type, the metaphor doesn't combine two incompatible metaphors. It is, however, original and strange. Though humans can die from infected chicken scratches, chickens never actually peck anyone to death.[7] Death by chicken-pecking is not a familiar bodily experience that will be useful in conceptualizing emotional and mental situations. Nevertheless, its ironic oddity is perfect for describing the surreal situation of dealing with teenage children.

Unique, monstrous source domains are not always a stylistic failure. Their strangeness itself can sometimes serve a purpose. Just as the chaotic thinking of mixed metaphors can sometimes express intense situations,

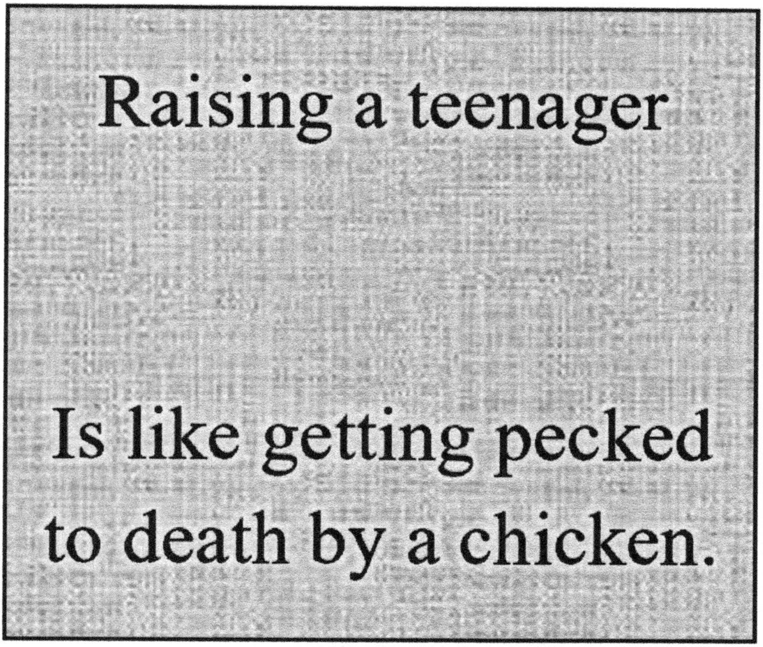

> **Raising a teenager**
>
> **Is like getting pecked to death by a chicken.**

FIGURE 30 This meme compares two horrific experiences.

sometimes unusual source domains can communicate the peculiarity of an experience or the impracticality of an opponent's ideas.

Novel image metaphors

Unusual source domains like Groening's 'snowmobile' passage have their uses. However, Groening's example is atypical of novel metaphors in that it plays around with a conceptual metaphor (LOVE IS A JOURNEY). If you're interested in creating a truly original source domain, it may be easier to use an image metaphor rather than a conceptual metaphor. Most image metaphors are created spontaneously in any case, so readers seem receptive to new ones, even if the source domains are unfamiliar. As long as readers can visualize the source domain, it will help them form a mental image of the target, even if they've never encountered a similar image metaphor before. This is why the description of a shop window as *a cunning, half-shut eye*, mentioned in the introduction, works so well. Its novelty is not a problem because a half-shut eye is easy to imagine.

The acceptability of novel image metaphors is also the reason that the 'drunken ballerina' example in the introduction is possible at all. If we're willing to put in the effort, we can probably imagine a lady in a tutu lurching around, even if we've never seen anything like it before. Of course, few readers want to go to so much trouble, so this example tests the limits of what is possible with image metaphor.

Skilled writers can push the boundaries a bit further, when they carefully lead us through the steps to understanding a novel image metaphor. P. G. Wodehouse, a master of novel image metaphors, employs this strategy in the following description.

> (He) was a tubby little chap who looked as if he had been poured into his clothes and had forgotten to say 'when!'[8]

Wodehouse is playing on the conventional image metaphor describing a woman's sexy, tight clothing as looking 'like she was poured into it'. If the character's body is not conventionally attractive, as in Wodehouse's passage, then the tight clothing might be less appealing. The novel variation works because most readers can visualize baggy clothes as if they were waterproof containers like plastic bags, stretched, and over-full with liquid. Wodehouse's description leads readers through this visualization and makes the novel metaphor easier to understand. The play on a conventional idiom and the inference that the fat character is to blame for his own situation (he forgot to say 'when') keep readers interested as they go through the process of understanding the novel image metaphor.

Wodehouse is scarcely the only author to use novel image metaphors to describe the familiar in terms of the fantastic, as in the following example:

> Turning, with my back to the hillside for a minute, I watch the red dragon of tail-lights slithering tightly down the valley.[9]

None of us has seen a dragon, but all of us have seen the tail-lights of cars on a highway. Describing the tail-lights as a dragon adds interest and arguably makes the mental image more vivid and concrete, even though we have no real-life experience with dragons.

Like other novel metaphors, image metaphors with unfamiliar source domains can be compared with more mundane examples using the format TARGET DOMAIN isn't (just/merely) (like) CONVENTIONAL SOURCE DOMAIN, it's (like) NOVEL SOURCE DOMAIN, described earlier in the chapter. Barnden provides the following example.

> This is a young woman with the best hair in town – lustrous, thick, swingy … So what did the network bozos do but stiff it up so that it looked not merely like a birds' nest, but one in which the birds had also shat?[10]

Messy hair is frequently compared to a birds' nest. By beginning with this conventional image metaphor, then moving on to the more extreme image of a birds' nest splattered with droppings, the author of the passage accentuates the terrible condition of the young woman's hair.

When we have actual experience with both the source domain and the target domain (or at least the general type of thing represented in the target domain, such as overweight people, vehicle tail-lights, or messy hair), an image metaphor can still be an effective way to evoke a mental image, as in these lines from William Blake:

> The children walking two and two, in red and blue and green …
> O what a multitude they seem'd, these flowers of London town![11]

Though some English speakers haven't seen children in London, everyone has seen kids in bright clothing. Everyone has also seen the target domain, flowers. Both domains are familiar, so the image metaphor simply encourages us to focus on the fresh, bright colours of the children's clothing by imagining them as flowers.

A familiar image can also make it easier to visualize something unfamiliar. In the following, a travel blogger describes a remote mountain lake that we will never see, in terms of a familiar shape that appears on every world map:

> We saw three lakes during day 3, one of them being an upside-down map of Australia. The view of that lake was so peaceful and beautiful, it was hard to believe it could get better.[12]

The following passage describes a momentary body stance assumed by a character that we can't see, in terms of a wishbone, something that many of us have seen regularly:

> The boys skidded across a big mat woven from pandanus leaves, Kimo's legs briefly akimbo, like a wishbone in mid-wish.[13]

Finally, this passage from Columbian writer Juan Gabriel Vásquez's latest book also describes a body position, this time in terms of an image that's familiar but also poignant:

> (The girls were) so drunk they were splayed out like pinned butterflies on the floor.[14]

This image metaphor not only helps us visualize the girls, but emphasizes their vulnerability. They not only look like colourful butterflies, but they're pinned helpless like collected specimens.

Either the source domain or the target domain of an image metaphor has to be familiar. If both domains are familiar, the metaphor can still be vivid and appealing. However, if both are unfamiliar, we may have trouble imagining the scene at all. In the following passages, the target domains of the image metaphors are unfamiliar fictional scenes, and the source domains are also things we've never seen. For most readers, these metaphors don't work as well as the ones with at least one familiar domain.

> Low could see him bobbing off through the crowd, his head rising and falling amid the suits like a sea otter in a bed of black and navy-blue kelp.[15]

> The edges of the ice field had a bluish tinge and was cracked along its surface like the parched tongue of a lost prospector.[16]

The next example describes electrical sparks in terms of two source domains that are both unfamiliar, drugged snakes and horny aliens:

> (Sparks) erupted and began to flash about the circumference of the mound like blue kraits overdosed on hormones. They jerked and twitched in an orgy of electric alien lust …[17]

Image metaphors seem to be more forgiving of inconsistencies than other metaphors. Nevertheless, little can be gained from comparing one unfamiliar sensory impression to another one. In the 'alien lust' example, we don't know what the blue sparks look like, and we also don't know what lustful aliens look like. Therefore, a comparison of the two is meaningless.

Even though no readers will have seen a lost prospector's tongue or horny aliens, some source domains may be familiar to some readers but unfamiliar to others. If an author's source domain is a movie, then the domain will be familiar only to readers who have seen that movie:

> His lips fastened on to her like a leech attaching itself to Katherine Hepburn's arm in *The African Queen*.[18]

Likewise, anyone who hasn't read about the Dark Lord Sauron in *The Lord of the Rings* will have trouble understanding the creepy sensation experienced by the narrator in this modern novel:

> Mr. Harmondsworth's voice seemed to be coming from far away, but I could feel his gaze on me, like the eye of Sauron searching out poor Frodo …[19]

It's relatively rare to find an image metaphor with a source domain that's familiar to everyone, but nevertheless so inappropriate for its target domain that it comes across as mixed. An example of this type was selected by the *Literary Review* for the 2017 Bad Sex in Fiction Award:

> The skin along her arms and shoulders are different shades of tan like water stains in a bathtub. Her face and vagina are competing for my attention, so I glance down at the billiard rack of my penis and testicles.[20]

Both the 'water stains' and the 'billiard rack' image metaphors are ill-suited for describing sexy bodies. Most of us are familiar with the idea of stains in a filthy bathtub, but it's difficult to associate this concept with the body of an attractive woman. The 'billiard rack' image metaphor is even more confusing. This metaphor caught the attention of the *Literary Review* judges in part because 'they were left unsure as to how many testicles the character in question has'.[21] The judges were correct in their diagnosis that 'there are parts in the book where Bollen goes overboard in his attempts to describe the familiar in new terms, leading occasionally to confusion'. Usually, original image metaphors that refer to an everyday target domain in terms of an everyday source, as in Blake's 'flowers of London town' metaphor, are easy to relate to. Bollard's confusing examples are noteworthy and apparently deserving of an award.

None of the metaphors described in this section are mixed in the sense of combining two incompatible metaphors, but this doesn't stop them from being useless or distracting. These examples show that unfamiliar or inappropriate source domains can be just as confusing as those that result from the combination of two incompatible domains.

There are many reasons for metaphors to be considered mixed, and this chapter has shown that there can be value to mixing them as well as motivations for keeping them apart. Mixed metaphors can be funny, incisive, or surprisingly vivid. Like any powerful tool, mixed metaphors should be treated with respect and set aside when they're not the right implement for the job. Sometimes, however, a mixed metaphor is exactly what's needed.

Notes

1   Sullivan and Sweetser, 'Is "Generic Is Specific" a Metaphor?'
2   Brian Tracy, *Eat That Frog! 21 Great Ways to Stop Procrastinating and Get More Done in Less Time* (Oakland, CA: Berrett-Koehler Publishers, 2001).
3   Semino, 'A Corpus-Based Study of "Mixed Metaphor"'.
4   Barnden, 'Communicating Flexibly with Metaphor', 448.
5   Jon Sopel, 'Is Donald Trump Now Unstoppable?' *BBC News*, 2016. Available online: http://www.bbc.com/news/world-us-canada-35388292 (accessed 11 December 2016).
6   Rafael Núñez and Eve Sweetser, 'With the Future behind Them: Convergent Evidence from Aymara Language and Gesture in the Crosslinguistic Comparison of Spatial Construals of Time', *Cognitive Science* 30 (2006): 401–50.
7   In one case, a man was killed by a rooster with a knife attached to its leg. Sarah Bee, 'Man Stabbed to Death by Chicken', *The Register*, 8 February 2011. Available online: http://www.theregister.co.uk/2011/02/08/man_bird_death_again_omg/ (accessed 29 January 2018).
8   P. G. Wodehouse, *Very Good, Jeeves* (New York: Double Day, Doran, 1930).
9   *The British National Corpus*.
10 Barnden, 'Communicating Flexibly with Metaphor', 448.
11 William Blake, 1789, 'Holy Thursday'. *Songs of Innocence*, 2016. Available online: http://www.tate.org.uk/learn/online-resources/william-blake/songs

-innocence-and-experience/transcript-songs-innocence-holy (accessed 11 December 2016).

12 Kevin Rowe, 'Days 6-11 – Inca-redible Scenes', *Rowe's Enterprises*, 21 October 2016. Available online: http://www.rowes-enterprises.org/blog/days-6-11-inca-redible-scenes/ (accessed 1 December 2016).

13 Alan Brennert, *Moloka'i*. New York: St Martin's Griffin, 2003, 5.

14 Juan Gabriel Vásquez, trans. Anne McLean, *Reputations* (New York: Riverhead Books, 2016).

15 Alan Dean Foster, *The Dig* (New York: Warner Books, 1996), 31.

16 Clive Cussler and Paul Kemprecos, *Lost City* (London: Penguin Books 2004): 38.

17 Foster, *The Dig*, 88.

18 Sarah Wisseman, *Burnt Siena (A Flora Garibaldi Art History Mystery)* (Farmington Hills, MI: Five Star Publishing, Kindle edition, 2015),Loc. 826.

19 Robert Hellenga, *The Sixteen Pleasures* (New York: Soho Press, 1989).

20 Christopher Bollen, *The Destroyers* (London: Scribner, 2017).

21 Alison Flood, 'Bad Sex Award Won by Christopher Bollen's Phallic "Billiard Rack"', *The Guardian*, 1 December 2017. Available online: https://www.theguardian.com/books/2017/nov/30/bad-sex-award-won-by-christopher-bollens-phallic-billiard-rack (accessed 3 December 2017).

9 MAKING THE MOST OF YOUR METAPHORS

When I was planning this book, I began asking random people what they thought about mixed metaphors. Almost all of them had strong opinions, and few could support their opinions with facts. I found it interesting that so many people disdained mixed metaphors while knowing so little about them.

I was equally interested to observe that many researchers in linguistics seemed eager to defend mixed metaphors. From a typical linguist's point of view, mixed metaphors are scarcely a problem. If anything, mixed metaphors offer 'testimony to the cognitive flexibility that is the hallmark of human intelligence and creativity'.[1] What, then, has caused this divide between linguists and non-specialists?

Certainly, the hundreds of years of prescriptions against mixed metaphor have played a role. When people have an opinion and can't explain why, it's usually because they've been told to believe it and haven't been given a good reason. Experts in an area, such as linguists, are more likely to question and reject prescriptions related to their topic of expertise. It's not surprising that linguists oppose linguistic prescriptions that most other people accept.

Prescriptivism also goes a long way towards explaining the universal reproach towards mixed metaphor in the writing community. Writers are expert language users and might be expected to question linguistic prescriptions. On the other hand, critics mock mixed metaphors, style guides abhor them, and English teachers warn students to avoid them at all costs. Once a phenomenon is stigmatized, writers have an incentive to avoid it regardless of whether there's anything wrong with it from a linguistic or cognitive perspective. For example, all sorts of prescriptions based on Latin grammar persist to this day, such as the injunctions against split infinitives (putting an adverb between *to* and an infinitive verb, as in *to boldly go*) and preposition stranding (as in *a preposition is a terrible thing to end a sentence with*). There's no inherent reason for these prescriptions, yet many writers don't want to risk violating long-established norms. Even if mixed metaphors have no negative effects on cognition or communication, many writers and speakers may want to avoid them because they worry about the ridicule that could otherwise result.

The fear of mixed metaphors may even stop some writers from experimenting with multiple metaphors. Sequences, combinations, and permutations of metaphors have been used to good advantage by Shakespeare, Hardy, Frost, and Einstein, to create memorable literature and witty aphorisms. It would be a pity if modern writers were discouraged from experimenting with metaphors due to concerns over mixing.

Clearly, the prescriptions against mixed metaphors have detrimental side effects. But are these prescriptions as baseless as the warnings against preposition stranding or split infinitives? Or are there legitimate reasons to avoid mixed metaphors, other than the fear of upsetting prescriptivists and their brainwashed adherents? In this book, I've suggested that there are social and cognitive motivations for minimizing mixed metaphors. Linguistics scholars are absolutely correct that mixed metaphors don't significantly hinder communication. For many linguists, this means that they are not a problem. Most writers and laypersons, on the other hand, are concerned with making a good impression, appearing competent, seeming knowledgeable, eliciting confidence, and so forth. Mixed metaphors can impede these goals.

Almost every kind of metaphor covered in this book can be competently used or completely abused. Many mixed metaphors have incompatible source domains that contradict each other when the metaphors are combined, for example. Usually, these metaphors seem sloppy. For example, *they're the barnacles on the wheels of progress* involves a contradiction, because a wheeled land vehicle cannot simultaneously be a boat. On the other hand, competing source domains can work beautifully when the writer makes it clear that the two source domains are alternatives. In the advice, *these mountains that you were carrying, you were only supposed to climb*, the metaphoric mountains are not simultaneously carried and climbed. The author presents the climbing and carrying as two alternative options.

Likewise, we've seen both bad and good examples of unfamiliar source domains. In *the placing of the lamp of truth near the seesaw of privilege and oppression*, the idea of seesawing by lamplight is imaginable, but odd. Nevertheless, when an author gently leads us through a novel source domain, we're prepared to accept it, as in P. G. Wodehouse's description of *a tubby little chap who looked as if he had been poured into his clothes and had forgotten to say 'when!'* Pouring a human body into its clothes is even stranger than midnight seesawing, yet because Wodehouse explains his source domain one step at a time, we can visualize it without too much work.

Even ambiguity between metaphoric and literal readings has positive as well as negative consequences. It's not helpful to say, 'I smell a rat around here', if it's not obvious whether you mean a literal rat or a metaphoric rat. Anyone listening to you won't know whether to get a rat trap or to check the books for embezzling. In other cases, however, it's valuable to refrain from explaining exactly what you mean. For example, allegorical poems and stories allow readers to muse on all the possible interpretations of the work.

When the literal and metaphoric meanings of an expression are similar, but not ambiguous, this can also make metaphoric language either more or less effective. When the Virgin Mary's suffering at watching Jesus's crucifixion is compared to Jesus's own suffering, for example, this belittles Mary's pain rather than accentuating it. On the other hand, in the title of the poem 'Light breaks where no sun shines', the metaphoric state is more surprising in contrast to the literal situation. Actual physical suffering or literal darkness can downplay metaphoric pain or metaphoric blackness, if the literal situation seems more dramatic than the metaphoric one. It can also accentuate the metaphoric meaning if it provides a contrast.

Like other metaphors, metaphoric idioms can be put together either well or poorly. Idiom combinations typically produce obvious mixed metaphors such as *that wet blanket is a loose cannon*. Sometimes, though, when the underlying metaphors and the idiomatic meanings are compatible, they can cleverly condense the meaning of two idioms into one idiomatic expression, as in the headline *Tony shoots fish in barrel, misses foot*.

All these comparisons illustrate how the most ingenious metaphors come perilously close to the most egregious misuses. The most praised and the most derided metaphoric passages sometimes differ only by a hair. These subtle differences underscore the proviso in the introduction, that there can be no hard-and-fast rules for avoiding mixed metaphors. You can't limit metaphors to one per paragraph, as a grammar guide recommended, nor is it always a good idea to use only one metaphor per sentence or clause. Any strategy that eliminates most mixed metaphors (as the one-metaphor-per-paragraph rule would do) would also prevent countless creative and beautiful metaphors. As a reader, I would personally rather suffer through any number of mixed metaphors than miss out on one of Wodehouse's clever descriptions or one of Dickinson's thought-provoking ambiguities.

The way to make the most of your metaphors is to understand them, not to censor them according to a rule. Look them up in the appendix of this book. See if they have the factors that will encourage them to combine. If they seem inclined to combine, check whether their source domains are compatible. Try visualizing the two source domains together to see if they make sense. Look for possible ambiguity or other ways that the literal meaning might detract from the metaphoric meaning. Check whether they involve metaphoric idioms, and if they do, make sure you understand their metaphoric origins. Consider the effect you are trying to achieve. Compare each metaphor combination to similar examples by authors that you admire or despise.

The mixed metaphors that will bother readers and critics will probably stand out to you once you identify the metaphors that are involved and understand how they're being used. If you know that you're mixing metaphors, but like the result, then go ahead! Trust your instincts. As in so many situations, once you know the rules you'll sometimes want to break them. The most meaningful metaphor combinations often veer the closest to mixing. Remember that if you're not living on the edge, you're taking up too much space.

In the case of mixed metaphors, the famous quotation from Shakespeare's *Hamlet* cannot apply: 'There is nothing either good or bad, but thinking makes it so.' Some metaphors *are* good or bad, but this depends on the thinking that has gone *into* them. Even the staunchest defenders of mixed metaphor will laugh or cringe at some of the examples repeated in this book. And even the strictest prescriptivists cannot criticize metaphors that fit together flawlessly. There are mixed metaphors that are simply bad, and there are metaphor combinations that are inherently well crafted. For the metaphors in the middle, those that neither stink nor shine – well, in those cases, you will simply have to step up to the plate and fish or cut bait. And try to score a touchdown.

Note

1   Gibbs, *Mixing Metaphor*, ix.

APPENDIX: INDEX OF METAPHORS

We can understand why metaphors are useful, and we can see why mixed metaphors might be a problem, even without the help of diagrams or technical language. However, in order to examine the details of a particular metaphor, it's necessary to introduce some new vocabulary and a visual system for representing metaphoric structure. This appendix begins with an introduction to a few of the more technical aspects of metaphors, followed by the basic structures of all the metaphors discussed in this book.

Additional metaphors can be viewed on the publicly available MetaNet Wiki (https://metaphor.icsi.berkeley.edu/pub/en/).[1] Throughout this book, whenever several possible names and analyses have been suggested for metaphors, the names and analyses closest to those employed in MetaNet have been chosen. This decision was made so that interested readers could easily find more information about these metaphors on the MetaNet Wiki. The metaphors in this appendix align as closely as possible with those on the Wiki, though for each metaphor I've provided example sentences and other information not included in the Wiki. Metaphor titles not included in the Wiki as of late 2017 are marked with an asterisk (*) in this appendix.

The list of metaphors in this appendix is alphabetical by target domain. First, it indicates whether each metaphor is primary or compound (see Chapter 2). If it's a primary metaphor, the listing notes one of the real-world correspondences that the metaphor is based on, such as the correspondence between adding items to a pile (MORE) and increasing the height of the pile (UP) underlying QUANTITY IS VERTICALITY (see Chapter 2). If the metaphor is a compound, the entry names one or more metaphors that are included in the compound. The entry then provides a few example sentences that use the metaphor and finally gives the diagram of the conceptual metaphor itself.

How to read metaphor diagrams

Conceptual metaphors are diagrammed as lists of correspondences between the source domain and the target domain. These correspondences, called *mappings*, are shown connected by arrows from the source domain to the target domain.[2] For example, in LIFE IS A JOURNEY, difficulties in life are understood as obstacles on a journey, as in expressions such as *she overcame her anxiety, they got through the divorce proceedings*, or *we have to find a way around these problems*. This correspondence is represented as a mapping from OBSTACLE to DIFFICULTY:

OBSTACLE → DIFFICULTY

The source domain is usually on the left and the target domain is on the right in metaphor diagrams.[3] Mappings are listed under the domain names, as in the following abbreviated list for LIFE IS A JOURNEY, which shows the mapping from a TRAVELLER (on a JOURNEY) to an EXPERIENCER (of LIFE), and the mapping from an OBSTACLE to a DIFFICULTY:

Source domain:		Target domain:
JOURNEY		LIFE
TRAVELLER	→	EXPERIENCER
OBSTACLE	→	DIFFICULTY
...		

In metaphor diagrams, the source domain is on the left and the target domain is on the right to show that mappings take information from the source on the left and move it to the target on the right. Since English speakers read from left to right, we expect information to move from left to right, too. However, this notation can be confusing because the titles of conceptual metaphors (such as LIFE IS A JOURNEY) name the two domains in the opposite order. That is, metaphor titles follow the pattern TARGET DOMAIN IS SOURCE DOMAIN, in which the target domain is listed first (on the left) and the source domain is second (on the right).

It's important to keep in mind that the source and target domains will appear in opposite orders in metaphor names (such as LIFE and JOURNEY in LIFE IS A JOURNEY) as opposed to metaphor diagrams (in which mappings from JOURNEY, on the left, follow the arrows to LIFE, on the right).

As you refer to the diagrams included here, also be aware that it's not practical to list all of the possible mappings of every metaphor, so these lists include only a selection of mappings. For example, the JOURNEY source domain of LIFE IS A JOURNEY sometimes includes a GUIDE who helps you 'find your way' in LIFE. This GUIDE is apparent in expressions such as *he helped me discover my life path, she led me every step of the way*, or *they showed me the road to success*. In the LIFE target domain, this GUIDE metaphorically maps to a life ADVISOR. The mapping from GUIDE to ADVISOR, like many mappings from JOURNEY to LIFE, is usually not included in diagrams of LIFE IS A JOURNEY, but can be added when it's relevant. Mostly, though, the mappings here should be sufficient to analyse the instances of these metaphors that you find in this book and in your daily life. Additional metaphors can be viewed on the MetaNet Wiki (https://metaphor.icsi.berkeley.edu/pub/en/).

List of metaphors cited in the text

ACHIEVING A PURPOSE IS ACQUIRING A DESIRED OBJECT
Primary.
Real-world basis: Getting an object and simultaneously fulfilling a need (Figure 31).
Examples: *They gave him a promotion. She was looking for love. He was trying to get attention.*

Source domain:		Target domain:
ACQUIRING A DESIRED OBJECT		ACHIEVING A PURPOSE
RECIPIENT	→	ACHIEVER
POSSESSABLE OBJECT	→	PURPOSE
SOURCE/GIVER OF OBJECT	→	FACILITATOR OF PURPOSE
ACQUISITION	→	CHANGE
POSSESSING AN OBJECT	→	EXPERIENCING FULFILMENT OF PURPOSE

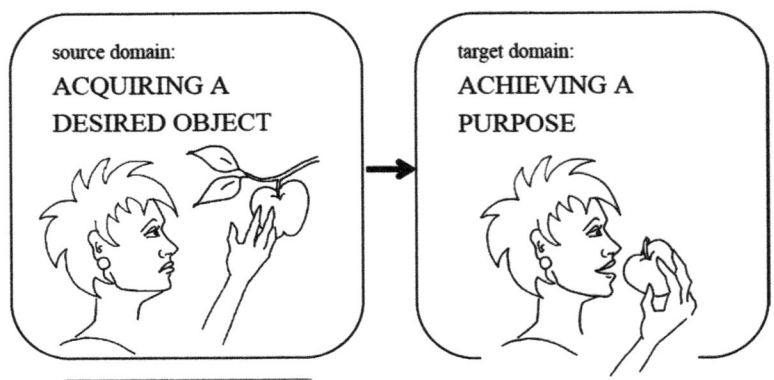

FIGURE 31 Information is mapped from a source domain, such as ACQUIRING A DESIRED OBJECT, to help understand a target domain, such as ACHIEVING A PURPOSE.

ACHIEVING A PURPOSE IS REACHING A DESTINATION
Primary.
Includes: MEANS ARE PATHS
Real-world basis: Going to a location and fulfilling a need (Figure 32).
Examples: *All his work got him nowhere. She's almost gotten to the next stage of her career, but she's not there yet. He's come a long way with improving his health. They reached their fitness goals.*

Source domain:		Target domain:
REACHING A DESTINATION		ACHIEVING A PURPOSE
MOVER	→	ACHIEVER
DISTANCE TRAVELLED	→	PROGRESS
DESTINATION	→	PURPOSE
PATHS TO A DESTINATION	→	MEANS TO ACHIEVE A PURPOSE
AIDS TO REACHING A DESTINATION	→	AIDS TO ACHIEVING A PURPOSE

AFFECTION IS WARMTH
Primary.
Real-world basis: Being embraced or held and feeling loved.
Examples: *She has a warm personality. Their kindness warmed his heart. She stared at him icily. He has a cold personality.*

FIGURE 32 ACHIEVING A PURPOSE can be understood as either REACHING A DESTINATION or ACQUIRING A DESIRED OBJECT. In our lives, we have to both go places and get objects, in order to achieve even simple goals such as eating.

Source domain: Target domain:
WARMTH AFFECTION
HEAT SOURCE → AFFECTIONATE PERSON OR ACTION
WARM → AFFECTIONATE
NOT WARM → NOT AFFECTIONATE
COLD → UNFRIENDLY

ALLIANCES ARE LOVE RELATIONSHIPS*
Compound.
Includes: EMOTIONAL INTIMACY IS PHYSICAL PROXIMITY, ALLIANCES ARE FRIENDSHIPS
Examples: *The politician courted big business for years. He's in bed with the mafia. The tobacco companies seduced the scientists. She's married to the media.*

Source domain: Target domain:
LOVE RELATIONSHIP ALLIANCE
LOVERS → POTENTIAL ALLIES
COURTSHIP → NEGOTIATION
MARRIAGE → COMMITTING TO ALLIANCE
SEXUAL INTERCOURSE → ALLIANCE

APPENDIX: INDEX OF METAPHORS

ANGER IS HEAT
Primary.
Real-world basis: Feeling angry and experiencing a resultant rise in body heat.
Examples: *Her rage burned. He was hot under the collar. She kept her cool.*

Source domain:		Target domain:
HEAT		ANGER
SOURCE OF HEAT	→	CAUSE OF ANGER
HEATING UP	→	BECOMING ANGRY
HOT	→	ANGRY
COOL	→	NOT ANGRY

ANGER IS THE HEAT OF FLUID IN A CONTAINER
Compound.
Includes: ANGER IS HEAT, ANGER IS PRESSURE IN A CONTAINER, THE BODY IS A CONTAINER FOR THE EMOTIONS
Examples: *He flipped his lid. She blew her stack. He was simmering for hours, then finally exploded. She was fuming. He was seething. Smoke was coming out her ears. He's just letting off steam.*

Source domain:		Target domain:
HEAT OF FLUID IN A CONTAINER		ANGER
CONTAINER	→	HEAD
LID	→	TOP OF HEAD
SOURCE OF HEAT	→	CAUSE OF ANGER
HEATING UP	→	BECOMING ANGRY
BOILING	→	DEMONSTRATING ANGRY BEHAVIOUR

ARGUMENT IS PHYSICAL COMBAT
Compound.
Includes: THE MIND IS A BODY, THEORIES ARE BUILDINGS
Examples: *He hurled accusations at her. Later, she threw his words back at him. The lawyer attacked his alibi, looking for a weak point, but it held fast.*

Source domain:		Target domain:
PHYSICAL COMBAT		ARGUMENT
COMBATANTS	→	ARGUERS

WEAPONS	→	WORDS
CAUSE OF COMBAT	→	TRIGGER OF ARGUMENT
ATTACKING	→	ARGUING
COUNTER-ATTACKS	→	REBUTTALS
FORTIFICATIONS	→	DEFENCES AGAINST ARGUMENTS
OUTCOME OF COMBAT	→	RESULT OF ARGUMENT

ARGUMENT IS WAR
Compound.
Special case of: ARGUMENT IS PHYSICAL COMBAT
Examples: *They duelled for years over that issue. She roused the troops, attacked his fortifications, and emerged victorious. He bombarded his opponent with vicious slander.*

Source domain:		Target domain:
WAR		ARGUMENT
ENEMIES	→	ARGUERS
ARMIES	→	SUPPORTERS
WEAPONS	→	WORDS
CAUSE OF WAR	→	TRIGGER OF ARGUMENT
ATTACKING	→	ARGUING
COUNTER-ATTACKS	→	REBUTTALS
FORTIFICATIONS	→	DEFENCES AGAINST ARGUMENTS
OUTCOME OF WAR	→	RESULT OF ARGUMENT

ASSISTANCE IS SUPPORT
Primary.
Real-world basis: Being helped by being held up.
Examples: *She supported her family. They depend on public donations. He doesn't need financial support. She's been leaning on her family members lately.*

Source domain:		Target domain:
SUPPORT		ASSISTANCE
SUPPORTER	→	HELPER
SUPPORTED PERSON	→	ASSISTED PERSON
BEING SUPPORTED	→	RELYING ON

ATTRIBUTES ARE POSSESSIONS
Primary.

Real-world basis: People who have certain possessions and also have certain attributes.

Examples: *He has a Roman nose. Her personality is lovely. His height is impressive. Doing yoga gave her good posture. He got a loud voice from working on construction sites.*

Source domain:		Target domain:
POSSESSIONS		ATTRIBUTES
OWNER	→	PERSON WITH ATTRIBUTE
ACQUIRING A POSSESSION	→	HAVING A NEW ATTRIBUTE
TRANSFERRING A POSSESSION	→	CAUSING AN ATTRIBUTE

THE BODY IS A CONTAINER (FOR THE EMOTIONS)
Compound.
Includes: IDEAS ARE OBJECTS
Examples: *Her happiness was overflowing. He was brimming with joy. Passion filled her. He could scarcely contain his excitement.*

Source domain:		Target domain:
CONTAINER		BODY
FLUID	→	EMOTION
LEVEL OF FLUID	→	INTENSITY OF EMOTION
CAPACITY OF CONTAINER	→	LIMIT OF ENDURANCE

BUSINESS COMPETITION IS BASEBALL*
Compound.
Includes: THE MIND IS A BODY
Special case of: BUSINESS COMPETITION IS A COMPETITIVE SPORT (Figure 33).
Examples: *Our company's at bat. They played hardball. Our company hit a home run with that project. This project never got to first base.*

Source domain:		Target domain:
BASEBALL		BUSINESS COMPETITION
TEAM	→	COMPANY
OPPONENT	→	RIVAL
BASEBALL PLAYER	→	EMPLOYEE
TURN AT BAT	→	OPPORTUNITY FOR THE COMPANY
HOME RUN	→	SUCCESSFUL OUTCOME

FIGURE 33 BUSINESS COMPETITION IS BASEBALL allows us to think about the workers in a company as the members of a baseball team.

BUSINESS COMPETITION IS AMERICAN FOOTBALL*
Compound.
Includes: THE MIND IS A BODY
Special case of: BUSINESS COMPETITION IS A COMPETITIVE SPORT (Figure 34).
Examples: *Let's make this touchdown for the company. Take the ball and run with it.*

FIGURE 34 BUSINESS COMPETITION IS AMERICAN FOOTBALL lets us consider employees in a company as a team in American football.

APPENDIX: INDEX OF METAPHORS

Source domain:		Target domain:
AMERICAN FOOTBALL		BUSINESS COMPETITION
TEAM	→	COMPANY
OPPONENT	→	RIVAL
FOOTBALL PLAYER	→	EMPLOYEE
TURN IN POSSESSION OF BALL	→	OPPORTUNITY FOR THE COMPANY
TOUCHDOWN	→	SUCCESSFUL OUTCOME

BUSINESS COMPETITION IS A COMPETITIVE SPORT
Compound.
Includes: THE MIND IS A BODY
Examples: *Let's win one for the company. They were playing for keeps, but we beat them in the end. The consultant is taking the ball and going home.*

Source domain:		Target domain:
COMPETITIVE SPORT		BUSINESS COMPETITION
TEAM	→	COMPANY
OPPONENT	→	RIVAL
PLAYER	→	EMPLOYEE
TURN TO PLAY	→	OPPORTUNITY FOR THE COMPANY
SUCCESSFUL PLAY	→	SUCCESSFUL OUTCOME

CAUSATION IS PROCREATION*
Compound.
Includes: CAUSING TO EXIST IS OBJECT CREATION
Examples: *They were the fathers of our country. She's the mother of Construction Grammar. They gave birth to a new era.*

Source domain:		Target domain:
PROCREATION		CAUSATION
PARENT	→	CAUSE
OFFSPRING	→	RESULT

COMMUNICATING IS OBJECT TRANSFER
Compound.
Includes: ACHIEVING A PURPOSE IS ACQUIRING A DESIRED OBJECT, UNDERSTANDING IS GRASPING
Examples: *He had trouble putting his feelings into words. She gave him an explanation, but it went right over his head. He took her advice. She got a*

recommendation from him. I finally got what she was saying. He got his point across. I didn't get much out of what he was saying.

Source domain:		Target domain:
OBJECT TRANSFER		COMMUNICATING
OBJECT	→	IDEA
CONTAINERS	→	LINGUISTIC EXPRESSIONS
DONOR	→	COMMUNICATOR
RECIPIENT	→	ADDRESSEE

DIFFICULTY IS HARDNESS
Primary.
Real-world basis: Experiencing difficulty while trying to physically affect a hard substance.
Examples: *This is a hard problem. It's a tough nut to crack.*

Source domain:		Target domain:
HARDNESS		DIFFICULTY
OBJECT	→	IDEA
DEGREE OF HARDNESS	→	LEVEL OF DIFFICULTY

ELECTRICITY IS A CROWD*
Compound.
Includes: IDEAS ARE OBJECTS
Examples: *The electrons are pushing and shoving and sometimes get in each other's way. Electrons rush along like an excited crowd.*

Source domain:		Target domain:
CROWD		ELECTRICITY
PERSON OR ANIMAL	→	ELECTRON
CORRIDOR	→	WIRE
GATE	→	TRANSISTOR
GETTING IN THE WAY	→	INHIBITING TRANSFER OF OTHER ELECTRONS

ELECTRICITY IS WATER*
Compound.
Includes: IDEAS ARE OBJECTS
Examples: *The electrons flow through the wires. The battery is full of electricity.*

Source domain:	Target domain:

WATER		ELECTRICITY
PIPE	→	WIRE
RESERVOIR	→	BATTERY

EMOTIONAL INTIMACY IS PHYSICAL PROXIMITY
Primary.
Real-world basis: People who know each other well, such as families and friends, tend to live closer together and spend time together.
Examples: *They're brothers, but they've never been close. Why are you acting so distant? He felt really close to her in that moment. Something was driving them apart.*

Source domain:		Target domain:
CLOSENESS		INTIMACY
CLOSE	→	INTIMATE
DISTANT	→	NOT INTIMATE

EXISTING IS BEING PHYSICALLY AT THIS LOCATION
Primary.
Real-world basis: We're aware of the existence of the things and beings that are located in our location.
Examples: *He's passed away. He's gone. The baby has arrived. Those days are gone. Her savings disappeared.*

Source domain:		Target domain:
BEING PHYSICALLY AT THIS LOCATION		EXISTENCE
ARRIVING	→	BEGINNING TO EXIST
DEPARTING	→	CEASING TO EXIST

EXPERIENCING A NEGATIVE STATE IS EXPERIENCING HARM
Compound.
Includes: THE MIND IS A BODY
Examples: *The discovery hurt him deeply. I died inside when I learned the truth.*

Source domain:		Target domain:
EXPERIENCING HARM		EXPERIENCING A NEGATIVE STATE
HARM	→	NEGATIVE STATE
DEATH	→	IRREVERSIBLE NEGATIVE OUTCOME

FRIENDSHIPS ARE FABRICS*
Compound.
Includes: EMOTIONAL INTIMACY IS PHYSICAL PROXIMITY
Special case of: IDEAS ARE OBJECTS
Examples: *They have a close-knit friendship. Their friendship is strong and never wears out. The argument tore their friendship to shreds.*

Source domain:		Target domain:
FABRICS		FRIENDSHIPS
TIGHTNESS OF WEAVE	→	INTIMACY
DURABILITY	→	POTENTIAL TO ENDURE

GENERIC IS SPECIFIC*
This cognitive structure is related to metaphor, but is not technically a metaphor itself.[4] GENERIC IS SPECIFIC allows any instance of a scenario to be conceptualized as one specific variant of the scenario.[5] GENERIC IS SPECIFIC is especially frequent in proverbs, as in *There's more than one way to skin a cat*, meaning 'There's more than one way to accomplish anything'. In this proverb, the SPECIFIC act of skinning a cat stands for a GENERIC activity, which makes the proverb applicable in many situations. The example in Chapter 3, *What father would anoint his child with such a leaden armour of expectations?*, also involves GENERIC IS SPECIFIC. Here, the SPECIFIC action of anointing a person for a sacred task stands for any GENERIC method of selecting a person for a task.

Although GENERIC IS SPECIFIC is a frequent structure that appears many times throughout this book, it deviates from the patterns laid out for conceptual metaphors in Chapter 2. For example, the source domain is not necessarily more concrete than the target domain. Skinning a cat is not more concrete than assembling a table, unblocking a drain, or performing many other tasks that can be described with the 'skinning a cat' proverb. Anointing someone for a task is not necessarily more concrete than assigning someone to a task in a different way.

Since GENERIC IS SPECIFIC is not a metaphor, the primary/compound distinction is not applicable.

Examples: *There's more than one way to skin a cat* 'There's more than one way to accomplish anything', *Better the devil that you know than the one you don't know* 'Better the familiar bad thing than the unfamiliar one', and many other idioms, proverbs, and sayings.

GOODNESS IS FAT*
Primary.
Real-world basis: Eating fatty foods and feeling good.
Examples: *There's a fat, juicy prize for the winner. That's just the icing on the cake. She's on the gravy train. That seems like thin gruel to me.*

Source domain:		Target domain:
FAT		GOODNESS
FATTY	→	GOOD
THIN	→	LACKING

GOODNESS IS LIGHT
Primary.
Real-world basis: Having sufficient light and benefitting from it.
Examples: *She has a brilliant future. He's a shining example for all of us. She's a star. He had a dark premonition. Beware the Dark Lord Sauron. Good guys wear white.*

Source domain:		Target domain:
LIGHT		GOODNESS
DARK	→	EVIL
BRILLIANCE	→	EXCELLENCE
POLISHING	→	IMPROVING

GOODNESS IS VERTICALITY
Primary.
Real-life basis: Being upright, awake, and healthy is a positive experience for humans because it allows for more useful activities.
Examples: *This coffee is excellent – it's right up there with the one we had last week. Heaven is up in the sky, and Hell is down underground.*

Source domain:		Target domain:
VERTICALITY		GOODNESS
UP	→	GOOD
DOWN	→	BAD
UPWARD MOTION	→	BECOMING BETTER
DOWNWARD MOTION	→	BECOMING WORSE

HAPPINESS IS BRIGHTNESS*

Primary.

Real-world basis: Being in the sunshine and feeling happy.

Examples: *'Sure,' she said brightly. He has a sunny personality. She felt gloomy and gray. The tragedy cast a shadow over the proceedings.*

Source domain:		Target domain:
BRIGHTNESS		HAPPINESS
BRIGHT	→	HAPPY
GLOOM	→	SADNESS

HAPPINESS IS VERTICALITY

Primary.

Real-world basis: Having an upright posture and facial expressions when feeling happy.

Examples: *He's high as a kite. She's on cloud nine. Don't do drugs – get high on life! He was in a depression. She was feeling down. He had a sinking feeling. Her spirits rose.*

Source domain:		Target domain:
VERTICALITY		HAPPINESS
UP	→	HAPPY
DOWN	→	SAD
UPWARD MOTION	→	INCREASE IN HAPPINESS
DOWNWARD MOTION	→	DECREASE IN HAPPINESS

IDEAS ARE OBJECTS

Primary.

Real-world basis: We interact with objects and learn new concepts from this interaction.

Examples: *Love is the most important thing in the world. The best things in life aren't things. Two hydrogens and an oxygen can be put together into a water molecule. You could string those stories together and have a novel.*

Source domain:		Target domain:
OBJECTS		IDEAS
TAKING APART OBJECTS	→	ANALYSING IDEAS
STRUCTURE OF AN OBJECT	→	STRUCTURE OF AN IDEA
CREATING AN OBJECT	→	COMING UP WITH AN IDEA
CONNECTIONS BETWEEN OBJECTS	→	RELATIONS BETWEEN IDEAS

IDEOLOGIES ARE ORGANISMS
Compound.
Includes: IMPORTANCE IS SIZE
Special case of: IDEOLOGIES ARE COMPLEX PHYSICAL SYSTEMS
Examples: *The book planted the seed of an idea in her head. They're cultivating all kinds of weird notions at their meetings. The germ of suspicion grew over the years. Once the idea took root in his mind, nobody could dissuade him.*

Source domain:		Target domain:
ORGANISMS		IDEOLOGIES
GERMINATING	→	BEGINNING
GROWING	→	INCREASING IN IMPORTANCE
CULTIVATING	→	CAUSING TO BECOME MORE IMPORTANT

IMAGE METAPHORS
Primary/compound distinction is not applicable.
Examples: *Her eyes are sapphires. Italy is a boot. His snoring thundered through the house. The cat's fur was velvety.*

IMPORTANT IS CENTRAL
Primary.
Real-world basis: More important people are often in the middle of a group. The most important part of a city is typically the city centre.
Examples: *This is my central point. Let's skip the peripherals. Let's get right to the core of the matter.*

Source domain:		Target domain:
SIZE		IMPORTANT
CENTRE	→	MOST IMPORTANT
PERIPHERAL	→	UNIMPORTANT

IMPORTANCE IS SIZE
Primary.
Real-world basis: Adults are bigger than children and important to children. Objects that are closer and more relevant appear bigger.
Examples: *He's a big man in the used car business. Think big. That objection is trivial. She felt small and ashamed. He's the big boss – we're just the little people.*

Source domain: Target domain:
SIZE   IMPORTANCE
BIG → IMPORTANT
SMALL → UNIMPORTANT

A LIFETIME IS A DAY*
Compound.
Includes: GOODNESS IS LIGHT, PASSION IS HEAT
Special case of: A LIFETIME IS A LIGHT/HEAT CYCLE*
Examples: *You should enjoy your sunset years. He's in the twilight of his life.*

Source domain: Target domain:
DAY   LIFETIME
EVENING → OLD AGE
NIGHTFALL → DEATH

A LIFETIME IS A FIRE*
Compound.
Includes: GOODNESS IS LIGHT, PASSION IS HEAT
Special case of: A LIFETIME IS A LIGHT/HEAT CYCLE*
Examples: *The fire of his life is dying. Her fire is going out.*

Source domain: Target domain:
FIRE   LIFETIME
BURNING → LIVING
GOING OUT → DYING

A LIFETIME IS A YEAR*
Compound.
Includes: GOODNESS IS LIGHT, PASSION IS HEAT
Special case of: A LIFETIME IS A LIGHT/HEAT CYCLE*
Examples: *She's a spring chicken. He's in the autumn years of his life. They have a December/May romance.*

Source domain: Target domain:
YEAR   LIFETIME
SPRING → YOUTH
AUTUMN → OLD AGE
WINTER → CLOSE TO DEATH

LIFE IS A JOURNEY
Compound.
Includes: ACHIEVING A PURPOSE IS REACHING A DESTINATION, MEANS ARE PATHS
Examples: *He finally got over his divorce. She overcame her problems. He's on the road to nowhere. She followed an academic path rather than going into law. Our business needs a roadmap for the next few years. She's at a good place in her life now.*

Source domain:		Target domain:
JOURNEY		LIFE
TRAVELLER	→	EXPERIENCER
PATH	→	MEANS
MAP	→	PLAN
FORK IN PATH	→	CHOICE BETWEEN MEANS
OBSTACLE	→	DIFFICULTY
BURDEN	→	(LONG-TERM) DIFFICULTY
DESTINATION	→	GOAL
VEHICLE	→	FACTOR THAT FACILITATES PROGRESS
FELLOW TRAVELLER	→	LIFE COMPANION

LOVE IS A JOURNEY*
Compound.
Includes: EMOTIONAL INTIMACY IS PHYSICAL PROXIMITY, ACHIEVING A PURPOSE IS REACHING A DESTINATION, RELATIONSHIPS ARE CONTAINERS
Special case of: LIFE IS A JOURNEY
Examples: *They've come so far together. Their marriage is on the rocks. They've hit a dead end. They tied the knot. They broke up and went their separate ways.*

Source domain:		Target domain:
JOURNEY		LOVE
TRAVELLERS	→	LOVERS
PATH	→	MEANS
FORK IN PATH	→	CHOICE BETWEEN MEANS
OBSTACLE	→	DIFFICULTY
BURDEN	→	(LONG-TERM) DIFFICULTY
DESTINATION	→	GOAL
VEHICLE	→	LOVE RELATIONSHIP
BONDS	→	MARRIAGE OR OTHER COMMITMENT

METONYMY

Although not a metaphor itself, metonymy is a process that can interact with metaphor. A metonymy extends a word's meaning to refer to a related concept. For example, the names of containers are often extended to refer to the containers' contents rather than the containers themselves. If you offer me coffee, I can answer, 'Yes, I'd like a cup,' and mean that I want a cup's worth of coffee. If you just brought me an empty cup, I'd be annoyed. As another example, authors' names are often extended to their books, so I can say, 'I have Jane Austen over there,' meaning that I have her works, not her actual body. There are many other types of metonymy. Some are listed in *Metaphors We Live By* by Lakoff and Johnson, and *Metaphor: A Practical Introduction* by Kövecses, for example.

THE MIND IS A BODY
Primary.
Real-life basis: Experiencing physical sensations at the same time as mental reactions.
Examples: *She hurt his ego. His feelings are wounded. Crosswords are good mental exercise. Her mental health has never been good. He has a mental illness. She's strong-minded.*

Source domain:		Target domain:
BODY		MIND
PHYSICAL CAPACITY	→	MENTAL CAPACITY
PHYSICAL STRUCTURE	→	MENTAL STRUCTURE
HEALTH	→	GOOD MENTAL FUNCTIONING
ILLNESS	→	IMPEDIMENT TO MENTAL FUNCTIONING

THE MIND IS A CONTAINER
Compound.
Includes: IDEAS ARE OBJECTS
Examples: *He's empty headed. She's scatter brained. Don't fill his head with rubbish! Her mind was brimming with new ideas.*

Source domain:		Target domain:
CONTAINER		MIND
CONTENTS	→	IDEAS
QUANTITY OF CONTENTS	→	NUMBER OF IDEAS
EMPTY	→	STUPID

THE MIND IS A MACHINE
Compound.
Examples: *The gears of her mind were turning. He's still processing that information.*

Source domain:
MACHINE
COMPUTING →
MACHINERY →

Target domain:
MIND
THINKING
COGNITIVE PROCESSES

THE MIND IS A PHYSICAL STRUCTURE
Compound.
Includes: IDEAS ARE OBJECTS
Examples: *She cracked up. He lost his mind. You need to get your head together. Spock performed a Vulcan mind-meld.*

Source domain:
OBJECT
PHYSICAL STRUCTURE →
PHYSICAL DAMAGE →

CONNECTIONS BETWEEN OBJECTS →

Target domain:
MIND
MENTAL STRUCTURE
IMPEDIMENT TO MENTAL FUNCTIONING
RELATIONS BETWEEN MINDS

MONEY IS FOOD*
Compound.
Special case of: MONEY IS A RESOURCE
Examples: *Many people blame the fat cats on Wall Street. We need to tighten our belts.*

Source domain:
FOOD
FAT →
POOR →
GLUTTONY →

Target domain:
MONEY
RICH
LEAN
GREED

MORALITY IS PURITY
Primary.
Real-life basis: Evaluating food, surfaces, etc., as clean and simultaneously evaluating their wholesomeness.

Examples: *She's having impure thoughts. He has a filthy mind. You need to clean up your act. There is some dirty language in this movie.*

Source domain:		Target domain:
<u>PURITY</u>		<u>MORALITY</u>
PURE	→	MORAL
IMPURE	→	IMMORAL
CLEANSING	→	IMPROVING MORALITY

THE NATION IS A FAMILY
Compound.
Examples: *He's the father of our country. Our government really takes care of us. Big Brother is watching.*

Source domain:		Target domain:
<u>FAMILY</u>		<u>NATION</u>
PARENT	→	NATIONAL LEADER
CHILDREN	→	CITIZENS
CARETAKING	→	GOVERNING

THE NATION IS AN OBJECT
Compound
Special case of: IDEAS ARE OBJECTS
Examples: *Syria is broken and nobody know how to fix it. Croatia is a hidden treasure.*

Source domain:		Target domain:
<u>OBJECT</u>		<u>NATION</u>
STRUCTURE OF AN OBJECT	→	STRUCTURE OF A NATION
CREATING AN OBJECT	→	FOUNDING A NATION
BREAKING AN OBJECT	→	HARMING A NATION
REPAIRING AN OBJECT	→	UNDOING HARM TO A NATION

PASSION IS HEAT
Primary.
Real-life basis: Experiencing increased body temperature caused by arousal.
Examples: *He's looking so hot today. She burned with desire. The heat between them was palpable.*

Source domain:		Target domain:
HEAT		PASSION
HOT	→	INDUCING PASSION
FEELING HEAT	→	EXPERIENCING PASSION
HEAT SOURCE	→	OBJECT OF PASSION

PERSISTING IS REMAINING ERECT
Primary.
Real-life basis: People, trees, many structures, etc., remain erect while they are living and/or functional.
Examples: *The law still stands. The world record was toppled.*

Source domain:		Target domain:
REMAINING ERECT		PERSISTING
ERECT	→	FUNCTIONAL
FALLING	→	ENDING

QUANTITY IS SIZE
Primary.
Real-life basis: Greater quantities are often also bigger. For example, a balloon is bigger if there is more air in it.
Examples: *Her monthly payments increased. Their dividend shrank. His interest diminished.*

Source domain:		Target domain:
SIZE		QUANTITY
LARGE	→	MORE
SMALL	→	LESS
GROWTH	→	INCREASE IN QUANTITY
SHRINKAGE	→	DECREASE IN QUANTITY

QUANTITY IS VERTICALITY
Primary.
Real-life basis: Adding objects or substances to a pile and seeing the pile become higher.
Examples: *Stocks rose. Funds are getting low.*

Source domain:	Target domain:
VERTICALITY	QUANTITY

UP	→	MORE
DOWN	→	LESS
UPWARD MOTION	→	INCREASE IN QUANTITY
DOWNWARD MOTION	→	DECREASE IN QUALITY

SIMILE

Similes are metaphors with the form *X is like Y*, as in *life is like a journey* or *the nation is like a family*. Similes involve the same conceptual metaphors as other metaphoric language. That is, the sentences *Life is like a journey*, *Life is a journey*, and *He made a wrong turn in the journey of his life* all involve LIFE IS A JOURNEY. However, only the first of these sentences is a simile.

SOCIAL GROUPS ARE COMPLEX STRUCTURES
Compound.
Examples: *The team fell apart. Part of the company broke off to form a start-up.*

Source domain:		Target domain:
COMPLEX STRUCTURES		SOCIAL GROUPS
(SMALLER) PARTS OF STRUCTURE	→	GROUP MEMBERS
(LARGER) PARTS OF STRUCTURE	→	SUBGROUPS
PHYSICAL CONNECTIONS	→	SOCIAL RELATIONSHIPS

SPORTING COMPETITIONS ARE BATTLES*
Compound.
Examples: *They're slaying the away team! He's defending the goal. They're being decimated.*

Source domain:		Target domain:
BATTLES		SPORTS COMPETITIONS
FIGHTERS	→	PLAYERS
ENEMY	→	OPPOSING TEAM
ATTACKING	→	PLAYING OFFENSIVELY
DEFENDING	→	PLAYING DEFENSIVELY

STATUS IS VERTICALITY
Primary.
Real-life basis: People dominate and control other people, animals, and objects that are physically beneath them or that have a lower position (Figure 35).

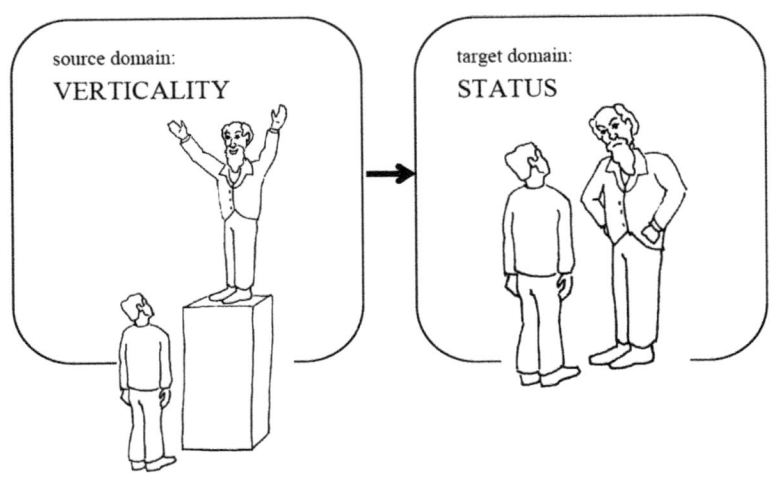

FIGURE 35 Status is verticality lets us think about dominance as being located 'above' other people.

Examples: *She's above me in the company hierarchy. He has twenty people under him. She's the top boss.*

Source domain:		Target domain:
VERTICALITY		STATUS
UP	→	MORE PRESTIGE
DOWN	→	LESS PRESTIGE
UPWARD MOTION	→	INCREASE IN PRESTIGE
DOWNWARD MOTION	→	DECREASE IN PRESTIGE
SEESAW	→	SYSTEM OF UNEQUAL PRESTIGE

SUSPICIOUS IS STINKY*
Primary.
Real-life basis: Food that stinks is suspicious.
Special case of: MORALITY IS PURITY
Examples: *I smell a rat. Something smells fishy here.*

Source domain:		Target domain:
STINKY		SUSPICIOUS
STINKY OBJECT	→	SUSPICIOUS IDEA/PERSON/SITUATION
SMELLING	→	SUSPECTING
DEGREE OF STINK	→	DEGREE OF SUSPICIOUSNESS

THEORIES ARE BUILDINGS
Compound.
Includes: PERSISTING IS REMAINING ERECT, IDEAS ARE OBJECTS
Examples: *She toppled his theory. He undermined her argument. That theory has a shaky foundation. Your philosophy is built on sand. Her theory collapsed under the weight of his arguments.*

Source domain:
BUILDINGS
FOUNDATION → BASIS
STRENGTH → LOGICALITY
ERECT → FUNCTIONAL
COLLAPSING → ENDING

Target domain:
THEORIES

THINKING IS MOVING
Compound.
Includes: ACHIEVING A PURPOSE IS REACHING A DESTINATION, THE MIND IS A BODY
Examples: *I was thinking in circles for a while, but I got there eventually. Let's think this through. Her thoughts were racing. His brain was moving sluggishly today.*

Source domain:
MOVING
MOVER → MIND
BEING IN A LOCATION → THINKING ABOUT A TOPIC
MOVING TO A NEW LOCATION → THINKING ABOUT A NEW TOPIC
SPEED OF MOTION → EFFICIENCY OF THINKING
GOAL-DIRECTED MOTION → PURPOSEFUL THINKING

Target domain:
THINKING

TIME IS A MOVING OBJECT
Primary.
Real-life basis: Watching objects approach you and experiencing time elapsing.
Examples: *Time flies. Christmas is coming. Election day is almost here. The week went by quickly; it's behind us now. Hold on to the good times, or they'll slip away from you.*

Source domain:		Target domain:
MOVING OBJECT		TIME
OBJECTS	→	EVENTS
OBJECTS IN FRONT	→	FUTURE EVENTS
OBJECTS BEHIND	→	PAST EVENTS
RESTRAINING AN OBJECT	→	PROLONGING AN EVENT

TIME IS A RESOURCE
Compound.
Subcase of: TIME IS AN ENTITY
Examples: *Time is money. We need to spend more time together. Don't waste time! Can I borrow a moment of your time?*

Source domain:		Target domain:
RESOURCE		TIME
OWNER OF RESOURCE	→	EXPERIENCER OF TIME
QUANTITY OF RESOURCE	→	DURATION OF TIME
GIVING UP RESOURCE	→	USING TIME

UNCERTAINTY IS VERTICALITY*
Primary.
Real-life basis: When an object is falling from above, it's uncertain where it will come down.
Examples: *The election is up in the air at the moment. My birthday fell on a Friday.*

Source domain:		Target domain:
VERTICALITY		UNCERTAINTY
UP	→	UNCERTAIN
DOWN	→	CERTAIN

UNDERSTANDING IS DIGESTING
Primary.
Real-world basis: Eating a food and digesting it, thereby knowing what it's like and whether it's good to eat.
Examples: *He swallowed that lie. She found the knowledge hard to digest. He needed to chew on that idea for a minute. That plan is half-baked. She's cooked up a crazy plan.*

Source domain:	Target domain:
DIGESTER	UNDERSTANDING

EATER	→	THINKER
FOOD	→	IDEAS
CHEWING	→	THINKING OVER
SWALLOWING	→	BELIEVING
DIGESTING	→	UNDERSTANDING
COOKING	→	PREPARING IDEAS FOR OTHERS
FEEDING	→	COMMUNICATING IDEAS

UNDERSTANDING IS GRASPING

Primary.

Real-life basis: Holding an object and understanding more about it (Figure 36).

Examples: *I get what you're saying. He has a good grasp of physics. The answers kept slipping away from her.*

Source domain:		Target domain:
GRASPING		UNDERSTANDING
GRASPER	→	THINKER
OBJECT	→	IDEA
ABILITY TO GRASP	→	ABILITY TO UNDERSTAND

FIGURE 36 UNDERSTANDING IS GRASPING supplements UNDERSTANDING IS SEEING by giving us another way of thinking about cognition.

UNDERSTANDING IS HEARING*

Primary.

Subcase of: UNDERSTANDING IS PERCEIVING

Real-world basis: We hear sounds and listen to speech, and learn information as a result.

Examples: *I'll have my ear to the ground. She sounds like a good boss.*

Source domain:		Target domain:
HEARING		UNDERSTANDING
HEARER	→	THINKER
OBJECTS	→	IDEAS
AUDIBILITY	→	COMPREHENSIBILITY

UNDERSTANDING IS SEEING

Primary.

Subcase of: UNDERSTANDING IS PERCEIVING

Real-world basis: We see the world around us and learn information as a result (Figure 37).

Examples: *I see what you mean. His argument is obscured by jargon. I'm in the dark about his intentions. The new candidate is a dark horse. She's a brilliant scientist. He's the brightest student this year. This book sheds light on that debate.*

Source domain:	Target domain:
SEEING	UNDERSTANDING

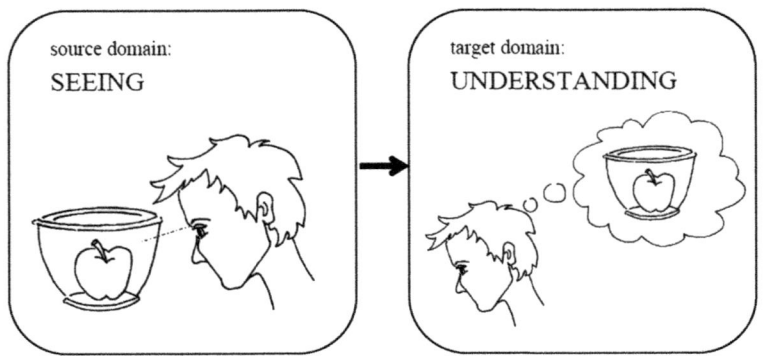

FIGURE 37 UNDERSTANDING IS SEEING is a frequently encountered metaphor in English.

VIEWER	→	THINKER
OBJECT	→	IDEA
VISIBILITY	→	COMPREHENSIBILITY
VISUAL ABILITY	→	CAPACITY FOR UNDERSTANDING
LIGHT SOURCES	→	SOURCES OF KNOWLEDGE
LIGHT EMISSION	→	INTELLIGENCE

Notes

1 MetaNet 'Category: Metaphor'.
2 Lakoff and Johnson, *Metaphors We Live By*. An excellent definition of *mapping* is formulated in: Barbara Dancygier and Eve Sweetser, *Figurative Language* (Cambridge: Cambridge University Press, 2014), 14.
3 Lakoff and Johnson, *Philosophy in the Flesh*.
4 Sullivan and Sweetser, 'Is "Generic Is Specific" a Metaphor?'
5 Lakoff and Turner, *More than Cool Reason*.

BIBLIOGRAPHY

Barcelona, Antonio and Cristina Soriano. 'Metaphorical Conceptualization in English and Spanish'. *European Journal of English Studies* 8 (2004): 295–307.

Barnden, John. 'Communicating Flexibly with Metaphor: A Complex of Strengthening, Compounding and Unrealism'. *Review of Cognitive Linguistics* 14, no. 2 (2016a): 442–73.

Barnden, John. 'Mixed Metaphor: Its Depth, Its Breadth, and a Pretence-Based Approach'. In *Mixing Metaphor*, edited by Raymond W. Gibbs Jr, 75–111. Amsterdam and Philadelphia, PA: John Benjamins, 2016b.

Black, Max. 'More about Metaphor'. In *Metaphor and Thought*, edited by Andrew Ortony, 19–41. Cambridge: Cambridge University Press, 1993.

Borges, Tarciso A. 'Mental Models of Electricity'. *International Journal of Science Education* 21, no. 1 (1999): 95–117.

Boroditsky, Lera. 'Metaphoric Structuring: Understanding Time through Spatial Metaphors'. *Cognition* 75, no. 1 (2000): 1–28.

The British National Corpus, version 3, BNC XML Edition. Distributed by Oxford University Computing Services on Behalf of the BNC Consortium, (2007). Available online: http://www.natcorp.ox.ac.uk/ (accessed 7 October 2017).

Brown, Theodore L. *Making Truth: Metaphor in Science*. Urbana and Chicago, IL: University of Illinois Press, 2003.

Burgers, Christian, Elly A. Konijn, and Gerard J. Steen. 'Figurative Framing: Shaping Public Discourse through Metaphor, Hyperbole, and Irony'. *Communication Theory* 26, no. 4 (2016): 410–30.

Cameron, Lynne. 'Mixed Metaphors from a Discourse Dynamics Perspective: A Non-Issue?' In *Mixing Metaphor*, edited by Raymond W. Gibbs Jr, 17–30. Amsterdam and Philadelphia, PA: John Benjamins, 2016.

Charteris-Black, Jonathan. 'Speaking with Forked Tongue: A Comparative Study of Metaphor and Metonymy in English and Malay Phraseology'. *Metaphor and Symbol* 18 (2003): 289–310.

Charteris-Black, Jonathan. *Politicians and Rhetoric. The Persuasive Power of Metaphor*. Basingstoke: Palgrave-Macmillan, 2011.

Charteris-Black, Jonathan. 'The "Dull Roar" and the "Burning Barbed Wire Pantyhose": Complex Metaphor in Accounts of Chronic Pain'. In *Mixing Metaphor*, edited by Raymond W. Gibbs Jr, 155–78. Amsterdam and Philadelphia, PA: John Benjamins, 2016.

Crisp, Peter. 'Allegory: Conceptual Metaphor in History'. *Language and Literature* 10, no. 5 (2001): 5–19.

Crisp, Peter, John Heywood, and Gerard J. Steen. 'Metaphor Identification and Analysis, Classification and Quantification'. *Language and Literature* 11, no. 1 (2002): 55–69.

Cutting, J. Cooper and Kathryn Bock. 'That's the Way the Cookie Bounces: Syntactic and Semantic Components of Experimentally Elicited Idiom Blends'. *Memory and Cognition* 25, no. 1 (1997): 57–71.

Dancygier, Barbara and Eve Sweetser. *Figurative Language*. Cambridge: Cambridge University Press, 2014.

Dancygier, Barbara and Lieven Vandelanotte. 'Internet Memes as Multimodal Constructions'. *Cognitive Linguistics* 28, no. 3 (2017): 565–98.

Deignan, Alice. 'Metaphorical Expressions and Culture: An Indirect Link'. *Metaphor and Symbol* 18 (2003): 255–71.

Deignan, Alice. *Metaphor and Corpus Linguistics*. Amsterdam and Philadelphia, PA: John Benjamins, 2005.

Denroche, Charles. *Metonymy and Language: A New Theory of Linguistic Processing*. New York: Routledge, 2015.

diSessa, Andrea A. 'Phenomenology and the Evolution of Intuition'. In *Mental Models*, edited by Dedre Gentner and Albert L. Stevens, 15–34. Hillsdale, NJ: Erlbaum Associates, 1983.

El Refaie, Elisabet. 'Reconsidering "Image Metaphor" in the Light of Perceptual Simulation Theory'. *Metaphor and Symbol* 30, no. 1 (2015): 63–76.

Enfield, Nicholas. 'Adjectives in Lao'. In *Adjective Classes: A Cross-Linguistic Typology*, edited by R. M. W. Dixon and Alexandra Aikhenvald, 323–47. Oxford: Oxford University Press, 2004.

Enfield, Nicholas. 'The Myth of Language Universals: Language Diversity and Its Importance for Cognitive Science'. *Behavioral and Brain Sciences* 32 (2009): 429–92.

Evans, Vyvyan. *The Emoji Code: The Linguistics behind Smiley Faces and Scaredy Cats*. New York: Picador, 2017.

Fainsilber, Lynn and Andrew Ortony. 'Metaphorical Uses of Language in the Expression of the Emotions'. *Metaphor and Symbolic Activity* 2, no. 4 (1987): 239–50.

Fauconnier, Gilles. *Mental Spaces*. New York: Cambridge University Press, 1994.

Fauconnier, Gilles and Mark Turner. 'The Origin of Language as a Product of the Evolution of Double-Scope Blending'. *Behavioral and Brain Sciences* 31, no. 5 (2008): 520–21.

Forceville, Charles. *Pictorial Metaphor in Advertising*. London: Psychology Press, 1996.

Forceville, Charles. 'Mixing in Pictorial and Multimodal Metaphors?' In *Mixing Metaphor*, edited by Raymond W. Gibbs Jr, 223–40. Amsterdam and Philadelphia, PA: John Benjamins, 2016.

Forceville, Charles and Eduardo Urios-Aparisi, eds. *Multimodal Metaphor*. Berlin and New York: Mouton de Gruyter, 2009.

Gentner, Dedre and Donald R. Gentner. 'Flowing Waters and Teeming Crowds'. In *Mental Models*, edited by Dedre Gentner and Albert L. Stevens, 99–129. Hillsdale, NJ: Erlbaum Associates, 1982.

Gentner, Dedre, Mutsumi Imai, and Lera Boroditsky. 'As Time Goes By: Evidence for Two Systems in Processing Space → Time Metaphors'. *Language and Cognitive Processes* 17, no. 5 (2002): 537–65.

Gibbs, Raymond W. Jr. *The Poetics of Mind: Figurative Thought, Language, and Understanding*. Cambridge: Cambridge University Press, 1994.

Gibbs, Raymond W. Jr, ed. *Mixing Metaphor*. Amsterdam and Philadelphia, PA: John Benjamins, 2016.

Geeraerts, Dirk. The Interaction of Metaphor and Metonymy in Composite Expressions. In *Metaphor and Metonymy in Comparison and Contrast*, edited by René Dirven and Ralf Pörings, 435–68. Berlin and New York: Mouton de Gruyter, 2003.

Goatly, Andrew. *The Language of Metaphors*. London: Routledge, 1997.

Grady, Joseph E. 'Foundations of Meaning: Primary Metaphors and Primary Scenes'. PhD diss., Department of Linguistics, University of California, Berkeley, 1997a.

Grady, Joseph E. 'THEORIES ARE BUILDINGS Revisited'. *Cognitive Linguistics* 8, no. 4 (1997b): 267–90.

Grady, Joseph E. 'The Conduit Metaphor Revisited: A Reassessment of Metaphors for Communication'. In *Discourse and Cognition: Bridging the Gap*, edited by John-Pierre König, 205–18. Stanford, CA: CSLI, 1998.

Grady, Joseph E. 'Primary Metaphors as Inputs to Conceptual Integration'. *Journal of Pragmatics* 37 (2005): 1595–614.

Grady, Joseph E. and Chris Johnson. 'Converging Evidence for the Notions of Subscene and Primary Scene'. In *Metaphor and Metonymy in Comparison and Contrast*, edited by René Dirven and Rolf Pörings, 533–54. Berlin and New York: Mouton de Gruyter, 2002.

Grady, Joseph E., Sarah Taub, and Pamela Morgan. 'Primitive and Compound Metaphors'. In *Conceptual Structure, Discourse, and Language*, edited by Adele E. Goldberg, 177–87. Stanford, CA: CSLI, 1996.

Grady, Joseph E., Todd Oakley, and Seana Coulson. 'Blending and Metaphor'. In *Metaphor in Cognitive Linguistics*, edited by Gerard J. Steen and Raymond W. Gibbs Jr, 101–24. Amsterdam and Philadelphia, PA: John Benjamins, 1999.

Harrison, Lawrence. 'Searching for "Malaphors"'. *The Washington Post*, 6 August 1976.

Hofstadter, Douglas and David Moser. 'To Err Is Human; To Study Error-Making Is Cognitive Science'. *Michigan Quarterly Review* 28, no. 2 (1989): 185–215.

Kimmel, Michael. 'Why We Mix Metaphors (and Mix Them Well): Discourse Coherence, Conceptual Metaphor, and Beyond'. *Journal of Pragmatics* 42 (2010): 97–115.

Koptjevskaja-Tamm, Maria, ed. *The Linguistics of Temperature*. Amsterdam and Philadelphia, PA: John Benjamins, 2015.

Kövecses, Zoltán. *Metaphor: A Practical Introduction*. Oxford: Oxford University Press, 2002.

Kövecses, Zoltán. *Metaphor in Culture: Universality and Variation*. Cambridge: Cambridge University Press, 2005.

Kövecses, Zoltán. *Language, Mind and Culture*. Oxford: Oxford University Press, 2006.

Kövecses, Zoltán. 'A View of "Mixed Metaphor" within the Conceptual Metaphor Theory Framework'. In *Mixing Metaphor*, edited by Raymond W. Gibbs Jr, 3–16. Amsterdam and Philadelphia, PA: John Benjamins, 2016.

Lakoff, George. *Women, Fire and Dangerous Things*. Chicago, IL: University of Chicago Press, 1987.

Lakoff, George. 'The Contemporary Theory of Metaphor'. In *Metaphor and Thought* (2nd edn.), edited by Andrew Ortony, 202–51. Cambridge, UK: Cambridge University Press, 1993.

Lakoff, George and Mark Johnson. *Metaphors We Live By*. Chicago, IL: University of Chicago Press, 1980.

Lakoff, George and Mark Johnson. *Philosophy in the Flesh: The Embodied Mind and Its Challenge to Western Thought*. New York: Basic Books, 1999.

Lakoff, George and Zoltán Kövecses. 'The Cognitive Model of Anger Inherent in American English'. In *Cultural Models in Language and Thought*, edited by Dorothy Holland and Naomi Quinn, 195–221. Cambridge: Cambridge University Press, 1987.

Lakoff, George and Mark Turner. *More than Cool Reason*. Chicago, IL: The University of Chicago Press, 1989.

Lee, Mark G. and John A. Barnden. 'Reasoning about Mixed Metaphors within an Implemented AI System'. *Metaphor and Symbol* 16, no. 1–2 (2001): 29–42.

Lonergan, Julia E. 'Understanding Mixed Metaphor and Conceptual Metaphor Theory'. PhD diss., University of California, Santa Cruz, 2009.

Lonergan, Julia E. and Raymond W. Gibbs Jr. 'Tackling Mixed Metaphors in Discourse: New Corpus and Psychological Evidence'. In *Mixing Metaphor*, edited by Gibbs Raymond W. Jr, 57–74. Amsterdam and Philadelphia, PA: John Benjamins, 2016.

Marks, Laura U. *Sensuous Theory and Multisensory Media*. Minneapolis, MN: University of Minnesota Press, 2002.

MetaNet. 'Category: Metaphor'. *MetaNet Metaphor Wiki*. 2015. https://metaphor.icsi.berkeley.edu/pub/en/index.php/Category:Metaphor (accessed 23 May 2017).

Moder, Carol. 'It's Like Making a Soup: Metaphors and Similes in Spoken News Discourse'. In *Language in the Context of Use: Discourse and Cognitive Approaches to Language*, edited by Andrea Tyler, Yiyoung Kim, and Mari Takada, 301–20. Berlin: Mouton de Gruyter 2008.

Moore, Kevin E. 'Frames and the Experiential Basis of the Moving Time Metaphor'. *Constructions and Frames* 24 (2011): 80–103.

Müller, Cornelia. *Metaphors Dead and Alive, Sleeping and Waking: A Dynamic View*. Chicago, IL and London: University of Chicago Press, 2008.

Müller, Cornelia. 'Why Mixed Metaphors Make Sense'. In *Mixing Metaphor*, edited by Raymond W. Gibbs Jr, 31–56. Amsterdam and Philadelphia, PA: John Benjamins, 2016.

Musolff, Andreas. 'What Role Do Metaphors Play in Racial Prejudice? The Function of Antisemitic Imagery in Hitler's Mein Kampf'. *Patterns of Prejudice* 41, no. 1 (2007): 21–43.

Musolff, Andreas. 'Dehumanizing Metaphors in UK Immigrant Debates in Press and Online Media'. *Journal of Language of Aggression and Conflict* 3, no. 1 (2015): 41–56.

Naciscione, Anita. 'Extended Metaphor in the Web of Discourse'. In *Mixing Metaphor*, edited by Raymond W. Gibbs Jr, 3–16. Amsterdam and Philadelphia, PA: John Benjamins, 2016.

Nayak, Naomi and Raymond W. Gibbs Jr. 'Conceptual Knowledge in the Interpretation of Idioms'. *Journal of Experimental Psychology: General* 119, no. 3 (1990): 315–30.

Newmark, Peter. *Approaches to Translation*. Oxford: Pergamon Press, 1981.

Nunberg, Geoffrey, Ivan A. Sag, and Thomas Wasow. 'Idioms'. *Language* 70, no. 3 (1994): 491–538.

Núñez, Rafael and Eve Sweetser. 'With the Future behind Them: Convergent Evidence from Aymara Language and Gesture in the Crosslinguistic Comparison of Spatial Construals of Time'. *Cognitive Science* 30 (2006): 401–50.

Ortony, Andrew. 'Why Metaphors Are Necessary and Not Just Nice'. *Educational Theory* 25 (1975): 45–53.

Pinker, Steven and Paul Bloom. 'Natural Language and Natural Selection'. *Behavioral and Brain Sciences* 13 (1990): 707–26.

Pritchard, William H. *Frost: A Literary Life Reconsidered*. Oxford: Oxford University Press, 1984.

Pritchard, William H. *Shelf Life: Literary Essays and Reviews*. Amherst, MA: University of Massachusetts Press, 2003.

Richards, Ivor Armstrong. *The Philosophy of Rhetoric*. Oxford: Oxford University Press, 1965.

Schäffner, Christina. 'Metaphor and Translation: Some Implications of a Cognitive Approach'. *Journal of Pragmatics* 36 (2004): 1253–269.

Semino, Elena. 'A Corpus-Based Study of "Mixed Metaphor" as a Metalinguistic Comment'. In *Mixing Metaphor*, edited by Raymond W. Gibbs Jr, 204–22. Amsterdam and Philadelphia, PA: John Benjamins, 2016.

Steen, Gerard J. *Finding Metaphor in Grammar and Usage*. Amsterdam and Philadelphia, PA: John Benjamins, 2007.

Steen, Gerard J. *A Method for Linguistic Metaphor Identification from MIP to MIPVU*. Amsterdam and Philadelphia, PA: John Benjamins, 2010.

Steen, Gerard J. and Raymond W. Gibbs Jr. 'Introduction'. In *Metaphor in Cognitive Linguistics*, edited by Raymond W. Jr. Gibbs and Gerard J. Steen, 1–8. Amsterdam and Philadelphia, PA: John Benjamins, 1999.

Stockwell, Peter. 'The Metaphorics of Literary Reading'. *Liverpool Papers in Language and Discourse* 4 (1992): 52–80.

Stockwell, Peter. *The Poetics of Science Fiction*. Harlow: Longman, 2000.

Stockwell, Peter. *Cognitive Poetics*. New York: Routledge, 2002.

Sullivan, Karen. 'Lexical Filledness and Metaphor in Idioms'. In *Collocations and Idioms 1: Papers from the First Nordic Conference on Syntactic Freezes*, edited by Marja Nenonen, Sinikka Niemi, and Jussi Niemi, 330–41. Joensuu, Finland: Joensuu University Press, 2007.

Sullivan, Karen. *Frames and Constructions in Metaphoric Language*. Amsterdam and Philadelphia, PA: John Benjamins, 2013.

Sullivan, Karen and Elena Bandín. 'Censoring Metaphors in Translation: Shakespeare's *Hamlet* under Franco'. *Cognitive Linguistics* 25, no. 2 (2014): 177–202.

Sullivan, Karen and Eve Sweetser. 'Is "Generic Is Specific" a Metaphor?' In *Meaning, Form and Body*, edited by Fey Parrill, Vera Tobin, and Mark Turner, 309–27. Stanford, CA: CSLI, 2009.

Sweetser, Eve and Karen Sullivan. 'Minimalist Metaphors'. *English Text Construction* 5, no. 2 (2012): 153–73.

Thibodeau, Paul and Frank H. Durgin. 'Productive Figurative Communication: Conventional Metaphors Facilitate the Comprehension of Related Novel Metaphors'. *Journal of Memory and Language* 58 (2008): 521–40.

Toury, Gideon. *Descriptive Translation Studies and Beyond*. Amsterdam and Philadelphia, PA: John Benjamins, 1995.

Van Den Broeck, Raymond. 'The Limits of Translatability Exemplified by Metaphor Translation'. *Poetics Today* 2, no. 4 (1981): 73–87.

Yu, Ning, 'Metaphor from Body and Culture'. In *The Cambridge Handbook of Metaphor and Thought*, edited by Raymond W. Gibbs Jr, 247–61. New York: Cambridge University Press, 2008.

INDEX

ACHIEVING A PURPOSE IS ACQUIRING A DESIRED OBJECT 56, 67, 76, 102, 109–10, 133, 142, 157, 193
ACHIEVING A PURPOSE IS REACHING A DESTINATION 76, 93, 101, 113, 194
acquisition. *See* child metaphor acquisition
AFFECTION IS WARMTH 33–4, 36, 194–5
allegory 103–5, 189
ALLIANCES ARE LOVE RELATIONSHIPS 69–70, 195
ambiguity 8, 10, 40, 85–116, 130, 142, 189, 190
Angelou, Maya 159–60
anger 36–7, 75–6, 87, 108, 112, 122, 127, 159–60, 171–2, 196
ANGER IS HEAT 36–7, 108, 159–60, 196
ANGER IS THE HEAT OF FLUID IN A CONTAINER 37, 127, 196
ARGUMENT IS PHYSICAL COMBAT 50, 78, 87, 108, 118–19, 134, 160, 177, 196–7
ARGUMENT IS WAR 80, 197
ASSISTANCE IS SUPPORT 66, 70, 87, 119, 197
ATTRIBUTES ARE POSSESSIONS 110, 197–8
Australia 11, 119, 122, 134, 163, 181
Aymara 177

bad writing 10–11, 14, 78, 171, 187–90
contests 79, 102, 171, 174, 183

Beckett, Samuel 135
Blake, William 181, 183
blending 105–12, 115, 116, 169
THE BODY IS A CONTAINER (FOR THE EMOTIONS) 36–7, 196, 198
business 17, 18, 47, 53, 76–7, 123, 134, 158, 198–9, 200
BUSINESS COMPETITION IS A COMPETITIVE SPORT 53, 77, 198–200

cannibalism 87
CAUSATION IS PROCREATION 166, 200
child metaphor acquisition 28, 31–4, 206
clashing metaphors. *See* incompatible metaphors
clauses 7, 8, 48–51, 54, 58, 63–4, 67, 95–6, 131, 140, 148, 189
combinations of metaphors. *See* compound metaphors
COMMUNICATING IS OBJECT TRANSFER 38, 109, 160–1, 200–1
compound metaphors 2, 7–8, 17–18, 22, 30, 36–7, 41–2, 47–8, 55–6, 63–4, 66–70, 75, 79, 81, 113–14, 147–9, 154–5, 161, 174–5, 191, 195–216
  idiomatic 49, 58, 117–34, 142
  metonymic 91–4
  unproblematic 5–6, 8, 15, 67, 76, 108, 148, 161–7
  with dead metaphors 40, 61
conceptual metaphor 2–6, 25–6, 29–32, 38, 44–5, 54, 61, 64, 112, 117, 135, 179, 192

contradictions in metaphor structures. *See* incompatible metaphors
correspondences between domains. *See* mappings

dead metaphors 38–41, 47, 59–61, 63, 80, 117–18, 160
descriptivism 11
dialects 11–13
Dickens, Charles 110
Dickinson, Emily 103–4
DIFFICULTY IS HARDNESS 59, 201
direct naming of incompatible elements 53–4

Einstein, Albert 162–3, 188
ELECTRICITY IS A CROWD 153, 201–2
ELECTRICITY IS WATER 153, 201–2
embodiment 27–8, 33–4, 38
emotional intensity 1, 15–16, 20, 64, 87, 122–3, 132, 171–3
EMOTIONAL INTIMACY IS PHYSICAL PROXIMITY 70, 172, 178, 195, 202–3, 208
Esperanto 12
EXISTING IS BEING PHYSICALLY AT THIS LOCATION 112, 202
EXPERIENCING A NEGATIVE STATE IS EXPERIENCING HARM 163, 202
extended metaphors 39, 68–72, 134–41, 175

Facebook 44, 70–1, 73, 113
Finnish 11
folk etymology 129–32
FRIENDSHIPS ARE FABRICS 71–2, 203
Frost, Robert 104–5, 161–2, 188

GENERIC IS SPECIFIC 48–9, 56, 62, 86–7, 94, 101, 134–5, 155, 158, 174, 203–4
GOODNESS IS FAT 124, 204
GOODNESS IS LIGHT 5, 164, 204, 207
GOODNESS IS VERTICALITY 113, 204

Hamlet (Shakespeare) 43, 190
happiness 99–100, 133, 148, 157–9, 162, 205
HAPPINESS IS BRIGHTNESS 99, 133, 175, 205
HAPPINESS IS VERTICALITY 162, 164, 175, 205
headlines 7, 18, 86, 93–5, 120–1, 134, 189
humour 5, 30, 49, 79, 89–90, 96, 99–103, 105, 107, 110–11, 125, 132–3, 142, 163, 171, 178

IDEAS ARE OBJECTS 79, 110, 152, 166, 198–3, 205, 209–11, 215
IDEOLOGIES ARE ORGANISMS 95, 165–6, 206
idiom blends. *See* mappings
idioms 5, 8, 10, 18–19, 38–9, 49, 56, 87, 96, 100, 107, 112, 117–42, 145, 180, 189, 204
ignorance 14, 17–20, 48, 64, 117–18, 122–3, 165–6, 171
image metaphors 5, 28–30, 52, 67, 73, 97–8, 163, 179–83, 206
IMPORTANT IS CENTRAL 206
IMPORTANCE IS SIZE 32–4, 94, 100, 120, 158, 164–5, 172, 206
inattentiveness 4, 19, 73
incompatible metaphors 2, 7–8, 39–40, 47–8, 53–4, 59–61, 63–4, 67, 78, 124, 142, 160, 172–3, 178, 184, 188
insults 5, 78–9, 133–4, 142
Internet 50, 72–3, 76, 89, 101, 105, 109. *See also* Facebook; Twitter

Japanese 37
jokes. *See* humour

Latin 38, 187
Lawrence, D. H. 1, 16, 172
lengthy metaphors. *See* extended metaphors

A LIFETIME IS A LIGHT/HEAT CYCLE 112, 151, 207
LIFE IS A JOURNEY 26–9, 39, 49, 52–6, 59–61, 64, 67, 87, 89, 93, 96, 104–5, 108, 121–2, 133, 148–9, 155–6, 161–3, 165, 175–8, 192–3, 208, 213
love 25–6, 36, 69–70, 87, 104, 149, 151, 159–60, 171–2, 178–9, 195, 208
LOVE IS A JOURNEY 178–9, 208

Macbeth (Shakespeare) 149–50
malaphors 5, 117–34
malapropisms 8, 124, 127
mappings 27, 33, 36, 72, 191–4, 219
marriage 25, 69, 136–7, 158–9, 178, 195, 208
memes 71–5, 82–3, 89–92, 105–6, 178–9
mental models 21, 136, 151–4, 168, 177
metaphor names 5, 26, 28, 191–3
metaphoric words 1, 3–4, 18, 25–7, 30, 37–40, 52–4, 59–61, 63, 80, 85–6, 92, 95, 97, 101, 109–10
metaphors presented as alternatives 154–61, 167, 171, 188
metonymy 22, 83, 91–4, 109, 125, 127, 209
THE MIND IS A BODY 39, 49, 70, 75, 89–90, 96–7, 100–1, 120, 122, 160, 162–3, 175, 178, 196, 198–9, 200–1, 209, 215
THE MIND IS A CONTAINER 139, 209
THE MIND IS A MACHINE 73, 79, 210
THE MIND IS A PHYSICAL STRUCTURE 160, 210
mixed metaphors causes 18, 37, 39, 47–8, 51–2, 63–4, 75–6, 120–2, 124–6, 128–9, 183
    definitions 2, 6–8, 10, 81
    intentional 5, 20, 61, 78, 132–4, 171–9
    involving only one metaphor 7–8, 81, 85–94, 123, 174–84

    types 3–4, 8, 30, 41–2, 75, 117, 123
    unwanted effects 14–20, 122, 142, 171, 187
    variations in perception of 9–10, 39–40, 55–6, 60, 77, 120
models. *See* mental models
MONEY IS FOOD 176, 210
MORALITY IS PURITY 5, 86, 103–4, 119, 140–1, 210–11, 214
multimodality. *See* visual imagery
THE NATION IS A FAMILY 78, 211
THE NATION IS AN OBJECT 66, 211

non-metaphoric 8, 22, 40, 59, 86, 89–90, 94–7, 101–2, 109, 125
non-standard English 11, 132
novel metaphors 29, 60–1, 67, 70, 85, 134–5, 140, 165, 174–6, 179–84, 188

old age 29, 94, 108, 112, 150–1, 163, 207
online. *See* Internet
1984 (Orwell) 12

pain 15, 20, 39, 96–7, 122, 131, 159, 171–2, 189
Parker, Dorothy 71–2
PASSION IS HEAT 30, 117, 158, 160, 207, 211
PERSISTING IS REMAINING ERECT 7, 73, 212, 215
physical experience. *See* embodiment
poetry 3, 15–16, 29, 99, 103, 112, 159
politicians 5–7, 12, 14, 16–17, 19, 50, 68, 79–80, 118–23, 128, 136, 165, 172
prescriptivism 11, 13, 15, 41, 187–8
primary metaphors 31–7, 42, 161, 191–219
proverbs 89–91, 163, 174, 203–4
proximity (of metaphors) 47–51, 57, 60, 97, 99, 149, 161

psychologists 6–7, 10, 16, 127
puns 30, 101, 103, 105

QUANTITY IS SIZE 87, 93, 95, 112, 212
QUANTITY IS VERTICALITY 32, 79, 191, 212

racism 11, 75–6
relatedness (of metaphors). *See* similarity
repetition (of metaphors) 15, 63–8, 102

school 14, 93, 99, 147, 151–3, 187
science 18, 77, 131, 149, 151–4, 169, 171
sexual intercourse 69–70, 80–1, 111, 147, 163, 172, 183, 195
Shakespeare, William 149–51, 188, 190
similarity (of metaphors) 47–8, 51–8, 100, 120–1
similes 1–2, 98, 111–12, 213
sleeping metaphors. *See* dead metaphors
SOCIAL GROUPS ARE COMPLEX STRUCTURES 7, 213
source domains 27–9, 31–2, 36, 40, 73, 94, 97–100, 102–3, 105, 112, 148, 158, 165, 167, 175, 181, 192–4
  incompatible 7–8, 41, 52, 60–1, 67–70, 96, 119–22, 124, 142, 188, 190
  unfamiliar 75–81, 130, 138, 162, 172–84, 188–9
special cases 49–50, 52, 56, 64, 73, 75, 77–8, 102, 113, 152, 165–6, 174–5, 178, 216–18
speech errors. *See* malaphors
SPORTING COMPETITIONS ARE BATTLES 213
sports 2–4, 17–18, 53, 64–6, 77, 94, 123, 135, 198–200, 213
STATUS IS VERTICALITY 53, 76, 164, 213–14

stupidity. *See* ignorance
style guides 6, 10, 13, 29, 48, 117–18, 142, 147
stylistics 10–13, 16, 75, 178
subcases. *See* special cases
subconscious metaphors 3–4, 29, 39
SUSPICIOUS IS STINKY 91, 214

target domains 27–32, 36, 40, 50, 61, 68–71, 73, 94, 97–100, 103–5, 112, 119, 124, 153, 159, 175, 181–3, 191–4
tautology 98–100
THEORIES ARE BUILDINGS 44, 167, 196, 215
THINKING IS MOVING 39, 89, 96–7, 215
TIME IS A MOVING OBJECT 55, 119, 149, 215
TIME IS A RESOURCE 111, 164–5, 216
Trump, Donald 66–9, 121, 135, 139–40, 177
Twitter 86, 89–90

UNCERTAINTY IS VERTICALITY 94–5, 216
UNDERSTANDING IS DIGESTING 40, 63, 216
UNDERSTANDING IS GRASPING 38, 40, 59–60, 200, 217
UNDERSTANDING IS HEARING 122, 218
UNDERSTANDING IS SEEING 31–2, 35–6, 40, 49, 59–60, 63–4, 70, 76, 91, 94, 100, 106, 108, 111, 118, 120, 122, 164–5, 167, 176–7, 218

visual images 30, 32, 72–5, 83, 87–9, 191

writing guides. *See* style guides

zeugma 30, 109–12, 134